A SECOND CHANCE

A SECOND CHANCE

The Making of Yiddish Melbourne

MARGARET TAFT AND
ANDREW MARKUS

A Second Chance: The Making of Yiddish Melbourne
© Copyright 2018 Margaret Taft and Andrew Markus
All rights reserved. Apart from any uses permitted by Australia's Copyright Act 1968, no part of this book may be reproduced by any process without prior written permission from the copyright owners. Inquiries should be directed to the publisher.

Monash University Publishing
Matheson Library and Information Services Building
40 Exhibition Walk
Monash University
Clayton, Victoria 3800, Australia
www.publishing.monash.edu

Monash University Publishing brings to the world publications which advance the best traditions of humane and enlightened thought.

Monash University Publishing titles pass through a rigorous process of independent peer review.

ISBN: 9781925495850 (paperback)
ISBN: 9781925495867 (pdf)
ISBN: 9781925495874 (epub)

www.publishing.monash.edu/books/sc-9781925495850.html

Series: Australian History
Series Editor: Sean Scalmer

Design: Les Thomas

Cover image: A group of new arrivals with David Abzac (centre), Fremantle Western Australia late 1940s. Permission to publish granted by Masha Fisher.

 A catalogue record for this book is available from the National Library of Australia

Printed in Australia by Griffin Press an Accredited ISO AS/NZS 14001:2004 Environmental Management System printer.

 The paper this book is printed on is certified against the Forest Stewardship Council ® Standards. Griffin Press holds FSC chain of custody certification SGS-COC-005088. FSC promotes environmentally responsible, socially beneficial and economically viable management of the world's forests.

Smugglers

We were met
By brisk efficiency.
Passport. Landing Permit.
Vaccination. Chest X-Ray.
Name. Nationality.
And, yes, –
Anything to declare?

Hands shuffled.
Fingers lifted,
Eyes looked,
Scanned.

Nothing was confiscated.
We were free to go.
Our bodies bent
Under the heavy cargo
Of our past.
We smuggled in
Values and slanted opinions.

We failed to declare
Ever-lasting nostalgia,
Memories of distant people,
Already fading cities
And lost sunsets.

Nobody asked, nobody cared.
We were left alone.
And wherever we go,
We leave a trail
Of unsuspected contraband,
Sometimes polluting, sometimes enriching
Our adopted home.

                Maria Lewitt, 1985

CONTENTS

Acknowledgements ix
Preface xiii
Introduction xv

PART ONE. A NEW HOME 1

Chapter 1. Arrival 3
Chapter 2. Where are we? 23
Chapter 3. Old world, new world 34
Chapter 4. Yiddish under the Southern Cross 54
Chapter 5. Politics – 'If everyone pulled in one direction,
            the world would tip over' 74
Chapter 6. Escape 90

PART TWO. REDEFINITIONS: THE HOLOCAUST AND ISRAEL 107

Chapter 7. 'In a moment of crisis ... divisions disappeared' ... 109
Chapter 8. Worst fears confirmed 132
Chapter 9. *She'erit hapletach* – the surviving remnant 143
Chapter 10. Australian responses 152
Chapter 11. Nightmares 172
Chapter 12. Ties that bind 180
Chapter 13. Israel: The game-changer 199

Part Three. Generations 221

Chapter 14. 'The pursuit of happiness' 223

Chapter 15. *Parnoseh* – earning a living 235

Chapter 16. Zenith 243

Chapter 17. Signs of change 259

Chapter 18. 'Yiddish has not yet said its last word' 276

Bibliography 301

Index 313

About the authors 347

ACKNOWLEDGEMENTS

This book began its life as a research project made possible by funding from the Australian Research Council under its Discovery Projects scheme in 2008, with additional funding in 2010 from the Pratt Foundation and the Hans Bachrach Foundation. The project was charged with researching, documenting and writing a history of the Yiddish speaking community in Melbourne, a community that flourished in the prewar and postwar years.

From the project's inception Dr Miriam Munz has been an invaluable member of the research team. Her organisational expertise came to the fore when contacting people and institutions, collecting information, photographs and documents, liaising with volunteers and sorting through a myriad of files. Her work provided the backbone of the project. Her gentle guidance and undertaking of the extensive interview process resulted in the collation of over sixty interviews with first, second and third generation members of the community. Throughout this entire process Miriam provided us with a steady hand and an unflinching commitment to complete the task. Without her, this book would not have been written.

We are extremely indebted to those individuals who gave of their time and allowed us to record their thoughts, delving into their memories, allowing us to share their love of and commitment to a community in which they lived and thrived. These interviews provided important insight into the way this small yet dynamic community functioned. We extend our heartfelt gratitude to them all.

We are greatly indebted to a number of institutions and individuals who provided support and assistance over the years. The Kadimah

A SECOND CHANCE

Jewish Cultural Centre and National Library was, and is, the heart of Melbourne's Yiddish world. The energetic Rachel Kalman and her team of loyal library volunteers maintain the books and documents that bear witness to Melbourne's Yiddish community. They were a willing and helpful partner in this project by providing access to reports and photographs, all of which gave us a window into the world that was.

The *Australian Jewish News* granted us space in their Melbourne office on several occasions to examine back copies of the newspaper. The paper is an invaluable record of community events. The State Library of Victoria also provided expert guidance in the exploration of print media and was a great asset in accessing back copies of the Jewish press.

We also extend our thanks to the Jewish Museum of Australia for giving us access to interviews they conducted in the early 1990s and their bank of photographs. The Holocaust Museum and Research Centre, the Lamm Library and the Australian Jewish Historical Society all provided assistance as required and we are indebted to them for their support of our project.

Danielle Charak was instrumental in shaping the first stage of the project and co-edited our first publication on Yiddish Melbourne, *Towards a History*. Danielle and Hinde Burstin were always on hand to offer expert advice on the intricacies of the Yiddish language and the community who spoke it; *a sheynem dank* to them both.

As part of this project Julie Meadows produced two wonderful books based on interviews with those Jewish immigrants who settled in Carlton prewar and postwar and who built a rich, vibrant life in this Yiddish enclave. Her books not only brought another time and

ACKNOWLEDGEMENTS

place to life, but also provided an important resource for our own work.

The Burstin brothers, David, Ben and Maurice, translated the articles and papers of their late father, an indomitable leader of the Yiddish community, Sender Burstin. Their book, which was published as part of this project, provided us with a rich source of accessible material.

To our colleague and lover of all things Yiddish, Dr Nathan Wolski, we thank him for his unwavering support, advice and counsel, much of which comes through in the book.

Adina Bankier Karp offered us a window into the ultra-orthodox *haredi* community, of specific relevance to the final chapter of our book. We thank her for sharing her knowledge and advice.

Michael Gawenda kindly accepted our invitation to read our manuscript and write the preface. Michael is a towering figure in the world of print media, an accomplished author and a lover of Yiddish. We are grateful to Michael for sharing his time and expertise.

Deb Rechter provided us with important insights and direction in the early stages of the manuscript's development. Nadine Davidoff was our talented editor who expertly guided the writing process and steered us towards commercial publication. We thank her for undertaking this project with us.

Photographs are reproduced with permission of the holding institutions or individuals. Permission was also obtained from individuals to include excerpts of their interviews.

The views expressed in the book are our own. They document a richly divergent, politically engaged community – replete with a range of perspectives. We do not expect all will agree with our interpretation but hope this book will be recognised as contributing to an ongoing discussion.

We acknowledge the support of Monash University's Australian Centre for Jewish Civilisation in the production of this book and to Nathan Hollier of Monash Publishing for having faith in it.

Finally, and perhaps most importantly, we are all indebted to those Yiddish pioneers who came to this remote corner of the globe and rebuilt an old world in a new land. Their legacy lives on.

PREFACE

Reading this fine and important book brought back so many memories. I lived in the world this book so vividly examines and describes. I knew all the men and women, the Holocaust survivors, who transformed the Australian Jewish community after the War and who created such a rich and vibrant Yiddish world in a place so far away from where they had come. I was a child of these people. They were my parents and my teachers and my early role models. Yiddish was my first language and not only in the sense that it was the language of our family. The first poems I heard and read were in Yiddish. My first songs were those classic Yiddish folk songs that my mother sang to me when I was a small child. Even the Torah I first encountered was in Yiddish because my father read it to me in Yiddish for a couple of hours every Sunday afternoon.

I was a pupil of both the Peretz Sunday School and later, the Sholem Aleichem Sunday School. It was at these schools that I was inspired to become a writer by some of the teachers mentioned in this book. I wrote my first Yiddish poems at Sholem Aleichem Sunday School because my teacher, Jacob Diner, encouraged me and challenged me to write them. Looking back, I think that the most intense educational experiences I had were in this Yiddish world which was so full of life, and yes, even joy. This book captures this world and describes it so well using interviews and profiles of its inhabitants.

This is the world I knew, and this book has brought back that world for me in all its richness and complexity. But it has also opened up for me the pre-war Yiddish world in Australia. I knew something about it but not as much as I thought. This part of the book, the first part, is rich with characters and events and stories of Yiddish life during the first four decades of the 20th century. It has great narrative strength. It tells a story of a time and of a people and of Yiddish that is now long gone but that should certainly not be forgotten.

Not just that. The book made me think about what Yiddish means to me today and what it means to my children. The book does examine the future for Yiddish and comes I think, to the right conclusion, that there is no real way of knowing its future. I am not so much concerned with that question. A few years ago, I did VCE Yiddish in a class that included the distinguished legal academic Louis Waller. We were taught by a wonderful teacher who reminded me of the Yiddish teachers of my youth.

Soon after that VCE year, I began to write Yiddish poetry again – more than half a century after I had written some poems in Yiddish at Sunday school. My son created songs from two of these poems and they were recorded by the Bashevis Singers – my daughter, my son and my great nephew – on an album of Yiddish songs, old folk songs and new songs that pays homage to the songs of the past but is firmly rooted in contemporary Jewish life and music.

My love for Yiddish, my connection to it, has grown over the years. I see that it has a future for me personally and for my children who have a love for Yiddish that is unlike mine but is nevertheless deep and I believe enduring. This book tells a story that has not been previously told. It is the story of a miracle I believe, of Jews who built a Yiddish world in far Australia, a world – their world – that had been all but destroyed in the Holocaust. This book captures that miracle, describes it, analyses it and I believe, brings that world to life.

Michael Gawenda
March 2018

INTRODUCTION

Most histories of immigrant groups are inward looking; the focus is on community leaders, organisations within the community, public events, achievements, progress and numbers. In this history, which focuses on a major segment of the Jewish community of Melbourne, the Yiddish-speaking immigrants from Eastern Europe, we initially share this interest in the inward perspective. We explore the realities and rich texture of immigrant life: the internal divisions within the immigrant community; the struggle for power and influence; the setting of community priorities; the right to determine who speaks on behalf of the community in interactions with the wider society; and the attempts to transmit cultural values across the generations. These facets of immigrant life are of little interest to the mainstream, which is content to see immigrant communities as homogeneous, without internal division.

This book takes its departure from other immigrant histories through its interest in the broad context, both international and national. We explore the background of the different waves of Jewish immigrants, from the first Jewish settlers to the unprecedented numbers arriving after the Second World War. We seek to understand the distinctive character of the community that emerged and coalesced in Melbourne.

We are also interested to understand the differences among immigrant settlers in Australia. We explore the distinctive background of the Jewish immigrants from Eastern Europe – the 'cultural baggage' that they brought with them to Australia. Communities have different characteristics and trajectories. The pre-war Jewish arrivals came from environments in which antisemitism determined their life opportunities. Their survival had in many cases depended on the establishment of their own communal organisations, cultural institutions and self-help societies. Those arriving after the Second World War brought with them the added trauma of the Holocaust, the lived experience of the physical destruction of a people and a civilisation.

Of the Jewish communities of the New World, the Melbourne community is among those in which the legacy of the Holocaust had the strongest impact. For most New World Jewish communities, the peak of growth occurred before 1930. While Holocaust survivors added to their numbers and knowledge of the Holocaust greatly influenced outlook and orientation to the non-Jewish world, the long-established communities were not transformed. But the arrival of survivors, who doubled the community's size between 1947 and 1954, in large measure came to define Melbourne Jewry. Also of major importance for this community was the struggle to establish the State of Israel in the immediate aftermath of the Holocaust and the pervasiveness of Zionism.

A further dimension differentiates this book from most immigrant histories. It seeks to provide insight into issues of broad significance for the understanding of Australian history. For example, it seeks to provide a deeper and grounded understanding of the working of post-1945 immigration policy, with specific reference to the effect of the White Australia policy on entry, not only from Asia but also from Europe. While Australia embarked on a bold and expansive post-war immigration program, Jewish immigration was only grudgingly tolerated by Australian authorities rather than actively pursued or supported. With regard to settlement policy, we provide insight

INTRODUCTION

into the so-called 'assimilation policy' that was at its height in the 1950s. With regard to the integration of Jewish settlers, this book explores the ways in which the first generation and their children became both a part of, and in some respects remained separate from, Australian society.

Part One

A New Home

Chapter 1

ARRIVAL

Sender Burstin's first night on Australian soil was hardly auspicious. The Melbourne winter of 1928 was not unduly cold, but Sender was chilled to the bone. He spent a restless night, tossing and turning. Thoughts whirled around him as he struggled to fully comprehend the enormity of his decision to come to this New World, this new *goldene medinah* (golden land), tucked into the farthest corner of the globe. As he looked out the window of his sparse, unheated hostel room this 25-year-old Polish Jew found nothing to cheer him. The wide roads and boulevards of Carlton stretched before him, desolate and devoid of the vibrant life he had known and loved yet felt compelled to leave. He was overwhelmed with despair.[1]

He ventured downstairs to the Café Lipski where the proprietor, Ezra Lipski, himself a recent immigrant, had shown considerable enterprise by establishing a migrant hostel to meet the needs of an increasing number of Jewish immigrants fresh off the boat, offering cheap rooms for rent above his restaurant on the edge of Drummond and Faraday streets in Carlton. While the hostel provided temporary accommodation for new arrivals such as Sender, the café had become

---

1   Sender Burstin, 'The Early Hardships of an Immigrant' (*Melburner Bleter (Melbourne Chronicle)*, March 1976), in his *Yiddish Melbourne Observed*, translated by Ben and David Burstin, Australian Centre for Jewish Civilisation, Monash University, 2013, p.16.

a central meeting place for young Jewish immigrant men searching for friendship as well as the familiarity and advice that only *landsman* (fellow countrymen) could provide. And of course there was the food, meals provided by Ezra who was both chef and waiter. For these young men, far from home and alone, chicken soup didn't just fill the belly, it warmed the heart. It was food for the soul.

As Ezra Lipski's regulars began pouring into the café, Sender scanned the tables for a familiar face. Was there anyone who had come on the ship with him? Not one. These men were all strangers and yet there was something that drew him closer. While they ate, drank coffee, played chess, he heard the familiar banter and conversation of the *mame loshen* (mother tongue) which harked back to a Yiddish world that lay at the heart of their existence, a world centred in Eastern Europe. This gave Sender some comfort and encouragement. At least the rumours he heard in Poland were true – there were some Yiddish speakers in this far-flung British outpost. Throughout the 1920s some 2,000 of Sender's compatriots had crossed the seas to *Oystralia*, a relatively small number, but constituting more than the total intake for any previous decade, two thirds of whom were to settle in Victoria.[2] They formed part of a small yet highly significant immigrant group that was at the vanguard of a migration story spanning the first half of the 20th century, one that saw the transposition of an entire way of life to this corner of the world. For it wasn't just the language they spoke that these Eastern European Jews brought with them. Yiddish represented far more.

While no country maintained Yiddish as its national language, for Jews like Sender Burstin and the other Lipski café regulars, the

---

2   Charles A. Price, 'Jewish Settlers in Australia', *Australian Jewish Historical Society Journal and Proceedings*, Vol. V, Part 8 (1964): p.375.

very essence of their being was closely tied to Yiddish culture that flourished in the large towns and cities of Poland and Lithuania and in which so many of these immigrants had lived – the metropolis of Warsaw, the textile centres and industrial cities of Bialystok and Lodz, and the culturally vibrant city of Vilna, known as the 'Jerusalem of Lithuania.' These cities had large Jewish populations; Warsaw alone, the capital of Poland, had over 300,000 Jews – one third of the town's population. While Sender Burstin's home town of Makow, 77 kilometres east of Warsaw was small in comparison, its Jewish population comprised 54 per cent of the total population. To put this into context, in 1921, Victoria's Jewish population numbered 7,677, just half of one per cent of the total Victorian population; and only a small percentage of them spoke Yiddish.

The Yiddish-speaking communities of Eastern Europe were able to cultivate and sustain a complex range of organisations, institutions and activities that became the bedrock of everyday life. Yiddish was heard in the streets and cafés, performed on the stage, read in daily newspapers and studied in schools. Yiddish had its own body of literature and its own academy, the scholarly YIVO institute of Vilna.[3] By the 1920s Yiddish had become a public, visible identity marker of an entire people.[4] Little wonder that provincial Melbourne jolted the senses, sending shock waves through men like Sender, whose lives had been and would remain steeped in a vast expansive Yiddish world.

It was a quirk of fate that propelled these Jews to settle in Carlton, a northern suburb of Melbourne. And it was no accident that the

---

3   David E. Fishman, *The Rise of Modern Yiddish Culture*, Pittsburgh: University of Pittsburgh Press, 2005, pp.83–137.
4   The 1931 Polish census reported that 80 per cent of Polish Jews claimed Yiddish as their mother tongue; Bernard Wasserstein, *On the Eve: The Jews of Europe Before The Second World War*, New York: Simon & Schuster, 2012, p.224.

Jewish boarding houses, kosher restaurants, kosher butchers, bakeries, grocers and communal hall were all concentrated in this one region of the city. Newly arrived Yiddish speakers in the 1920s gravitated to the suburbs north of the Yarra, particularly Carlton and North Carlton which had a strong connection to Jewish settlement since the 1870s and already contained the nucleus of a Yiddish-speaking community.[5]

> Everybody knew everybody else, the businessman and the man who worked on the job. It was a village, if you like, a ghetto, but a voluntary one, without walls. . . . They had settled in Carlton so they could live with fellow Jews, people who understood who they were.[6]

South of the Yarra was where the Englishe Yidn lived. Carlton was home to the Yiddishe Yidn.[7]

Carlton was more than a Yiddish enclave; it was also an area in which Jews mixed with and lived amongst other immigrants.[8] The Carlton streets were playgrounds for a cosmopolitan bunch of kids. Bialystok-born Leon Grodski, whose parents opened a boarding house on Rathdowne Street, didn't resent being a 'Jewboy' because everyone carried an ethnic label. The niceties of political correctness were unheard of; 'Catholics were Micks, the English were Pikes, Italians were Dagos and we were Jewboys.'[9] Taibella Hain (Tess Schwartz)

---

[5] Price, 'Jewish Settlers in Australia', Hilary Rubinstein, *The Jews in Australia: A Thematic History, Volume 1: 1788–1945*, Melbourne: William Heinemann Australia, 1991, p.157.

[6] Yankel Pushett in *A Shtetl in Ek Velt: 54 Stories of Growing up in Jewish Carlton*, edited by Julie Meadows, Australian Centre for Jewish Civilisation, Monash University, 2011, p.79.

[7] Yankel Rosenbaum, 'Religiously Carlton, Jewish Religious Life in Carlton 1919–1939', *Australian Jewish Historical Society Journal*, Vol. XII, Part 3 (1994): p.523.

[8] Price, 'Jewish Settlers in Australia', p.400.

[9] Leon Grodski in *A Shtetl in Ek Velt*, p.115.

ARRIVAL

played with children of different religious backgrounds: 'We played with an old tennis ball and "skippy" with a bit of rope . . . I played with Marjorie Pritchard, Howard Egan and Shirley Gordon. They were all Protestants. One day, I played with Moira, who was Catholic.'[10] Her mother Chaya Hain (Chayin) never washed clothes or cleaned outside on Sundays in deference to her Christian neighbours.

From the 1920s Jewish Carlton was centred in and comprised an area bordered by Faraday Street in the south, Park Street in the north, Nicholson Street in the east and Lygon Street in the west. 'Living in Elgin Street meant you were literally in the centre of Jewish Carlton life.'[11] The northern ends of Rathdowne and Drummond Streets comprised the centre of Jewish residency.[12] 'Drummond Street housed many Jewish families, and in our block alone there must have been ten to fifteen families. This was typical of most of the streets around Carlton and North Carlton.'[13]

While Sender and his new acquaintances talked and *schmoozed* (gossiped), they shared vital information, mostly about their daily experiences, but more importantly about their desperate search for a job. This was networking of a most crucial kind, one in which immigrants were particularly adept. Sender learnt a great deal about how to survive and build a new life in this new country from other Jews, mostly through word of mouth. Jews were no strangers to this type of self-help. Jewish immigrants not only brought with them to the New World the physical trappings of life in Eastern Europe but also, more importantly, the cultural baggage of centuries of Jewish

---

10   Tess Schwartz in *A Shtetl in Ek Velt*, p.61.
11   Jack Hansky in *A Shtetl in Ek Velt*, p.195.
12   Price, 'Jewish Settlers in Australia', Appendix IXa.
13   Theo Weisberg in *A Shtetl in Ek* Velt, p.229.

existence – an existence that not only thrived and flourished but was marred by deadly pogroms fuelled by religious fervour bent on destroying the 'Christ killers.' Self-reliance and self-governance were survival traits embedded in communities in the period before European Emancipation, when the lifting of restrictions on Jewish life in Europe that gradually occurred between the late 18th century and the beginning of the 20th century enabled Jews to live fuller and freer lives. While this form of fully self-contained communal/religious organisation broke down under the impact of the Enlightenment (an intellectual and scientific movement of 18th-century Europe characterised by a rational and scientific approach to religious, social, political and economic issues) and capitalism, it inculcated a type of resilient, independent, self-determining lifestyle that could be felt for centuries to come.[14] Self-help organisations were therefore key to the survival of Jewish communal life and, as we will see, their subsequent growth in Melbourne would help to reshape and redefine the Jewish community for decades to come.[15]

Sender Burstin understood the need for Jews to be self-reliant. He had experienced first-hand life under oppressive regimes that exploited and restricted their Jewish communities and did nothing to support them. With steely determination he set out to do something about it. He turned his back on traditional Orthodox Judaism and became a political activist, a radical. He embraced a new secular, socialist Jewish political party, the Bund. Founded in Czarist Russia in 1897, the Bund's ideology appealed to Sender, with the vision of

---

14   Peter Medding, *From Assimilation to Group Survival: A Political and Social Study of an Australian Jewish Community*, Melbourne: F.W. Cheshire Publishing, 1968, pp.10–11.
15   H. Rubinstein, *The Jews in Australia*, p.39.

improving the lives and working conditions of Jews everywhere and to defend them against the ravages of antisemitism. These guiding principles were intrinsically bound to the centrality of Yiddish language and culture to Jewish life. In opposition to a rival secular political movement, Zionism, which supported the establishment of a Jewish homeland in Eretz Yisrael, the Bund subscribed to the concept of *doykeit* (the 'here and now'). In Poland the Bund became a significant political force in the interwar years.[16] Although his political position would change over time, Sender's passion for the Bund's ideals and its humanist values never left him. These ideals and values would involve him in numerous disputes and heated debates with other members of the community over the ensuing decades, but they remained his moral compass and would guide his philanthropic and communal work for the rest of his life.

Although the economic crisis of the Great Depression was yet to engulf the world, its impact was beginning to be felt. In 1920s Victoria, factories came to surpass rural industries as the main generators of wealth, but jobs for immigrants were hard to find.[17] Sender was desperate to find work. Not only did he have to repay a loan that covered his travel expenses and the cost of the landing permit the Australian government required, but he had to save enough money to bring out his young bride, Fayge. It would be a year before he saw her again.

As a former union official, Sender had a wealth of experience in administration and organisation, but as he walked the streets of Carlton he saw little need for his type of skills. He weighed up

---

16 Wasserstein, *On the Eve*, pp.68–9.
17 Geoffrey Blainey, *A History of Victoria*, Melbourne: Cambridge University Press, 2013, p.181.

his options. His 'new' friends offered advice. 'Try your hand as a hawker, a door-to-door salesman. It's easy work. You don't need to speak English. You just point!' But the thought of knocking on doors and forcing his foot in the doorway in order to cajole a poor housewife into buying his wares did not appeal.[18] For many, such as Moses Freedman, a former student of Torah in Warsaw with no other employment prospects, it was the only option.[19] Another offer came by way of a café regular who ran towards him clutching a telegram, 'Burstin, I have a job for you!' It was as a farm labourer, a job the café regular had secured but no longer needed as he had found employment in the city. Most of these new immigrants had been city dwellers, more familiar with life on the streets, in the bustling marketplace or working in the burgeoning textile factories of Poland, than behind a plough. Sender was no exception. But he was desperate and Sender was prepared to try his hand at almost anything.[20]

Sender Burstin's foray into farming lasted one day. Was it turning up at the country train station for labouring work without overalls and wearing a white shirt and cufflinks that raised the farmer's suspicions? Or was it the chessboard Sender produced after dinner to try and impress his boss and prove his mettle? The next morning Sender dutifully chopped the pile of wood, as he was instructed (white shirt and cufflinks notwithstanding), then sat down to write his wife a letter full of promise that his luck had changed. At the end of the day the farmer burst into his room with a return train ticket and money for the day's work. Although Sender's command of English was poor, he came to understand that the farmer's concerns were the

---

18 Burstin, 'The Early Hardships of an Immigrant', p.18.
19 Leon Freedman in *A Shtetl in Ek Velt*, p.93.
20 Burstin, 'The Early Hardships of an Immigrant', p.20.

lack of communication between them. 'You don't understand me and I don't understand you,' the farmer seemed to be saying, shrugging his shoulders. Sender never again attempted to make his fortune on the land.[21]

Sender returned to Melbourne despondent. Six weeks had passed since his arrival and still he had no employment. He had £50 left to his name and after sending £40 back home to his wife, £10 was left to cover living expenses. He needed at least £1 per week.[22] But there was no going back. Unlike some immigrants, such as the British, Jewish immigrants had little to return to and rarely went back to live in their country of origin.[23] Sender eventually found work in a factory, again through a Jewish support organisation, the Welcome Society, run by a group of former immigrants who took responsibility for meeting new arrivals and helping them with resettlement. This group really had their hands full, reporting that it had met 67 boats in 1926![24] The day that Sender got his first pay packet of £2 was one of the happiest of his life. He promptly sent half of it back to Poland.

Sender's decision to leave Poland was not taken lightly. Like so many other men of his generation he had to leave behind a wife, family, friends and a way of life. But these were exceptional times for Jews in Europe. Life was becoming increasingly perilous. Like other Jewish families, the Burstin family had felt the full brunt of

---

21 Burstin, 'The Early Hardships of an Immigrant', p.21.
22 Burstin, 'The Early Hardships of an Immigrant', p.22.
23 Gur Alroey, 'Out of the Shtetl: In the Footsteps of Eastern European Jewish Emigrants to America, 1900–1914', *Leidschrift*, Vol. 22, No. 1 (2007): p.91–2. Alroey estimates that between 1908 and 1924, about 33 per cent of all immigrants to America returned, compared with only 5.2 per cent of the Jews.
24 *Australian Jewish Herald*, 10 March 1927.

the calamities besieging Europe in the first decades of the century, political crises, wars and rising antisemitism. Nationalist movements were on the rise, and the pall of fascism was beginning to cast its ugly shadow. Jew hatred in Poland was systemic and brutal. As one immigrant explained to family in New York, 'In Poland Jews are not hated, they are despised . . . Antisemitism in Poland is not just a matter of politics but also a deep reflection of national psychology.'[25] Sender had felt the full physical force of this hatred while on his way to a Bund meeting, just before he went to Warsaw to collect his visa. A couple of Polish thugs he recognised from the local high school accosted him in the street, shouting 'Burstin Pythagoras', a nickname he acquired at school because of his skill at mathematics. They punched and pushed him to the ground, badly hurting his hand as he fell. His glasses lay on the footpath. He reported the incident to the principal of the Polish high school, who did nothing. As he left the principal's office, he was surrounded by Polish youths who resembled a lynch mob, and was forced to beat a hasty retreat.

Career prospects were also poor, particularly for Jews. Fayge's aspirations to be a teacher were quashed when her application to undertake a teacher-training course was rejected because she was a *zhidovska* (Jewess). Sender and Fayge came to the bitter and painful realisation that Poland, the home of their ancestors, held no future for Jewish life.[26] So with heavy hearts they made the momentous decision to cut their ties with the land of their birth. Although Sender had a brother and sister living in America, the National Origins

---

25 Dovid Frishman, *Briv fun Poyln* [A letter from Poland] early 1920s, YIVO Institute for Jewish Research (New York) RG 108.
26 Burstin, 'The Early Hardships of an Immigrant', pp.22–3.

Immigration (Johnson-Reed) Act of 1924 effectively shut down Jewish immigration there.[27] The only visa Sender could get to leave Poland was to Australia. With that in hand, he set sail for a land down under.

Chain migration

It was in Lipski's café that Sender met another Yiddish-speaking Polish Jew who had recently immigrated, the energetic Leo Fink. While Leo and Sender differed politically – Sender was a passionate Bundist, while Leo a committed Zionist – both men were Yiddishists whose lives over the years would continue to cross paths. Both were leaders, radicals whose impact on the community would be transformative. Leo's journey to Melbourne, however, took a different trajectory than that of Sender Burstin.

Bialystok-born Leo Fink had a great sense of adventure. By the time he was 27 years old, Leo had already tasted life beyond Polish borders. Before setting foot on Australian soil, he spent two years in Palestine in a pioneer corps, studied civil engineering for four years in Berlin and Altenburg and worked in a family start-up textile business with his three brothers and father in Galatz, Romania. In Romania Leo stumbled upon a Viennese newspaper that extolled Australia as the country of the future. The business in Galatz was not thriving, so when new horizons beckoned, Leo seized the opportunity. One of the Fink brothers was immediately despatched to the British consulate in Bucharest. Three permits were obtained. A bold new adventure was unfolding.

---

27   Jonathan D. Sarna, *American Judaism*, New Haven: Yale University Press, 2004, pp.215–16.

A SECOND CHANCE

Leo and two of his brothers, Simche (later called Sid) and Wolf, landed in Melbourne in 1928. Like all immigrants, the Fink brothers were desperate to find work. When a Jewish agricultural settlement in Berwick offered them farm work they tried their luck on the land. Their encounter with the Aussie bush lasted a year, but bush life didn't hold any great appeal or success for the Fink boys. The turning point came with the arrival of the fourth brother, Jack, in 1929. Armed with an innovative textile machine known as a 'ragger', which shredded knitted fabric back into yarn for reuse (an early recycling device), the brothers embarked on yet another enterprise. This time they made good. The Fink family business was formed, which led to the creation of United Woollen Mills Pty Ltd and United Carpet Mills Pty Ltd.

Like many other Jewish immigrants, the Fink brothers were committed to bringing other family members to Australia. Chain migration was a common pattern of immigration, enabling large families to immigrate together or in clusters. Pre-war Jewish families utilised the same process. The government offered assistance only to British immigrants, so Jews simply had to look after their own. For Jewish families to settle in Australia, sponsorship had to be provided by familial connections or through people who came from the same town or region. In many cases the main breadwinner would travel first, providing the first link in the chain. Others would be brought out as soon as the first family member was established and financially secure.[28] And so it was with the Finks.

In the early 1930s the brothers sponsored their Uncle Velvl and his family, who in turn sponsored his brother Michael and wife

---

28   Price, 'Jewish Settlers in Australia', pp.377–78.

ARRIVAL

Hinde with children Ben and Sara in 1933. The Fink brothers went to extraordinary lengths to bring their parents, Mordechai and Masha, and disabled sister Zina to Australia after their visa applications were initially refused. Never one to take no for an answer, Leo seized the initiative. Endowed with a fair amount of enterprising *chutzpah* (audacity) Leo travelled to Canberra to put the family's case to immigration officials. By guaranteeing that their elderly parents and disabled sister would not be a burden on the State, permits were obtained. They arrived in 1936. The brothers' cousin, Laibl Fink, arrived shortly before the outbreak of war.

Between the years 1928 and 1939 some twenty members of the Fink family arrived in Melbourne as a result of direct family sponsorship. Stories tell of help and support from other Eastern European Jewish immigrants who had arrived earlier. Wine merchant and ex-Lodzer Sammy Wynn acted as guarantor for Leo Fink when the bank would not extend a loan. Michael Pitt (formerly Pitkowski), a fellow well-connected Bialystoker who had arrived just one year earlier in 1927, offered advice and support. Yasha Taft (formerly Tafipolsky), a Russian Jewish émigré who arrived as part of the chain migration of a large extended family in 1922, was an electrical contractor who helped the Finks set up their first textile machine under a 'pay me when you can' agreement. As there was little charitable assistance, immigrants were mostly reliant upon relatives or friends who were already established and could, and did, provide the sort of help they needed most in their resettlement. It wasn't only financial help; sometimes it would just be putting in a good word with a landlord, or passing on useful information about jobs, or giving tips on how to negotiate a loan or set up a new business. On reflection, Leo's daughter, Freda Freiberg, recalled that her family's successful resettlement was partly attributable to the simple fact that 'people helped each other' back then.[29]

Throughout the 1920s this pattern of chain migration was the direct result of people with family or regional connections helping each other. Jewish immigrants arriving in Melbourne in this period came from a small number of towns. In the 1920s the most significant in order of actual numbers were Warsaw, Bialystok, Lodz, Kalisz, Cracow and Lublin. They formed clusters that developed into collaborative networks based on regional allegiances that would remain steadfast for decades to come. Their work ethic and independence were often lauded by representatives of the Jewish establishment. 'They are not *schnorrers* [beggars],' Rabbi Israel Brodie of the Melbourne Hebrew congregation wrote on the front page of the *Australian Jewish Herald* on the 23 September 1926.

> No application for relief has been made by any recent arrival. Our brothers have come here to work and work hard. They will and do, undertake any kind of work . . . Australia has need of such men. Australian Jewry will be rendering a service to their country as well as to the community, by assisting and encouraging our new arrivals to settle here.

While these immigrants came from a specific geographic region, they nevertheless came from different walks of life and brought different life experiences with them. They also brought their ideological differences and rival political agendas. They would argue heatedly over politics and remonstrate over differences in religious practice, from varying degrees of orthodoxy to secular non-observance. All of this took place within the colourful, often combustible, world of Yiddish.

---

29   Freda Freiberg, interview 22 July 2015.

Encounters

When Sender Burstin was greeted in the street by his Australian neighbour with a friendly 'Good morning, nice day isn't it?', he felt the warmth of acceptance. In his first year in Australia it signalled his status as an equal. A *goy* (gentile) speaking to him in such a familiar way? Ah *Oystralia*! Ironically it was when Sender went in search of a religious service on Yom Kippur, the Day of Atonement, the holiest day in the Jewish calendar, that he felt most alienated. He was a secular Jew but felt overwhelmed with nostalgia. He longed to be near his orthodox father and to see and feel once more how the Jews in Makow prepared for Kol Nidre, on the eve of Yom Kippur. Entering the Bourke Street *shul* he was confronted with a prayer service and liturgical music that shook him to the core. It wasn't just the *davening* (praying) that was different and the music that was strange. Here were men dressed in suits and hats, with a short *talles* (prayer shawl) draped over their shoulders. Who was this clean-shaven cantor whose attire and head covering were more suitable for a priest conducting a church service? Where was his long beard, his white *kitl* (ceremonial gown) and broad, sweeping *talles* edged in silver? These were not his *shtetl* Jews. He left the service early, feeling disconnected, cut off from his past. His former life seemed an eternity away. Disheartened, disillusioned, he was again reminded that some things would never be the same.[30]

As Sender walked from the *shul* along Bourke Street, he encountered a political rally organised by the Communist Party. He heard

---

30 Sender Burstin, 'Adapting to the Environment in Australia' (*Melburner Bleter (Melbourne Chronicle)* September-October 1978), in his *Yiddish Melbourne Observed*, translated by Ben and David Burstin, Australian Centre for Jewish Civilisation, Monash University, 2013, pp.32–4.

the familiar cries for 'revolution', 'dictatorship of the proletariat', warnings against the evils of capitalism, none of which surprised him. Fearful of his experiences in Poland he expected violence to erupt when police would routinely arrive and use brute force to disperse the crowd. A brawl usually followed. Instead he witnessed an orderly, peaceful meeting. The only policeman present was one of the crowd, attentively listening to the speaker.[31] Thank God that some things were not the same!

Sender came to Australia with some knowledge of the Australian Labor Party and the union movement. He was impressed with the improvements made to the working conditions of all Australians, the eight-hour day and the role that unions played in establishing a legally binding minimum wage. He eagerly joined his own factory workers union, paid his union dues and attended his first meeting with great expectations of active involvement. In Poland union meetings were lively and volatile, with heated debates and discussions and fierce arguments over political factions wanting to control the union. These meetings always attracted a large number of members. Sender knew many of them. With great anticipation, Sender arrived at his first Labour Day parade in Melbourne ready for action. His expectations and hopes were soon dashed. Of the 1,000 or so union members only about 20 were there. He knew none of them. No-one from the factory where he worked was there. There were no young men, no red flags to wave proudly, the march was well organised but uninspiring. The spirit of the Eureka Stockade that Sender had so admired, 'as a symbol of the struggle for democratic rights' was

---

31   Burstin, 'Adapting to the Environment in Australia', pp.34–5.

gone, as was the passion.[32] Similarly, when he attended his union's annual general meeting, only a few members were present, all elderly, orderly and passive. The meeting was over in no time and they all went home. Sender came to the realisation that economic prosperity and social advances that made life easy and affordable also brought political apathy. Despite the fact that there were bitter industrial disputes in the 1920s, Sender's impression was that there was no appetite for open confrontation. He came to understand that the Australian people expressed their disapproval in a different way – at the ballot box. They did so in the Federal election of 1929. As Sender recalled later in life, 'I was to learn that the Australian working masses were not altogether politically indifferent. When there was an attempt to change one of the foundations of Australian democracy, something stirred.'[33] The Bruce government was resolutely defeated, because of its controversial handling of industrial relations at a time of growing unemployment. The Scullin Labor government was swept into power.[34] This was democracy at work. This was freedom. 'This was the reply of the Australian people.'[35] Sender liked what he saw.

Once Sender had found steady employment and had a roof over his head, there was still an unfulfilled need, a yearning deep in his soul – *Yiddishkeit*. The word meant more than an ideology or a set of Jewish beliefs. *Yiddishkeit* was an all-embracing way of life that

---

32　Sender Burstin, 'Reflections on the Australian Labour Movement' (*Melburner Bleter (Melbourne Chronicle)* December 1975), in his *Yiddish Melbourne Observed*, translated by Ben and David Burstin, Australian Centre for Jewish Civilisation, Monash University, 2013, p.37.
33　Burstin, 'Reflections on the Australian Labour Movement', p.40.
34　Burstin, 'Reflections on the Australian Labour Movement', pp.36–40.
35　Burstin, 'Reflections on the Australian Labour Movement', p.40.

emanated from the popular culture and folk practices of Yiddish-speaking Jews who inhabited the small towns, or *shtetlekh*, of Eastern Europe. If Sender closed his eyes he could see it, smell it, hear it, he could transport himself in time and place to a distant world. But here in Melbourne? In *ek velt* (this corner of the world)? Not far from Lipski's café, in the same building on Drummond Street that housed the Welcome Society, he found the Kadimah. Here in the middle of what he thought was a cultural wasteland was a Yiddish heart beating strong. There were books, journals and newspapers from all corners of the Yiddish world. Sender was overcome with emotion. The Kadimah was a thriving cultural hub. There were Yiddish literary discussion groups, folk concerts and Yiddish theatre. Within a few short weeks he was fully immersed in the centre's activities. He became a dedicated member of the working committee, spending every spare hour he had at the Kadimah. He began by helping to organise the Sunday functions, but soon found himself busy in the library. Books needed repair, cataloguing was virtually non-existent, borrowing systems were ad hoc. Without any library experience but his usual determination and considerable administrative skill Sender set about reorganising the library, putting in place a system that was used for decades.[36] Sender had found his spiritual home. He again felt a fire and a passion to work for a cause.

It was in the Kadimah in those early days that Sender met a number of influential individuals, like-minded men, activists and radicals, who had immigrated in the years before him. Aron Patkin,

---

36 Sender Burstin, 'How My Involvement with the Kadimah Began' (*Melburner Bleter (Melbourne Chronicle)* April 1976), in his *Yiddish Melbourne Observed*, translated by Ben and David Burstin, Australian Centre for Jewish Civilisation, Monash University, 2013, pp.26–31.

ARRIVAL

President of the Kadimah in 1928–9, a lawyer from Moscow who arrived in Melbourne in 1926, who was knowledgeable in all aspects of Yiddish folk culture. Three men from Lodz, Samuel (Shloyme) Wynn, Israel Sher and Simche Brilliant, all of whom carried the mantle of leadership at the Kadimah over a number of years. Aaron Bar-Cohen, the secretary of the Welcome Society, who had arrived in Australia decades earlier, was conversant in both Yiddish and Hebrew and involved in Jewish education. Sender also met some of the earlier pioneers of the Kadimah: Reuben Rothberg, Isaac Hurwitz and Aaron Newmark. He was most impressed with teacher, writer, research scientist and Yiddishist Hirsch Munz, who arrived in Melbourne in late 1927 from the industrial town of Krynki, not far from Bialystok.[37] There were so many others whose story will be told in the chapters to follow.

These were Jews who felt comfortable in their own skin, had lived full cultural Yiddish lives in large cities in which high visibility was not only the social norm but a badge of honour. As we will see, the arrival of these Yiddish-speaking 'newcomers', with their strange mannerisms, European dress code and boisterous demeanour, did not go unnoticed. Elements of the established Jewish hegemony were certainly unsettled by these 'noisy north of the Yarra' Jews.[38] In large measure the 'north of the Yarra' Jews lived separate lives, cultivated separate institutions and developed their own cultural organisations. However, there would be disputations and ongoing arguments between the different sectors of the community over the advancement and use of Yiddish and conflict over issues of representation

---

37 Burstin, 'How My Involvement with the Kadimah Began', pp.26–31.
38 Trevor Rapke, 'The Pre-War Jewish Community of Melbourne', *Australian Jewish Historical Society Journal*, Vol. VII, Part 4 (1973): p.297.

and identity. There were battles to be fought. But these Jews were up for it.

These Yiddish speakers from Eastern Europe, men like Sender Burstin and Leo Fink, who met at the Kadimah, ate meals at kosher cafés, greeted each other loudly and demonstratively on the streets of Carlton, shared rooms at the boarding houses, worked in the factories, shops and in the marketplaces, these men felt no compulsion to assimilate and blend into their surroundings. They pushed against the conservative Jewish establishment, donned the cloak of modernity and steered the community towards a non-congregational, secular *Yiddishkeit*. These radicals were men who had found their place in time. These were the disruptors.

Chapter 2

WHERE ARE WE?

When his boat docked in Port Phillip Bay on a July morning in 1933, renowned Warsaw-based Yiddish writer Melech Ravitch sensed he was encountering something unique: 'I felt with all my senses something which I had never felt up until then – a new world, a different world, a strange world – the world at the southern sphere of our planet.'[1] Melbourne's small but vibrant Yiddish-speaking community flocked to the public readings and lectures given by Ravitch, the first of two visits he made to Melbourne in the course of a few years. It was a community with which he had much in common: language, culture, a shared history.

But the Yiddish speakers were only a small part of a thriving Jewish community with which Ravitch had little in common. Its seeds had been planted in Australian soil some 145 years earlier and was a community that had no interest in or empathy with the Yiddish world of Eastern Europe. When Yiddish speakers from Eastern Europe began arriving in Melbourne in significant numbers in the 1920s, they joined a group of proactive, energetic Yiddishists, who at the time were just a small part of a community whose leadership had developed a distinct way of life and an Australian-Jewish way of

---

1 Melech Ravitch, 'Australia and I', *Yiddishe Almanac 1942*, translated by Dvora Zylberman.

doing things that was deeply influenced by British traditions. This community, while of diverse origin, had evolved through a process of adaptation, taking full advantage of the liberties and opportunities this country afforded its citizens. The arrival of these Yiddish speakers from the *shtetlekh* and towns of Eastern Europe, who brought their different ways and their own expectations, contributed to and often challenged the established patterns of Jewish life in Victoria.

The first Australian Jews

Eastern European Jews were preceded firstly by Jews from Britain and, by the time of the gold rush in the 1850s, central Europe particularly from German lands, who, for the most part, melded well with their British counterparts.[2] The first Jews to settle in Australia did not come of their own volition. At least 14 Jewish convicts, mostly petty criminals, arrived on the First Fleet in 1788.[3] This assortment of Jewish pickpockets and thieves who were cast off at Sydney Cove had the dubious honour of being the founding members of Australia's Jewish community. Brought here in iron chains and shackles, they would, however, become part of the most egalitarian society in the British Empire. By the end of the transportation era in 1868, some 1,000 Jews had arrived as convicts – 'guests' of Mother England. Jewish free settlers, in search of a better life, began arriving after 1816, less than 30 years after the First Fleet cast its colonial footprint at Botany Bay.[4]

---

2   Price, 'Jewish Settlers in Australia', pp.369–76.
3   John S. Levi and G.F.J. Berman, *Australian Genesis: Jewish Convicts and Settlers 1788–1860*, Melbourne: Melbourne University Press, 2002, p.19.
4   Levi and Berman, *Australian Genesis*, pp.12–13.

WHERE ARE WE?

From 1881 to 1914 approximately 2,400,000 Jews left Eastern Europe, including the Russian empire, which encompassed Poland, Lithuania and the Baltic countries, the eastern regions of the Austrian Hungarian Empire, most notably Galicia, and Romania. About 85 per cent of these emigrants went to the USA; other countries to receive them were, in descending numerical order, Canada, Argentina, Eretz Israel and South Africa. They formed the basis of what became large, vibrant diasporic communities in the countries they emigrated to. Very few came to Australia during this period.

Blending in

Although Australia offered many freedoms and opportunities to migrants, ethnic diversity was not encouraged or welcomed. It was a monocultural and insular Christian world, in which difference was not particularly advantageous to one's social status. Like all Jews who had learnt to survive in diasporic communities, Jews from Britain and those who arrived from central Europe came to understand both the opportunities available to them and the need to blend into their host Australian, largely British, environment. They achieved this blending in a number of ways. They avoided the often-derogatory term 'Jew', preferring 'Hebrew', 'Israelite', or persons of the 'Mosaic persuasion'.

In Britain, Freemasonry enabled Jews to associate and integrate with Christians from the early 18th century. Freemasonry, the oldest, largest, and most widely recognized fraternal institution in the world, can trace its origins to the stonemasons' guilds. Founded in London in 1717, Freemasonry sought to unite men of good character who, though of different religious, ethnic and social backgrounds, shared a belief in God and the brotherhood of mankind. Freemasons are beholden to render assistance to one another unless they have broken the law. In the 19th century, Freemasonry was largely a Protestant middle-class organisation. For Jews, admission as a Freemason was a powerful symbol of acceptance and equality and an important part of their emancipation.[5] In Australia, Freemasonry was extremely popular with leading members of the established Jewish community, as it enabled Jewish males to form mutually beneficial social relationships with gentiles, while remaining openly Jewish.[6] Prominent rabbis Jacob Danglow and Israel Brodie were practising Freemasons; Moses Rintel, Melbourne's first rabbi, became the first Worshipful Master of Melbourne's Lodge of Judah in 1858, a Lodge that, despite its Old Testament name, did not only have Jewish members. Community and political figures were also members of the order.[7]

The established community gained acceptance through deliberate adoption of British customs and protocols, through their promotion to positions of public office and their loyalty and patriotism to the British Empire in times of crisis. For example, a large proportion of young Jewish men answered the call to arms with the outbreak of the First World War in 1914. Thirteen per cent of the eligible male Jewish population voluntarily enlisted at a time when there was no conscription, compared to nine per cent of the total population.[8] The death toll from the First World War had a devastating impact on the Australian population, also leaving its mark on the Jewish community. Fifteen per cent of the Jewish soldiers lost their lives,

---

[5] Jacob Katz, 'Freemasons and Jews', *Jewish Journal of Sociology*, Vol. 9, No. 2 (1967); Jacob Katz, *Jews and Freemasons in Europe 1723–1939*, Cambridge: Harvard University Press, 1970.

[6] Suzanne D. Rutland, *Edge of the Diaspora*, Sydney: Brandl & Schlesinger, 1997, p.127.

[7] H. Rubinstein, *The Jews in Australia*, p19. Even though some congregational leaders held the title of 'Reverend', in this work the general term 'Rabbi' is applied to all.

[8] Rutland, *Edge of the Diaspora*, p.133.

with many families touched by the cost of war. Some were lauded for their leadership, such as General Sir John Monash, corps commander on the Western Front, Lieutenant-Colonel Eliezer Margolin, and Lieutenant-Colonel Harold Cohen. Monash, the son of German immigrants and regarded by many as the leading military strategist of the war, was knighted by King George V at Bertangles in France in 1918, while two Jews, Leonard Keysor from Sydney and Issy Smith from Melbourne, were awarded the Victoria Cross. Approximately 100 received military honours or were mentioned in despatches.[9] Their courageous efforts on the blood-soaked battlefields gained for the small Australian Jewish population a degree of respect, but they were not freed from the growing influence of antisemitism, which had its impact in Australia, as it did across the Western world.

The egalitarianism of early 20th-century Australia afforded many Jews opportunities that were not available in their countries of origin. Jews wanted equality and, to a large extent, they obtained it.[10] They were free of the legal restrictions that hindered participation in civil society; they could hold public office, enter the professions, engage freely in commerce and the arts, get a full education and own property. Here they could aspire to social recognition. Men of exceptional talent, such as John Monash and Isaac Isaacs, were able to reach the highest leadership positions.

In contrast, in the United States of America and Canada discrimination against Jews was often institutionalised. There were university quotas, restrictions on the number of Jewish medical interns in many teaching hospitals, restrictive covenants that prohibited Jews

---

9 H. Rubinstein, *The Jews in Australia*, pp.28–9, 401.
10 Israel Getzler, *Neither Toleration nor Favour: The Australian Chapter of Jewish Emancipation*, Melbourne: Melbourne University Press, 1970.

from living in certain residential areas, as well as bans on Jews at many resorts and private clubs. The Chancellor of Queen's University in Ontario noted that 'the presence of Jews tended to lower the tone of Canadian universities', while a prestigious hotel in America announced in its advertising that 'no Hebrews or tubercular guests were received.'[11]

By the early 20th century, Australian Jewry had attained a high degree of social standing, political status and commercial success. In politics Australian Jews, who comprised less than 0.5 per cent of the population, punched above their weight. The first Jew was elected to the Victorian Parliament in 1860. By 1895 there were seven Jewish Members of Victoria's Legislative Assembly and two Members of its Legislative Council.[12] In 1930 Sir Isaac Isaacs, a former Attorney-General of the Commonwealth and Judge of the High Court, became the first Australian-born Governor-General. Isaacs, the Jewish son of a Polish tailor who had settled in London before emigrating to Melbourne in 1854, had grown up in country Victoria.[13]

The many accomplishments of Australian Jewry gained prominent notice in the *Australian Jewish Herald*, the leading community newspaper that reflected the social values and mores of the Jewish establishment. Imperial honours granted to Jews were celebrated, civic duty was praised and valued, social and cultural organisations flourished, always within the protocols and practices adopted from their British counterparts. High teas were served at charity functions, musical soirees were performed, and balls were attended.

---

[11] Gerald Tulchinsky, *Canada's Jews: A People's Journey*, Toronto: University of Toronto Press, 2008, pp.283–327; Jonathan Sarna, *American Judaism*, New Haven: Yale University Press, 2004, p.221

[12] Rutland, *Edge of the Diaspora*, p.112.

[13] Zelman Cowen, *Isaac Isaacs*, St Lucia: University of Queensland Press, 1993.

Dancing was obligatory! The social columns effused with the antics of the glitterati, the hoi polloi of this new society who enjoyed all the trappings of a good life in the colony. On the marriage of Sir John Monash's daughter the paper devoted two gushing paragraphs to descriptions of the bridal gown.[14] When a certain Madame Frances Alda Simonsen was to return home from her time abroad, the paper delighted in telling its readership that she had played Peep-Bo in Gilbert and Sullivan's *Mikado*.[15]

Yet these effusions did not denote a one-way street to assimilation. There was also encouragement of attendance at Hebrew classes and the newspaper publicised the formation of Jewish welfare and self-help organisations integral to the survival of the community, celebrated Jewish religious festivals, and advertised suppliers of kosher food. The *Jewish Herald* did not shy away from challenges facing either the local community or Jewish populations across the world. One local problem that was recognised was the rate of out-marriage. In 1911, 27 per cent of Jewish husbands in Australia had non-Jewish wives and the proportion was increasing.[16] Halacha (Jewish religious law) dictated that when a Jewish male married a gentile woman the children were not considered Jewish. Rabbi Danglow lamented this state of affairs, commenting that 'of all the evils that can descend upon Jewish lives, intermarriage is undeniably one of the worst and most to be feared and guarded against.'[17]

The *Jewish Herald* featured a plethora of articles discussing the Jewish world, including the emergence of Zionism as a political force

---

14 *Australian Jewish Herald*, 22 April 1921.
15 *Australian Jewish Herald*, 4 February 1921.
16 Rutland, *Edge of the Diaspora*, pp.141–2.
17 *Australian Jewish Herald*, 21 October 1921.

and the plight of East European Jews. Fundraising drives for victims of the Ukrainian pogrom in 1920 saw the Jewish establishment take the lead in organising donations. As Ukrainian Jewish Relief Fund President, Rabbi Danglow called upon 'each and every member of the Jewish community to respond to the call for help'.[18]

In 1928, in an attempt to address the growing number of Yiddish speakers in the community, the newspaper experimented with a one-page Yiddish supplement. Poorly executed in a hotch-potch of German, English and Yiddish words, with sections printed in different fonts, the supplement lasted just one edition.[19] Nevertheless, it was a recognition, albeit flawed, of the changing community.

Australian antisemitism

Despite its many advantages, life in the antipodes was not free of prejudice. Fierce sectarian tension between Protestants and Catholics was commonplace and to some extent displaced animosity directed at Jews. Heightened antisemitism throughout Western culture in the first decades of the 20th century did, however, have an impact on Australia, but in a benign form compared to Europe.

Australian antisemitism remained largely social and populist, tied to a distrust and dislike of the foreigner in a largely Anglo Saxon country. Aspects of European antisemitism influenced mainstream Australia. Leading literary figures Marcus Clarke, Henry Lawson and Norman Lindsay depicted stereotypical Jews as unsavoury characters with unscrupulous motives concerning money and profit. Unflattering depictions of Jews in cartoons and derogatory

---

18   *Australian Jewish Herald*, 24 June 1920.
19   Pinchas Goldhar, 'The Press of the Jewish Community in Australia', *Yiddishe Almanac 1937*, translated by D. Charak.

articles appeared in a number of newspapers and magazines, such as *Smith's Weekly*, *The Bulletin* and *Melbourne Punch*. In the 1890s, the Victorian and New South Wales trade unions opposed the immigration of Russian Jews fleeing pogroms, fearing that an influx of Jews would erode living standards. The stereotype of the Jew as archetypal capitalist, unscrupulous financier, money-lender and war profiteer gained some traction in the early Australian Labor Party. During the First World War, prominent Australian Labor Party parliamentarian Frank Anstey published a notorious pamphlet, *The Kingdom of Shylock*, in which he argued that international Jewish financiers had orchestrated the war for their own profit.[20] The blackface stage character of Mo' McCackie, the vilest parody of a long-nosed, ugly Jew, grew in popularity at the height of the Great Depression, although its working-class following may in part be explained by his mockery of the establishment and his proclivity for blue jokes. Ironically, Mo' McCackie was the creation of an Australian Jewish comedian, Roy Rene.[21]

Following the 1917 Bolshevik Revolution, antisemitism gained a further dimension. Sections of the Australian establishment and the political right grew progressively more hostile towards Jews, particularly towards recent immigrants from Europe who were feared to be Bolshevik sympathisers.[22] This dimension of antisemitism remained largely covert. John Monash experienced resentment and personal attacks towards him in the army because he was a Jew and because of his Prussian parentage. While some attacks did impede his career,

---

20   Philip Mendes, *Jews and the Left*, Basingstoke: Palgrave Macmillan, 2014, p.46.
21   John S. Levi, *Strike Me Lucky! Judaism in Australia*, Adelaide: Charles Strong Memorial Trust, 1998.
22   W.D. Rubinstein, *The Jews in Australia*, Melbourne: Australian Ethnic Heritage Series, 1986, pp.57–60.

Monash's extraordinary talents enabled him to prevail. By the 1920s he was one of the most respected Australians of the day, holding office as Chairman of the State Electricity Commission of Victoria and Vice-Chancellor of Melbourne University. It was Monash who was called upon to restore order during the bitter police strike of 1923. The appointment of Sir Isaac Isaacs to the post of Governor-General was opposed initially by King George V, but not primarily because he was a Jew. The King's concern was that he was a local, and not a member of the British aristocracy, as his predecessors, such as the Earl of Hopetoun, Baron Tennyson, Baron Northcote, the Earl of Dudley, Baron Denman, Baron Forster and Baron Stonehaven had been. Prime Minister Scullin stood his ground and the appointment was confirmed.[23]

There was limited institutional antisemitism in Australia. The Australian Stock Exchange did not elect its first Jew, Herbert Baer, until 1960. A few elite social and sporting clubs, such as the Union Club, the Australian Club, the Royal Sydney Golf Club and the Melbourne Club, refused Jewish members. Right-wing antisemitism grew in the 1930s, reflecting trends in Britain, where the British Union of Fascists had been formed under the leadership of Sir Oswald Mosley, a member of the upper class. In Australia the forerunner of the antisemitic League of Rights was founded in 1934.[24] While some opportunities were denied to Jews in Australia, it is unlikely that our Yiddishists from Eastern Europe would have cared greatly about being refused entry to the Melbourne Club.

---

23 Zelman Cowen, 'Isaacs, Sir Isaac Alfred (1855–1948)', *Australian Dictionary of Biography*, National Centre of Biography, Australian National University, http://adb.anu.edu.au/biography/isaacs-sir-isaac-alfred-6805/text11773.

24 W.D. Rubinstein, *The Jews in Australia*, p.60.

WHERE ARE WE?

Melech Ravitch, the writer, dreamer and wanderer, left Melbourne for the last time in July 1937. On his first visit he had explored the possibility of a Jewish settlement in the Kimberley region of Western Australia; on his second he had helped establish the I.L. Peretz Yiddish School. He gave his two adult children, Ruth Bergner and Yosl Bergner, who remained in Melbourne, what he thought was the greatest gift of all – Australia – so regarded despite the many challenges that faced immigrant arrivals in times of economic turmoil. He told his son: 'My job is done. I can now go further on my own. I brought you to this beautiful world, and here I opened for you the door to the most beautiful garden – the door of the Australian continent, the youngest and most beautiful of them all.'[25]

---

25 Ravitch, 'Australia and I'.

Chapter 3

OLD WORLD, NEW WORLD

In Yiddish they called it *der alter heym* – the old home. For Eastern European Jews it meant more than bricks and mortar. The 'old home' was the land of their birth, where their ancestral roots were firmly planted. *Der alter heym* pulled at the very heart of a life once lived.

The home town where Yiddish journalist Shmuel Benet (later Bennett) spent his formative years was Radom, a hive of Jewish activity. Ninety-three kilometres south of Warsaw, Radom was no great metropolis; by 1931 it was home to 25,159 Jews, constituting 32 per cent of the total population of 77,902. But it was a far cry from Melbourne at the time, with its population of less than 9,000 Jews. By all accounts Radom was a lively, bustling city of considerable Jewish commercial and industrial enterprise, one that was also steeped in orthodox Chasidic tradition. While the Jews always faced challenges, Jewish life flourished. As Bennett recalled, 'The Jews of Radom formed a world in miniature. Among their number were writers, musicians, scholars, rabbis, painters, artisans, doctors, rich and poor Jews; in the words of a Yiddish saying, "Jews for every day of the week".'[1] It was a world that stood for all its Jews: 'Ordinary, poor, working Jews, right down to the pack-carriers and slaughterhouse

---

1   Shmuel Bennett, *Chronicles of a Life*, Melbourne: S. Bennett, 1999, p.47.

workers, took part in the daily traditional life of the community.'[2] It was a world that encompassed 1,000 years of often-turbulent Jewish existence on Polish soil; until it was obliterated by the Nazi onslaught, Jewish Radom was, like so many towns and cities where Jews lived, a world that had endured.

Throughout the 1920s and 1930s Radomer Jews were employed in the trades and small crafts; they were hairdressers, cap-makers, jewellers, tailors, shoemakers, saddlers, painters, box-makers, carpenters, sheet-metal workers, watchmakers and printers. There were shopkeepers too: haberdashers, businesses that sold household commodities, butchers, bakers and grocers. Most cake shops were owned by Jews. Industrial plants such as tanneries and brickyards were also owned by pioneering Jewish entrepreneurs. There were Jewish doctors, lawyers and officials. By 1925, Jewish Radom boasted its own merchant and artisan banks, trade unions, welfare organisations, a hospital, a Jewish orphans' home and an aged-care home. In the interwar period Radom Jewry sustained over 100 organisations and social institutions, a Yiddish theatre, as well as an artistic and literary society.[3]

In Radom political rivalries played out against the backdrop of Jewish nationalist movements that had swept through Poland. There were Zionist organisations, notably the Orthodox Agudas Yisroel, which supported religious Zionism and in the interwar period organised training camps for life in Palestine, the socialist organisations, including the Bund, and the Poale Zion. The first *yeshivah*, an institution of Jewish religious learning, was founded in 1908. There were twelve private prayer houses (*shtiblekh*), several primary and

---

2 Bennett, *Chronicles of a Life*, p.19.
3 'Radom', *Jewish Virtual Library*, http://www.jewishvirtuallibrary.org/radom, accessed 2 April 2018.

secondary schools and five libraries. Yiddish newspapers included the daily *Radomer Tsaytung* (until 1925), the weekly *Radomer Lebn* (later *Radomer-Keltser Lebn*), the *Radomer Shtime*, and there was a Polish paper, *Trybuna*, as well.[4] Radom represented a microcosm of what life was like for religiously observant, cultural Jews such as Shmuel Bennett. A full and rich life immersed in *Yiddishkeit*. A world within a world! A world borne of necessity. It all had to do with survival.

Antisemitism in Poland

While Jewish life flourished in Poland, it was also subject to virulent antisemitism. Shmuel Bennett's memories of Polish antisemitism were from his earliest school days, when the classroom atmosphere was 'full of hate', particularly following the Catholic priest's visit. He remembered assaults in the streets 'when Polish boys took it into their heads to seek us out for "fun".'[5]

By the late 19th century, political groups throughout Europe sought to restrict the roles that Jews could undertake in economic and cultural life. This was to a large extent in response to Jewish emancipation and heightened Jewish visibility in many walks of life. The antisemitic groups that formed in Germany rapidly moved east to engulf the Hapsburg and Russian empires. Government-sanctioned political parties pledging action against Jewish 'infiltration', the consequences of the rights and freedoms of emancipation, fed into a broad spectrum of deep-seated anti-Jewish prejudice. The popularity and political influence of these parties grew. The result was widespread riots, street

---

4 'Radom', *Virtual Shtetl*, POLIN Museum of the History of Polish Jews, https://sztetl.org.pl/en/towns/r/601-radom/99-history/137920-history-of-community, accessed 2 April 2018.

5 Bennett, *Chronicles of a Life*, pp.66–7.

violence and boycotts of Jewish businesses, charges of blood libel in which Jews were accused of using Christian blood for their rituals, and the distribution of poisonous antisemitic publications such as the notorious 1905 *Protocols of the Elders of Zion* which helped fuel conspiracy theories concerning Jewish global domination. A murderous wave of pogroms followed the assassination of Czar Alexander II on 13 March 1881, predictably blamed on the Jews. The Kishinev Passover pogrom of 1903 was particularly brutal. Nearly 50 Jews were murdered and hundreds injured; some 1,500 homes and businesses were looted or destroyed.[6] Kishinev caught world attention and brought home the perilous circumstances in which Jews lived. It was headlined in *The New York Times* and inspired Chaim Nachman Bialik's epic poem 'In the City of Slaughter.'[7]

During the First World War and the years following, the Jews of Eastern Europe were caught in a catastrophic period of political upheaval, devastating economic conditions, civil wars, and the fall of empires. Pogroms in Eastern Europe between 1917 and 1921 caused the death of approximately 60,000 Jews and resulted in the significant movement of displaced Jewish populations. Between 1921 and 1925, 400,000 Jews left Europe, 280,000 of them going to the United States of America. In 1921, 120,000 Jews arrived in the United States, constituting 15 per cent of all immigrants for that year. Between 1919 and 1926 nearly 100,000 Jews immigrated to the British Mandate of Palestine.[8]

---

6   Dan Cohn-Sherbok, *Anti-Semitism*, Stroud, Gloucestershire: History Press, 2009, pp.231–49.
7   H.N. Bialik, 'The City of Slaughter', in *Complete Poetic Works of Hayyim Nahman Bialik* edited by Israel Efros, Vol. I, New York: Histadruth Ivrith of America, 1948, pp.129–43.
8   'Pogroms', *The YIVO Encyclopedia of Jews in Eastern Europe*, http://www.yivoencyclopedia.org/article.aspx/Pogroms, accessed 2 April 2018; *Encyclopaedia*

Immigration to Australia

Jewish communal organisations around the world responded to Jewish suffering with aid programs and fundraising campaigns to alleviate the hardships endured by Eastern European Jews. In general, their assistance took the form of sending money and supplies to communities trapped in devastating circumstances. Leaders of the Jewish community in Great Britain took further action. On 6 May 1921, a joint committee of British Jewry wrote to Britain's Secretary of State, Winston Churchill, imploring the British government to assist with the 'grave emergency which has arisen in connection with the emigration of Jews from the devastated regions of Eastern Europe'. The memorandum went on to describe the desperate plight of some 40,000 Jewish refugees from the Ukraine flooding into Poland awaiting further resettlement. Its writers assured Churchill that these Jews were 'anti-Bolshevik' and 'predominantly traders', and asked if there was the possibility of 'opening some of the British dominions and colonies to a fixed number of selected emigrants under suitable guarantees.' Further to this, the joint committee was prepared 'to organise the necessary machinery for sheltering, transporting, receiving and settling the emigrants', clearly emphasising that Jewish agencies would bear the cost of resettlement.[9]

The British government simply passed the request to the Dominions, without making any recommendations. The memorandum reached the Australian Prime Minister's Department from the High Commissioner

---

Judaica, edited by Michael Berenbaum and Fred Skolnik (2nd ed.), Detroit: Macmillan Reference USA, 2007, Vol. 16, pp.279–282.

[9] Joint Foreign Committee of the Jewish Board of Deputies and the Anglo-Jewish Association, London, Memorandum to Secretary of State, 6 May 1921 (National Archives of Australia (NAA), Series A434, 1949/3/3196).

in London. The government's response was a flat refusal, on grounds that Australia did 'not permit the entry of Russians' and therefore 'no encouragement can be given to the immigration of these people to Australia.' On 1 June 1921 the High Commissioner's office received further notice from the Prime Minister's Department that:

> the immediate requirements of the Commonwealth are being met by immigration of ex-servicemen whose passages are paid by the British government, in addition to large numbers of British immigrants which are being nominated by relatives and friends. Immigration of refugee Jews would involve exclusion of some of these British emigrants. Commonwealth Government therefore regrets inability to co-operate.[10]

While Australia was a free and open society, it sheltered behind strict immigration controls and exclusions under the White Australia policy. Throughout the 1920s and 30s the Australian Government not only controlled the number of immigrants it allowed into the country but also policed their nationality and race.

Racial understandings formed the basis of immigration policy; a racial hierarchy determined eligibility for entry and priorities.[11] In the 1920s the government was increasingly concerned to stem the flow of southern and eastern Europeans.[12] Jewish immigration, in particular of the Yiddish speakers of Poland, was greatly impacted by this. Despite there being no official quota limiting Jewish immigration to Australia in the 1920s, there was a preference for immigrants

---

10 Prime Minister's Dept to High Commissioner's Office, London, Cablegram, 1 June 1921 (NAA, Series A434, 1949/3/3196).

11 James Jupp, *From White Australia to Woomera: The Story of Australian Immigration*, Melbourne: Cambridge University Press, 2002, pp.6–10; Andrew Markus, *Australian Race Relations*, St. Leonards, NSW: Allen & Unwin, 1994.

12 Charles A. Price, *Southern Europeans in Australia*, Melbourne: Oxford University Press, 1963, pp.83–139.

of British and northern European stock. In the mid-1920s unofficial restrictions were exercised on Australia's behalf by British consular staff in Poland to restrict what was seen as a potentially large flow of Polish Jews to Australia.[13] Australian authorities gave discretionary power to British passport control officers to vet prospective Polish Jewish immigrants who represented a 'peculiarly backward class' and to subjectively gauge their suitability before their applications were received by Australian representatives.[14]

Without enforcing a numerical quota, three priorities were stipulated for possible visa approval. These were: agriculturalists with capital and/or skilled labourers with a working knowledge of English; those with Australian guarantors for employment and financial support; and those with sufficient landing money (£40 in 1925) who were deemed persons of 'superior standing' with a good education and a working knowledge of English. Persons who could not comply with one or more of these requirements could be refused a visa. In addition, while assisted passages were provided to many immigrants from England, all non-British migrants had to pay their own fares.[15]

Thus under this policy, visas to Australia were restricted to those who were either able to prove financial independence, were of superior standing or were sponsored by family members or friends already living here. Jewish immigrants who came to Australia in the 1920s did so under these terms. As was always the case, Jews had to fall back on their own resources and that of their fellow Jews to meet official

---

13   H. Rubinstein, *The Jews In Australia*, p.146; Paul Bartrop, '"Good Jews and Bad Jews": Australian Perceptions of Jewish Migrants and Refugees, 1919–1939', in *Jews in the Sixth Continent*, edited by W.D. Rubinstein, Sydney: Allen & Unwin, 1987, pp.169–184; NAA, Series A434, 1949/3/3196.

14   F.J. Quinlan, Prime Minister's Dept, Memorandum to Official Secretary, Australian High Commission, London, 3 October 1925 (NAA, Series A434, 1949/3/3196).

15   F.J. Quinlan, Memorandum.

and unofficial government requirements for resettlement. Some 2,000 Jews, the vast majority of whom were Yiddish speakers from Eastern Europe, managed to jump these hurdles in the 1920s.

The increasing number of new Jewish arrivals in the 1920s put significant pressure on philanthropic organisations. The need to house, feed and find accommodation for these new Eastern European immigrants prompted members of the community to spring into action. This time it was European Jews who had found refuge in Melbourne in an earlier period who took the reins. 'When in 1922 another wave of immigrants appeared, Kadimah did not stand idly by', Samuel Wynn, President of the Kadimah at the time, himself a Yiddish-speaking immigrant who had arrived in 1913, recalled:

> Partly under its control the Jewish Welcome Society came into existence ... Its task was to meet every ship, to find work and accommodation for the new arrivals (a course for learning basic English was also organised) and in general to make the new immigrant who has no one to look after him a little more at home.[16]

By 1926 the small band of volunteers was struggling to cope with the load. Indicative of how the community could pull together in spite of inherent differences, tireless community worker Lucy Hallenstein, a member of the Jewish establishment who had lost a son in the First World War and was often to be seen in Melbourne's affluent suburbs in her chauffeur-driven green Rolls Royce, stepped in and formed the Women's Auxiliary to assist the Welcome Society with its workload.[17] The Welcome Society remained an effective relief organisation

---

16 Samuel Wynn, 'The Melbourne Kadimah', *Yiddishe Almanac 1937*, translated by M. Lipkies.
17 Rapke, 'The Pre-War Jewish Community of Melbourne', p.295.

assisting new arrivals until 1930 when, as the Great Depression decimated the economic life of the country, immigration came to a virtual standstill.

Building a community

The Poylishe Yidn brought with them to this distant land an understanding of how their communities in Poland had functioned and survived through the ages. The fiercely independent, self-contained communities that thrived in pre-war Poland were a direct result of conditions of life as a subject people; their lives had to be self-sustaining, resilient and independent, lived in conditions of enforced separation from many of their Polish compatriots. It was almost impossible to be both a Pole and a Jew at the same time.

Born of necessity, Eastern European Jews were great institution builders. They created their own space in their parallel world. In the major centres of population they sustained a remarkable number of organisations that looked after the young and the old, the religious and the secular, the political and the non-political. They created a range of associations that sought to take care of the most urgent needs from the cradle to the grave. In the interwar period in Cracow, the 60,000 Jews of the city ran more than 300 institutions. They invested heavily in what one historian described, using the concept of 'social capital', as relationship networks among people who lived and worked in a particular society, enabling that group of people to function and survive.[18] These organisations had their origins in the Middle Ages when Jews were prohibited to live amongst the gentile population. Their *kehilot* were governing councils whose main

---

18   Wasserman, *On The Eve*, p.20.

responsibilities were collecting taxes and securing military recruits. Even though the need for such governance broke down by the middle of the 18th century, the tradition of self-governance remained an entrenched feature of Jewish life well into the 20th century.

The *kehile* of Western Europe functioned differently to their Eastern European counterparts. The *kehilot* of France, Italy, the Netherlands and Britain were controlled by congregational organisations. The synagogue hierarchy was the ruling authority. In the East, the modern *kehile* was a municipal council elected in what was an often fiercely contested election. This enabled and empowered a range of Jewish political parties, both religious and secular. While it also fostered political rivalries, it promoted political ambition. These *kehilot* quickly became a hotbed of political ideologies and activism. In the interwar period, the *kehilot* were reinstated in Poland's Second Republic as all-embracing modern, secular and religious institutions.

Some 900 *kehilot* operated in Poland.[19] They had recognised legal status and were able to tax their constituents. They operated with limited autonomy but were able to support religious institutions and after 1928 were allowed to fund a number of social welfare associations. The *kehile* of Warsaw, a particularly robust, volatile and dynamic organisation, consisted of fifty elected representatives from a number of political parties, including Agudas Yisroel, three different Chasidic parties, Zionists, Mizrahi, Revisionist Zionists, the Bund, Folkspartei, Poale Zion Right, Poale Zion Left, and assimilationists and philanthropic organisations. Polish Jews were clearly uninhibited in promoting and prosecuting their varying views and contested ideologies. Smaller towns and *shtetlekh* had *kehilot* that operated on more

---

19   Wasserman, *On The Eve*, p.21.

limited lines than those of the larger cities; although their source of revenue was often the same, it was smaller, their primary concern being the maintenance of religious institutions and the rabbi's salary.[20]

The Jews who came to Australia in the interwar period were predominantly from the larger towns and cities with well-established democratically elected *kehilot*, which managed and addressed the religious, political, social and communal needs of its constituents. These Jews had tasted the freedom and diversity that stemmed from democratically elected institutions where Jews could be equal partners amongst themselves in the decision-making processes that directly affected them. It also provided a highly transportable template for governance and communal organisation. Sender Burstin explained the effectiveness of the *kehile* as a political and communal model. He also hinted at its rather volatile nature:

> In *der alter heym* the *kehile* was a public and legal institution that was recognised by the state. Whether he wanted to or not, every Jew was obliged to belong to it. The *kehile* had the authority to impose taxes on the Jewish population and to incur expenses as it deemed appropriate. So it is obvious that the various Jewish parties and groups would seek election to the *kehile* in order to influence its actions.[21]

Jewish immigrants from Eastern Europe arriving in Australia throughout the 1920s and 1930s brought these communal traits with them. Initially they did not challenge the existing Jewish hegemony;

---

20 Samuel Kassow, 'The Interwar *Shtetl*', in *The Jews of Poland Between Two World Wars*, edited by Yisrael Gutman et al., Hanover, NH: University of New England, 1989, p.211.

21 Sender Burstin, 'Towards a Democratically Elected *Kehile*', in his *Yiddish Melbourne Observed*, translated by Ben and David Burstin, Australian Centre for Jewish Civilisation, Monash University, 2013, p.139.

rather, they developed a number of parallel communal structures as they had in Poland, ones that best suited their needs and their lifestyle and that reinforced their own regionality. They brought with them an understanding and experience of their highly organised *kehilot*. The implications of transplanting such a communal model into the Australian environment led to inevitable conflict. The newcomers chose the path of secular, democratic communal governance in what could be a fiercely competitive environment, rather than the more conservative, exclusive form of synagogue-based representation promoted by the established, uncontested and self-elected Melbourne Jewish community. This form of democratic governance gave the Yiddishists a voice and a means of exercising control over their own affairs. It was an entirely different way of doing things, and it would have considerable consequences.

Not only did the Yiddishists seek to do things differently. In Jewish Melbourne after 1918 there was a proliferation of social and political organisations and a growth of communal networks that reflected an expanding and extremely diverse, often secular, community that saw various ways in which to express Jewish identity. It was the beginnings of a struggle for supremacy, in which control of the community by religious organisations was challenged and ultimately defeated by secular communal bodies. Each group had a vested interest in deciding how the community was run and how to control and coordinate their various activities. The Yiddishists were experienced in living within such a diverse community while retaining their own distinct ethos. They thrived in such a competitive environment. The origins of Melbourne's pluralist Jewish community of today can be traced to this period.

Yiddishists find a communal home

The Kadimah (a Hebrew word meaning 'forward') was founded in 1911 by 14 newly arrived Jews from Eastern Europe and Russia, who undertook the task of establishing a Jewish library, initially in central Melbourne at 59 Bourke Street. What began as a relatively modest pursuit started by a handful of cultural enthusiasts attracted 200 Jews with divergent backgrounds and opinions to its first annual meeting in the following year. Not all those attending were enamoured with the cultural milieu that the Yiddish language and those who spoke it represented. The majority were establishment Jews, the 'top hats' as they were called, who preferred a Jewish centre that reflected them and in which English was the preferred *lingua franca*. As the number of Yiddish-speaking Jews was still small, the majority view prevailed.

Eastern European Yiddishists found in the Kadimah an organisation that addressed their many needs. It was no *kehile*, but it did provide a secular oasis for the culturally starved immigrant; it offered the familiar, a home, a part of *der alter heym*. It had a governing body with elected office-bearers. It provided the gateway to the type of institution that could be shaped and moulded to represent them – an institution that was relevant to their lives, that was for them and by them. Over the years the Kadimah would undergo a process of change and adaptation. In a relatively short time the Yiddishists made it their own and never relinquished its tenure. As Shmuel Bennett recalled, 'The old and the new immigrants came to the Kadimah for a serving of Yiddish culture in the form of a lecture or a play, or to sit in the library over a Yiddish book or Yiddish newspapers and magazines from overseas.'[22]

---

22 Bennett, *Chronicles of a Life*, p.278.

Even in the early years the Yiddish presence was evident. In 1921 the illustrious Yiddish writer Peretz Hirshbein visited Melbourne with his wife, Yiddish poet Esther Shumiatcher Hirshbein, for a series of lectures. He recalled the vibrant atmosphere of the Kadimah: 'I was taken from the train straight to a library and large lecture hall. Modern books. Yiddish, Hebrew, Yiddish newspapers, from all corners of the world. The language is a lively one. The questions are also lively, relevant, topical ones, bound up intimately with Jewish life throughout the world.'[23]

But ownership is often won through struggle, and so it was with the Kadimah. What initially began as a power struggle between the establishment and the Yiddish-speaking newcomers was resolved in 1917 with the election of Zionist advocate and Lodz-born Yiddishist Samuel Wynn as president, a position he held twelve times between 1917 and 1933. Although small in stature, Wynn, a tenacious leader and combative activist, had a personality that was larger than life. He was also a rebel. At the age of 14 he thumbed his nose at the religious orthodox establishment by openly smoking a cigarette on the Sabbath. He was attracted to liberal and radical writers, especially Tolstoy. Wynn was no stranger to political struggles, his older brother having been a militant socialist who was imprisoned during the failed 1905 Russian revolution.[24]

Once the Kadimah had rid itself of the 'conservative' establishment elements in its ranks it was faced with a new battle concerning language and ideology. It was a battle between the Zionists, who agitated for Hebrew, and the Yiddishists, who felt that Yiddish would provide the

---

[23] Peretz Hirshbein, 'Travel Stories: Pictures', in *Australian Yiddishe Almanac, 1937*, p.84.

[24] David Dunstan, 'Wynn, Samuel (1891–1982)', *Australian Dictionary of Biography*, National Centre of Biography, Australian National University, http://adb.anu.edu.au/biography/wynn-samuel-9207.

best means for building a new community in this far-flung corner of the globe. In an act of compromise, the Kadimah made room for all languages; there were English lessons for new arrivals, alongside lectures on Yiddish and Hebrew literature and on various aspects of Australian life. Dealing with conflicting ideologies was another matter altogether.

The Kadimah sealed its place in the Yiddish community when, in 1915, it relocated to 313 Drummond Street Carlton, the pulsating heart of Yiddish life in Melbourne, where the sweet smell of freshly baked onion rolls, *pletslekh*, mixed well with the 'hard bread of an immigrant in a strange faraway country'.[25] But this did not spell the end of disputation, as there were more battles to be fought.

1917 was a momentous year in Jewish life. The Bolshevik Revolution captured the imagination of Melbourne's Jewish left-wing activists. The Balfour Declaration on Palestine, in the same year, energised the Zionists and, as was to be expected, the Kadimah became the battleground for the contest of ideas. Both factions fought for the allegiance of the Kadimah, testament to its growing communal influence and status. The Zionists won a battle in 1919 when the Kadimah amalgamated with the Zionist movement *Hatkhia* (The Revival), an alliance that held until 1926. From then on, the growing number of Yiddishists heralded a new era of renewal for the Kadimah and fomented its place as an institution for Yiddish culture, increasingly reflecting and addressing the growing educational, social and cultural needs of the expanding Yiddish-speaking community.

In an attempt to involve the younger generation in cultural life, the Kadimah Younger Set was founded in 1928. Activities, largely conducted in Yiddish, included hikes, sporting competitions, amateur

---

25   Pinchas Goldhar, cited in *Yiddish Melbourne: Towards a History*, edited by Andrew Markus and Danielle Charak, Melbourne: Monash University, 2008, p.16.

theatre, dances and other social events. The Younger Set ran regular Friday night functions at the upper Kadimah hall. Jewish writers such as Pinchas Goldhar and Herz Bergner would often visit as guest speakers on these evenings. Also appearing at the Friday night functions were young Australian writers, including Alan Marshall, who later won fame for his book, *I Can Jump Puddles*, and formed a close bond with Shmuel Bennett.

The Kadimah once again outgrew its premises and the foundation stone for a new centre was laid in Lygon Street, North Carlton in September 1932, in the middle of the Great Depression. This too courted controversy; in an act that trumpeted the Kadimah's secular stance, no Jewish prayer was recited at the laying of the foundation stone, which drew the ire of Rabbi Brodie of the Melbourne Synagogue. Notwithstanding the lack of rabbinic blessing, the Kadimah celebrated the opening of its new expanded premises on 25 March 1933 and renamed itself the Jewish Cultural Centre and National Library "Kadimah". The opening celebrations also sparked fierce criticism of another kind – this time from one of their own. The lack of spoken Yiddish at the inauguration angered the Yiddish writer Pinchas Goldhar, a very vocal advocate of Yiddish in Melbourne at the time. As he recalled,

> The Kadimah opening was nothing other than a bitter disappointment for the friends of the Yiddish language and culture. Yiddish is much more than the means that carries the new Jewish awareness, Yiddish is not only the forum, it is the content, the very soul of our current work and being. Yiddish is not only our tool, but it is the hand that scratches out our existence.[26]

---

26   Quoted in Pam Maclean, 'Pinchas Goldhar: His Yiddishist Vision – a Flawed Nationalism?', *Australian Journal of Jewish Studies*, Vol. 5, No. 1 (1991): p.21.

Samuel Wynn responded to Goldhar's criticisms by arguing that pragmatism demanded that the Kadimah broaden its horizons beyond its Yiddish language base. This did not imply the dilution of Yiddish, which formed the bedrock of the Kadimah's operations. Wynn argued, 'This does not mean, God forbid, that Yiddish is to be treated like some sort of stepchild at the Kadimah. Quite the opposite, Yiddish functions and books hold the most highly honoured place in our halls, libraries and our calendar of activities.'[27]

The use of Yiddish in public forums would be a recurring point of contention for years to come, but it was a fight the Yiddishists refused to concede. Between 1912 and 1932 the Kadimah annual reports were published in English. In 1933, the report was published in both English and Yiddish for the first time, and much of its activity was conducted in Yiddish thereafter. By the late 1930s, the paid membership of the Kadimah had grown to 360. A great many more attended its functions – public lectures, literary and musical evenings, concerts, Yiddish theatre, community groups, and an annual fundraising bazaar. Its much-used library housed more than 2,000 books and its reading room received the major Jewish newspapers and periodicals from overseas.[28] As we shall see, many of the cultural, artistic and literary initiatives that enriched the community sprang from the Kadimah's precinct.

The newcomers

A number of exceptional individuals arrived in Melbourne from the 1910s to the outbreak of the Second World War; they were to

---

27   Maclean, 'Pinchas Goldhar'.
28   Kadimah Annual Report 1938.

exercise an influence on the community far beyond their numbers. Many of them would not have considered leaving Europe but for the exceptional circumstances that made life there perilous. Some were forthright political leaders and tenacious activists – game-changers and disruptors who were able to create and adapt their environment to reconstruct the type of communities they knew in *der alter heym*, in the lands they had been forced to leave. Among them were Kadimah president and State Zionist Council president Samuel Wynn who arrived in 1913, Kadimah presidents Samuel (Simche) Brilliant and Israel Sher in 1914, Bundist and founding member of the I.L. Peretz School Myer Silman in 1922, Kadimah presidents and Zionists Aron Patkin and Yehuda Honig in 1926, Jewish Welfare stalwart Jonas Pushett and Bialystok community leader and mediator Michael Pitt in 1927, Kadimah president, Jewish Welfare leader and staunch Zionist Leo Fink, and Bund leader, community activist and welfare advocate Sender Burstin in 1928.

Yiddishkeit sat at the core of these newcomers' being. Amongst those who sought new horizons far from the turmoil of Eastern Europe were Yiddish writers, actors and teachers. They not only created new spaces for cultural enhancement, but also challenged the standards and norms of what was considered entertainment, literature and art. Literature and theatre were not just superficial indulgences or optional extras, but the life-blood of their existence. As will be discussed, they developed a thriving theatre and a Yiddish school, expanding and enriching the community. The writer Pinchas Goldhar arrived from Lodz in 1928. Yitzhak Kahn who arrived in 1937, Herz Bergner in 1938, and Yiddish journalist Shmuel Bennett in 1939 joined the ranks of writers before the outbreak of war. Yiddish theatre was enlivened with the addition of professional actors such as

Yankev Ginter who arrived from Lodz in 1928, Abraham Braizblatt who arrived from Warsaw in 1937, the legendary Yankev Waislitz and Rachel Holzer both former members of the Vilner Trupe who came to Australia from Warsaw as part of world tours in 1938 and 1939 respectively, and the actor and teacher Yasha Sher in 1939. Yiddish education was spearheaded by a leading educator from Vilna, Joseph Giligich, who arrived in 1938.

These Yiddish-speaking Jews from the *shtetlekh* and cities of Eastern Europe were a highly distinctive immigrant group, a group that could not be defined simply as economic immigrants nor, strictly speaking, as refugees. What we witness here is the transplantation of an entire civilisation that had adapted, survived and flourished under circumstances that were often abysmal and threatened life and livelihood. By 1939 these immigrants had left their mark in laying the foundations for the communal structures, organisations and cultural institutions that came to define the Melbourne Jewish community for decades to come and were embraced and further developed by the next wave of eastern European immigrants, the Holocaust survivors.

A new Yiddish consciousness

By the mid-1930s conditions and circumstances in Melbourne were conducive to the creation of several key Yiddish institutions – a Yiddish school, a Yiddish newspaper and a broader offering of Yiddish theatre and literature. While these cultural institutions formed the backbone of this community of newcomers, its Yiddish consciousness, its *Yiddishkeit* was something more intangible. This community embraced a full sense of being, a sense that the richness of cultural and political life that they had known in Poland could also find expression here in Melbourne; it was an old civilisation in a new land.

Shmuel Bennett recalled, 'For the Jewish newcomers of those times, Australia was the land of dreams, yet the Carlton reality was as close to their old life as they could achieve.'[29]

When Shmuel Bennett's family arrived in Carlton in 1939, his enterprising mother immediately established in their home a kosher community restaurant and boarding house for single Jewish men, which quickly became something of an institution – 'Before we knew it, a restaurant attracting many customers every day was in full swing.'[30] Here at Mrs Bennett's dining tables, set up in the midst of a modest Jewish home, sat Yiddish writers, thinkers, political activists and even rabbis. Herz Bergner would sit alongside Rabbi Wishkowski. Here, Samuel Wynn, by then a Jew of considerable wealth and reputation, would regularly come for 'a homely kosher meal.'[31] Here, Wynn and his compatriots were reminded of another time and place. In a corner of Melbourne, in Carlton, they could dream of *der alter heym*.

---

29 Bennett, *Chronicles of a Life*, p.277.
30 Bennett, *Chronicles of a Life*, p.287.
31 Bennett, *Chronicles of a Life*, p.287.

Chapter 4

YIDDISH UNDER THE SOUTHERN CROSS

Picture this. The year was 1938; the scene, the Princess Theatre in Spring Street, Melbourne. There, on the stage, in front of a capacity audience of 1,500 theatregoers, the Yiddishe Bine players presented S. Ansky's mystical four-act play, *The Dybbuk*, one of the most celebrated plays in Yiddish theatre. The audience was transfixed. The staging was innovative and the settings majestic. This was Yiddish theatre at its best. Here was a blend of myth and Chasidic legend in modern form – an expressionist pageant of dancing beggars, choral speeches and choreographed choruses. The show was a sensation.[1]

Subtitled *Tsvishn Tsvey Veltn* (Between Two Worlds), the play tells the tale of a young Chasidic bride who is possessed by the spirit of her former dead lover, a *dybbuk*. The *dybbuk* is a creature of Jewish folklore, a disembodied soul that wanders relentlessly until it finds a haven in a living person. The only way to rid the body of its possessed spirit is through an act of exorcism. *The Dybbuk* is a tragic story of unrequited love, of wandering souls who move between the living and the dead, forced to inhabit two irreconcilable worlds.[2]

---

1   Arnold Zable, *Wanderers and Dreamers: Tales of the David Herman Theatre*, Melbourne: Hyland House, 1998, p.16.
2   'Dybbuk, The', *The YIVO Encyclopedia of Jews in Eastern Europe*, http://www.yivoencyclopedia.org/article.aspx/Dybbuk_The, accessed 3 April 2018.

The production was a showcase for its director and lead performer, the recently arrived world-famous professional Yiddish actor, Yankev Waislitz. The play struck a chord with the audience, predominantly made up of Jewish wanderers who themselves straddled two worlds: the *shtetl* world of their past and the new world of Australia.

The resounding success of *The Dybbuk* was a clear indication that a new, culturally diverse Jewish community was thriving in Melbourne, as a result of a repositioning of Jewish cultural life that took place in a remarkably short period of time. The Yiddishist newcomers had carved out a new cultural space within a highly organised, long-established Jewish community that had very different cultural needs from its own. Here was a radical reimagining of the way Jewish life could be lived through different cultural enactments. In weaving its old-world sensibilities into the Australian Jewish landscape, these new immigrants created a new space in which they could uphold their cherished culture and language.

A distinctive feature of this Yiddish-speaking immigrant community was their drive to recreate the world they had left behind in Eastern Europe. No other European immigrant group in Melbourne had ever attempted the transplantation of an entire civilisation. These Yiddish immigrants imported an all-inclusive way of life in which their Jewishness was expressed through their cultural identity, an identity that was conveyed through secular rather than religious channels. This identity was articulated through Yiddish theatre, Yiddish literature, a Yiddish press and Yiddish education. Cultural expression embraced every facet of their lives. It was how they defined themselves. There was no delineation between their daily existence and forms of cultural expression. Everything was entwined and encased in the world of Yiddish. Yiddish was the language of life.

This nexus between Yiddish culture, identity and daily life was not shared by all Jews living in Melbourne. The established Jewish community did not express their Jewishness in the same all-embracing manner. There were distinct demarcations between how they expressed their Jewish identity and their Australian sensibilities. Indeed, many Jews compartmentalised their religion so as not to disrupt the flow of daily life. Adelaide-born industrial chemist Isaac H. Boas, doyen of the established Jewish community, was remembered as someone who 'regarded himself as a Jew from 10 to 12 on a Saturday morning. The rest of the week he was an Australian and a man's religion in his daily life was irrelevant. He deplored any form of public attention being attracted to the Jewish community.'[3]

For Jews such as Boas, Yiddish language and culture were totally irrelevant; they were indeed, an unwelcome distraction that drew public attention to a point of difference. In the minds of others, you were a Jew when you went to synagogue and prayed in Hebrew, and that was it. Otherwise you spoke the King's English, read English-language newspapers, enjoyed local theatre, a recital or soiree, and, if you preferred light comic opera, Gilbert and Sullivan was a favourite. If you wanted to entertain your young children, a Cinderella pantomime was just the thing. The established Jewish community never attempted to transpose a radically different cultural heritage onto Melbourne society. Instead, they adapted to and integrated with their Australian compatriots and, broadly

---

[3] Throughout the 1920s and 1930s Isaac Boas was a Treasurer and President of the St Kilda Hebrew congregation and a Chairman of the Victorian Advisory Board; see Trevor Rapke, 'The Prewar Jewish Community of Melbourne', pp.296–7.

speaking, their assimilation was successful. Religious ritual and religious observance was the only feature that set these Jews apart. But with the arrival of the Yiddishists, Jews began to express their culture and religion in vastly different ways. As a consequence, the cultural fabric of Jewish life in Melbourne became richer, more diverse and more complex.

The vibrancy of Yiddish theatre

Yiddish theatre in Melbourne played the greatest role in creating this new cultural space. It was highly visible, accessible and its reach was extensive. Following trends in Yiddish culture in Poland, the Melbourne Yiddish cultural scene in the interwar period underwent a process of professionalisation and internationalisation. Specifically, Yiddish plays represented the finest traditions of modern European theatre, in both content and performance. More than half of the repertoire of the Warsaw Yiddish Art Theatre consisted of translations that included the works of Molière, Chekhov and Dostoevsky.

Yankev Waislitz invigorated and expanded Melbourne's theatrical repertoire and lifted the performance standard of Yiddish productions. Waislitz was part of a Yiddish theatrical tradition that broke new ground in Poland. In 1919, he joined the modernist Vilna Troupe, founded during the First World War. This group of actors transformed Yiddish theatre, performing in a standardised Lithuanian (Litvish) Yiddish and employing the innovative Stanislavsky method of characterisation, which relied on actors living the experience rather than merely representing it. The Vilna Troupe performed plays from the greatest Yiddish writers, bringing contemporary and topical issues to its audiences, enthralling them with their professionalism and the high standard of production. Waislitz remained with the Troupe until it disbanded in 1935.[4]

On 26 January 1938, Yankev Waislitz disembarked at Port Melbourne as part of a world tour. He had no intention of staying in Melbourne permanently, but the winds of change were blowing and he would be swept up in them. Towards the end of 1938, following a 10-month schedule of 37 one-man shows and theatrical performances in Melbourne and Sydney, Waislitz sailed for Brazil to continue his world tour. It was his good fortune that he did not make it back to Europe; the outbreak of war forced him to cut his tour short and he returned to Melbourne in 1940, to the city that had taken him to its heart. Waislitz was impressed with the openness of this new, free society and how his fellow Yiddishists had managed to forge a new life steeped in *Yiddishkeit*. He decided to call Melbourne home. By 1940 Europe was burning.

Cracow-born Rachel Holzer arrived in Melbourne for a series of shows on 2 April 1939. A renowned professional Yiddish actress of international standing, Holzer instilled a new awareness of what the very best of European Yiddish theatre could offer. She preferred plays that grappled with relevant contemporary issues, plays that resonated with her audience. In some respects she was ahead of her times.[5] Holzer's one-woman show on 15 April was lauded by her audience and by Melbourne's theatre critics. Writing in *The Argus*, George Hutton pronounced her 'an artist of distinction and the product of a

---

[4] Debra Caplan, 'The Sun Never Sets on the Vilna Troupe', *Pakn Treger: Magazine of the Yiddish Book Center*, Summer 2014, http://www.yiddishbookcenter.org/language-literature-culture/pakn-treger/sun-never-sets-vilna-troupe, accessed 4 April 2018; 'Vilna Trupe', *The YIVO Encyclopedia of Jews in Eastern Europe*, http://www.yivoencyclopedia.org/article.aspx/Vilner_Trupe, accessed 4 April 2018.

[5] Arnold Zable, 'Queen of the Yiddish Stage', *Australian Jewish News*, 4 December 1998, p.18.

great theatrical tradition . . . with a quality in her work which roused the greatest admiration of all.'[6] *The Sydney Morning Herald* noted that, 'Even listeners who knew no word of the Yiddish tongue could appreciate her great emotional range, her feeling for character, her swift expressiveness of gesture . . . she has a charming appearance and manner, and her voice, no matter how vehemently she uses it, preserves a remarkable richness.'[7]

Holzer was accompanied on her trip to Australia by her husband, Yiddish writer, translator, and theatre critic Chaim Rosenstein. In 1939 she performed in the modern play *Froy Advocate* (Lady Lawyer), a comedy by Louis Verneuil about a woman's right to an independent career, translated from French to Yiddish by her husband. As well as playing the lead, Holzer produced and directed the play, earning her the distinction of being the first woman to direct a Yiddish play in Australia. The couple only intended to stay in Australia for six months, but the outbreak of war forced them to change their plans.[8]

By the late 1930s, the Melbourne Yiddish cultural scene was well and truly on the Yiddish world map. So what happened in Melbourne between the First and Second World Wars to create this rich cultural environment?

The cultural tipping point

The interwar years were extraordinary times for the Melbourne Jewish community. Although small in number, the arrival of immigrants who fled an ever more hostile Eastern Europe created a distinctive

---

6   *The Argus*, 17 April 1939, p.4.
7   *Sydney Morning Herald*, 31 July 1939.
8   Serge Liberman, 'Seventy Years of Yiddish Theatre in Melbourne (1909–1979)', Part 2, *Melbourne Chronicle*, January 1981.

demand, a spontaneous cultural synergy that coalesced in a relatively short time. This created a new market for cultural production – for Yiddish theatre, for Yiddish literature, for Yiddish press, and for the next generation of consumers to be nurtured by a Yiddish school and political activity. Among the new arrivals were performers, writers and artists, who brought with them not only considerable skills, professionalism and passion, but also steadfast determination to shape and define the new cultural space they now inhabited. They were pioneering individuals who had fled unprecedented, rapidly worsening circumstances in Eastern Europe. Once in Melbourne, they channelled their energy into fashioning a Yiddish world under the Southern Cross.

Yankev Waislitz and Rachel Holzer were not the first professional Yiddish actors to grace the Melbourne stage, but they took theatre to a new level in its development. Waislitz and Holzer were preceded by actors and theatrical pioneers who settled in Australia in the first decades of the 20th century, and in larger numbers in the 1920s and 1930s. They followed the lead of Shmuel Weissberg, often named the grandfather of Yiddish theatre in Melbourne. Weissberg, an actor and theatrical impresario, arrived in Australia in November 1908 and was the first to bring the more serious works of Jacob Gordin, known for introducing naturalism and realism to the Yiddish stage, to Yiddish audiences.[9]

By the mid-1920s Yiddish theatre had started to take off. Yankev Ginter, a professional Yiddish actor from Lodz, arrived in 1927. It didn't take Ginter long to find his theatrical feet in Melbourne. He immediately joined a nascent Kadimah troupe in a production of

---

9   Liberman, 'Seventy Years of Yiddish Theatre in Melbourne'.

Sholem Aleichem's *Tevye the Milkman*. The Kadimah was instrumental in sponsoring a number of ensembles to produce Yiddish plays. The first, the Kadimah Drama Circle, was formed in 1925 and underwent at least six confusing name changes before 1939 as it amalgamated, regrouped and split. Its first production, on 5 October 1925, was Sholem Aleichem's drama *Tsezeyt un Tseshpreyt* (Scattered and Dispersed). The play depicts the disintegration of a Russian Jewish bourgeois family; one child converts to Christianity, one becomes a revolutionary, another becomes a Zionist and the fourth an outspoken hedonist. Containing all the elements of contemporary high drama, the play resonated with its audience.

In the year that he joined the Circle, Ginter also performed in David Pinski's *Yankl the Blacksmith* and Gordin's *The Slaughter*, a daring play bordering on the grotesque with its depiction of a young girl who is forced to marry a rich man whom she despises. After enduring violent abuse at his hands, she is driven to murder. By all accounts, the play both shocked and enthralled theatregoers. In a display of pure audacity, Yankev Ginter bucked the trend to have playbills printed mostly in English and went to great lengths to print the posters for *The Slaughter* at least partly in Yiddish. As no Yiddish typeface was yet available, the posters were printed by an obliging Australian printer who used letters cut out from Yiddish newspapers that had been printed in Poland as the basis of his type. The posters were riddled with errors but Grinter nevertheless distributed them proudly at his stall at Victoria Market. These playbills were probably the first Yiddish-language items to be printed in Melbourne.[10]

---

10   Liberman, 'Seventy Years of Yiddish Theatre in Melbourne'.

The entrepreneurial Ginter quickly went on to form his own theatre group, the Yiddishe Bine. He continued to shift Yiddish performances in Melbourne away from *shund* (trashy melodramas) to works by great contemporary Yiddish playwrights. This was not only in keeping with current trends in Europe and New York, but also addressed the changing needs of a fast-growing, culturally attuned audience. The Yiddishe Bine's first production was in 1927 – Gordin's *Chasie the Orphan*.

The Ginter home at 167 Albert Street, Brunswick, was a focal point for newly arrived Yiddishists. It became a central meeting place, a home away from home for visiting and newly arrived thespians, writers and activists, where rowdy play rehearsals were accompanied by heated political discussions and the obligatory table of food and drink. Yankev Ginter nurtured other Yiddish actors, mostly amateurs; he raised the bar for stage performance and expanded the repertoire. It was the Ginters who played host to Yankev Waislitz as soon as he set foot in Melbourne, meeting him at the dock and providing accommodation.[11] Yankev Ginter's younger brother Nosn, also a professional actor, joined the Ginter clan in Melbourne in 1936. The 'Ginter family company', as the Yiddishe Bine came to be called, produced a roll call of Yiddish classics, including Friedrich Wolf's anti-Nazi play *The Yellow Patch* and Sholem Aleichem's *Two Hundred Thousand,* a play about bourgeois excess and working-class morality. Yankev Ginter remained a central figure in Melbourne Yiddish theatre for the next twenty years.[12]

---

11   Zable, *Wanderers and Dreamers*, p.8.
12   Liberman, 'Seventy Years of Yiddish Theatre in Melbourne', p.6.

Adding to this burgeoning group of theatrical professionals was the arrival in 1937 of Abraham Braizblatt, a young Warsaw-born professional actor, folk singer and recitalist who came to perform at a number of cultural evenings hosted by the Kadimah. He toured Sydney and Melbourne, produced revue evenings and several Yiddish plays, including Itzik Manger's adaptation of Goldfaden's *Di Kishefmacherin* (The Witch) in which he played the lead. It would remain Braizblatt's best-known work. The play was reprised both during and after the Second World War.[13]

The arrival of talented actors Rachel Levita in 1938 and Yasha Sher in 1939 added to the professionalisation and expansion of pre-war Yiddish theatre in Melbourne. Both were seasoned performers, Sher in his native Riga and Levita in Lomza, and both made quite an impression in Melbourne. Sher was described by Pinchas Goldhar as 'a new and important talent from Latvia',[14] and Waislitz was so impressed with the budding young actress that he took her under his wing, teaching her 'how to speak, to act, to think'.[15]

By the end of the 1930s audiences had grown, repertoires were enhanced and productions became increasingly professional. Rehearsals were held regularly, lines had to be memorised in a standardised Yiddish, without prompting, rather than in a hotch-potch of regional dialects, and the Kadimah hall in Lygon Street, with a capacity of 400, was regularly filled to overflowing. In order to satisfy the growing demand for theatrical performances, at the urging of Yankev Waislitz, the Kadimah ensemble merged with the

---

13 Zable, *Wanderers and Dreamers*, p.71.
14 Zable, *Wanderers and Dreamers*, p.22.
15 Peter Kohn, 'Levita – a Star Remembers: the Peter Kohn interview, *Australian Jewish News*, 17 February 1989, p.11.

Yiddishe Bine to form the David Herman Theatre, named in honour of Waislitz's mentor and inspiration and one of the founding directors of the Vilna Troupe.

The David Herman Theatre group was responsible for over 130 independent theatrical productions before it was disbanded in 1992. Up until the outbreak of war in 1939, over 30 recent Yiddish immigrants – professional and amateur actors, set designers, makeup artists, wardrobe and props managers – made the David Herman Theatre their spiritual home. Out of necessity most held daytime jobs and would arrive for rehearsals at the Kadimah's cavernous hall fatigued from work. But here they were transformed. Here they lived a different life. As Rachel Levita recalled, 'There was no heating in winter, no air-conditioning in summer, but we were idealists. We lived for the performances.'[16] And their audiences, who crammed into the halls to watch every performance with baited breath, were also transformed.

Yiddish theatre offered all the elements that made theatre compelling: plays that made you laugh, cry, ponder moral dilemmas, appeal to your social sensibilities and deliver polemics on the political issues of the day. For many Yiddish lovers it was the theatre they turned to for respite from the day's toil. Here they could leave behind the worries of the daily grind of earning a living and the growing concerns of family they'd left behind in Europe. Here they were uplifted and transported to another time and place. While many may not have read Ansky's *The Dybbuk* or Sholem Aleichem's *Tsezeyt un Tseshpreyt*, they could experience their overwhelming impact on the stage.

---

16   Kohn, 'Levita'.

As well as providing entertainment, Yiddish theatre satisfied a great psychological need. Not only did it fill its audience with nostalgia, it also had a restorative effect, providing comfort to the immigrants treading a line between the old world and the new. Yiddish theatre was the gateway through which they could re-enter the cultural world they had left behind, and they did so through a Yiddish *vort* (word), through their *mame loshen* (mother tongue). Herein lay the connection between Yiddish theatre and Jewish folk life. As Chaim Rosenstein recalled, '[Yiddish] theatre is a living reflection of our past and present and a guide to our future. Theatre does not speak with the dead letters of the newspaper or the book. Quality Yiddish theatre speaks to us in the living language of our grandfathers, grandmothers, parents, brothers and sisters.'[17] At a time when the very essence of European Jewish life was being stamped out of existence, Rosenstein's observation was particularly poignant. Yiddish theatre was piercingly relevant to these new immigrants in this new world.

Australian Yiddish literature

Like theatre, Yiddish literature was integral to the modern Yiddish arts movement, and central to the creation of a new cultural milieu in Melbourne. Yiddish publishing houses flourished in Poland during the interwar period. In 1934, 281 Yiddish books were printed. Owing to the professionalism of Yiddish publishing in Poland, American Yiddish writers, such as Joseph Opatoshu and H. Leivik, chose to publish their books in Poland rather than America. Poland's Yiddish

---

17 Chaim Rosenstein, 'Yiddish Theatre in Australia', *Yiddish Almanac 1942*, translated by Dvora Zylberman, p.305.

publishing houses served a worldwide market, thereby granting Yiddish writers a global readership.[18]

Lodz-born writer and journalist Pinchas Goldhar arrived in Melbourne in May 1928, heralding a new beginning for Yiddish literature in the antipodes. Goldhar brought with him literary expertise, professionalism, and a journalist's sharp eye for observation and detail. Often cited as Australia's most significant Yiddish writer, he was to show just how far contemporary Yiddish writing could be taken within an Australian milieu.

Before Goldhar's arrival, there was virtually no Yiddish publishing in Melbourne. He became the first editor of a Yiddish newspaper in 1931; he contributed to the first Yiddish book published in Melbourne, *The Australian Yiddish Almanac*, in 1937; he was the first to publish a Yiddish anthology of short stories in 1938; he was the first Yiddish writer to be included in an Australian anthology, and the first to translate Australian writers into Yiddish.[19]

Unlike writers such as Sholem Aleichem, whose realism often provided positive messages about Jewish life, Goldhar's Australian Yiddish stories of impoverished immigrant life were dark and pessimistic. They highlighted the everyday struggles of new migrants – isolation and cultural dissonance in an alien land. His work was a product of the desperate and uncertain times in which he lived and which had propelled him, his widowed father and siblings to flee Poland and find refuge in Melbourne. Goldhar's characters were, in every way, Yiddish-speaking Polish Jews, but it was their displacement

---

18 David Fishman, *The Rise of Modern Yiddish Culture*, Pittsburgh: University of Pittsburgh Press, 2005, p.85.

19 Serge Liberman, preface to *The Collected Stories of Pinchas Goldhar*, Melbourne: Hybrid Publishers, 2016, p. vii.

within the Australia environment that interested him most, and in this his work broke new ground. His work can be seen as the transition point, the space between pre-war Australian Yiddish writing and the post-war era – a shift from optimism to despair. A newcomer writing about contemporary fellow newcomers was an innovation.[20]

Goldhar was a pioneer in another respect, too. By forging close ties with Australian writers and artists, he carved out a new cultural space for Jewish immigrant writers. He established affiliations with left-leaning writers, such as Vance and Nettie Palmer, Frank Dalby Davison and Brian Fitzpatrick, and with social realist artists, such as Noel Counihan, Vic O'Connor and Jewish immigrant Yosl Bergner, the son of Melech Ravitch. By 1944 Goldhar was translating into Yiddish and publishing abroad stories by Henry Lawson, Vance Palmer, Frank Dalby Davison and Alan Marshall. He learnt a great deal through his association with Australian writers and artists. He developed and shared their interests in the literature of minority groups and a belief that culture should be outward-looking, with an international perspective. In return, he provided his Australian colleagues with a fresh European perspective, new insights and a Yiddishist's sensibility, particularly the link between language and cultural identity. He helped them break down their own sense of cultural isolation and entrapment in what was, to them, a stifling monocultural British colony.[21]

Goldhar also nurtured a group of up-and-coming younger Yiddish writers who would go on to achieve great acclaim, such as Herz Bergner, Hirsh Munz and Judah Waten. Waten, although conversant

---

20 Pam Maclean, in *The Collected Stories of Pinchas Goldhar*, Melbourne: Hybrid Publishers, 2016, pp.1–17.

21 Maclean, in *The Collected Stories of Pinchas Goldhar*.

in Yiddish and a fine translator of Yiddish stories, wrote only in English. His translation of Herz Bergner's Yiddish novel, *Between Sky and Sea*, won the Australian Literature Society's Gold Medal for the best book published in 1946. Through a short and intensely productive period – Goldhar's life was tragically cut short in 1947 – Goldhar set a new standard for Yiddish literature by reimagining Yiddish writing within an Australian context. In doing so, he opened up new cultural opportunities for Melbourne's Yiddishists and for Australian writers.

Emergence of a Yiddish press

In Poland Yiddish speakers had been well served by a vibrant Yiddish press. In 1934 there were 14 daily Yiddish newspapers and some 58 Yiddish periodicals, through which Yiddish speakers kept abreast of topical social and political issues and events.[22] In Melbourne, Yiddish newspapers sourced from overseas were available in the Kadimah library's reading room or through private subscriptions. A Yiddish newspaper was a Yiddishist's cultural and social lifeblood.

Until the 1930s the Melbourne Jewish community only had one English-language newspaper, published fortnightly. The *Jewish Herald*, established in 1879 and renamed the *Australian Jewish Herald* in 1920, was a high-quality newspaper that mainly served the more established community. As such, it was not attuned to the specific cultural needs of a Yiddish readership. As Sender Burstin recalled,

> The Yiddish-speaking immigrant did not know English. The English press was foreign and closed. He was cut off from the Jewish and outside worlds. The best he could do was to

---

22 Fishman, *The Rise of Modern Yiddish Culture*, p.85.

subscribe to a Yiddish newspaper from Poland which would reach him five to six weeks later. It was technically not possible for a Yiddish paper to appear as there was no Yiddish printing press or Yiddish type.[23]

With the arrival in Melbourne of David Altshul in 1927, things began to change. Originally from Russia and already in his mid-50s, Altshul brought with him some Yiddish type and the drive to establish a Yiddish newspaper. Burstin remembered him as possessing 'all the best qualities of a modern Russian Jew, which included a consciousness of Jewish nationhood in its fullest sense'.[24]

Even with the best will in the world, establishing a Yiddish newspaper was no easy task. Not enough readers, not enough money to fund the venture and, prior to Altshul's arrival, no Yiddish typeface for printing it. Some eight attempts were made to launch a Yiddish newspaper in the late 1920s and 1930s. After a number of false starts, Altshul, with Pinchas Goldhar as editor and the backing of the Kadimah committee, launched *Oystralyer Lebn* (Australian Life) in 1931. It lasted until 1934. In 1935 *Di Yiddishe Nayes* (The Yiddish News) was launched and circulated with the *Australian Jewish News*, published weekly in Melbourne by Chaim Rubinstein. The *Australian Jewish Herald* attempted to resurrect its Yiddish weekly in 1936 with a four-page supplement, but it folded after seven issues. The Yiddish-speaking market could not yet sustain two Yiddish weekly papers, but this would change with the arrival of many more Yiddish speakers after 1945.

---

23 Sender Burstin, *Yiddish Melbourne Observed*, translated by Ben and David Burstin, Melbourne: Australian Centre for Jewish Civilisation, Monash University, 2013, p.46.
24 Burstin, *Yiddish Melbourne Observed*, p.47.

By the end of the 1930s, the Yiddish speakers of Melbourne had laid the foundations for their own cultural world. There was a thriving Yiddish theatre, two Yiddish books had been published, and a Yiddish press was emerging. The next priority was the education of their children. It was one thing to fulfil your own aspirations for a Jewish life centred in *Yiddishkeit* but quite another to ensure its survival for the generations to come. For this to happen, the children needed to be schooled in Yiddish language and culture to ensure continuity. They needed a Yiddish school.

A Yiddish school is launched

The push for a structured Yiddish education program was given impetus by the arrival of renowned Yiddish writer and adventurer Melech Ravitch, and champion of Yiddish language and literature, educator Joseph Giligich, both of whom initially came to Melbourne on temporary missions to raise funds in support of Polish Jewry.[25] Ravitch made two separate trips, the first to investigate prospects for a Jewish settlement in the Kimberley region of Western Australia, and the second to raise funds for Yiddish schools in Poland. Both men were exceptional individuals caught up in extraordinary times.

The visits of Ravitch and Giligich were the catalyst for the establishment of the I.L. Peretz School, named in honour of one of the greatest Yiddish writers of the late 19th and early 20th centuries. It was one thing to support Jewish causes abroad, but now it was time to look after one's own. Their influence provided leadership and the

---

25   'Joseph Giligich (1891–1977)', *Yiddish Melbourne*, http://future.arts.monash.edu/yiddish-melbourne/biographies-joseph-giligich/, accessed 5 April 2018; 'Melech Ravitch (1897–1976)', *Yiddish Melbourne*, http://future.arts.monash.edu/yiddish-melbourne/biographies-melech-ravitch/, accessed 5 April 2018.

right kind of synergy. Before the I.L. Peretz School was established there had only been part-time institutions giving Jewish students a rudimentary grasp of the Hebrew language and religious instruction. Some of them were run by the United Jewish Education Board in the classrooms of state schools and others operated as Talmud Torah schools (religious schools) under the auspices of the synagogues. They offered nothing in the way of Yiddish language or literature.

Ravitch's reception at the Kadimah attracted a record crowd. Some 700 people crammed into the hall to hear him speak, filling the corridors and every entrance and spilling onto the stage. Ravitch was a celebrity in the Yiddish literary world and a progressive thinker. His effusive descriptions of the relatively recent flourishing of Yiddish schools in Eastern Europe and the United States prompted the Melbourne Yiddishists to forge ahead with their own plans to establish a local Yiddish school.[26]

The I.L. Peretz School, initially known as the Yiddish Sunday and Afternoon School, was formed after a meeting on 1 October 1935 by a group of Yiddish activists, many of whom had been enthusiasts of the Yiddish schools in Poland. The meeting took place at the home of Yankev Ginter, whose influence in the community stretched beyond the stage door. The following day the group sent a letter inviting interested members of the community to attend a public meeting. The letter outlined the aims and values of the proposed school, which were based on those underpinning the CYSHO (Central Yiddish School Organisation) schools in Poland. They included spoken and written knowledge of the Yiddish language, knowledge of Yiddish literature, an introduction to Jewish history, and an assurance that

---

26 Burstin, *Yiddish Melbourne Observed*, p.52.

the school would be apolitical. The public meeting was held on 8 October at the Kadimah, and the dream to create a Yiddish school in Melbourne modelled on those in Vilna and Warsaw became a reality.

The Kadimah housed the school, which opened its doors to students on 3 November 1935, with classes on Wednesday afternoons and Sunday mornings. Melech Ravitch, the principal, and teachers B. Star and L. Szabinski began their classes with 30 students.[27] The establishment of the I.L. Peretz Yiddish School heralded a new form of sustainable Jewish education that was secular, Yiddish, and removed from the grip of the synagogues, which promoted religious instruction, orthodox observance, and the Hebrew language. It signalled a break from the type of religious education fostered by the established community and was the first attempt at founding a Jewish school in Melbourne since the late 19th century.

When the eternal wanderer Ravitch left Australia in 1937, Joseph Giligich was appointed his successor. Although he had already accepted a job as principal of a Jewish day school in Canada, Giligich changed his mind and decided to settle in Melbourne. It was a city that inspired him with its Yiddish heart and soul, but, more importantly, its bold way of doing things. An experienced educator, teacher and scholar, Giligich had established and run Yiddish schools in Latvia and Lithuania. He was also a Yiddish activist, prepared to fight for the right to teach Yiddish under oppressive regimes and at great risk to himself. By the time he arrived in Melbourne he was a well-known advocate for Yiddish education.

By 1938, when Giligich began as principal of the school, there were four classes and 45 students. The new principal consolidated

---

27 David Burstin, 'I.L. Peretz Yiddish School 1935–84', *Australian Jewish Historical Society Journal*, Vol. X, Part 1 (1986): pp.15–27.

the foundations of the young school, which soon thrived under his guidance, passion and dedication. Holding his post for over 30 years, Giligich did far more than nurture the children and steer them through the world of Yiddish literature. He remained the guardian of Yiddish culture in Melbourne. Throughout the war years the school flourished, increasing its enrolment to 140 students by war's end. During the same period the Yiddish-speaking children of Europe were being systematically annihilated. Here, in a far-off land, at the southernmost edge of a large continent, a small group of Yiddishists were endeavouring to save a whole world. As Pinchas Goldhar proclaimed in 1933, 'Only through language can the secrets of the deepest inner recesses, of our essence, be elevated to immortal value.'[28]

---

28 Quoted in Pam Maclean, 'Pinchas Goldhar: His Yiddishist Vision – A Flawed Nationalism?', *Australian Journal of Jewish Studies*, Vol. 5, No. 1 (1991): p.25.

Chapter 5

POLITICS – 'IF EVERYONE PULLED IN ONE DIRECTION, THE WORLD WOULD TIP OVER'

There is an old Yiddish saying, 'One Jew, one opinion; many Jews, many arguments.' Jewish politics was, and remains, complicated and fractious; passionate commitment to causes is one factor explaining the dynamism of Jewish communities. Even before the arrival of significant numbers of Yiddishists, the Melbourne Jewish community in the interwar period was neither united nor cohesive. In 1921, the *Australian Jewish Herald* described it as a community with 'schisms, cliques and conflicting communal organisations quite out of all proportion to its size'.[1] A major line of division at the time was between Bundists and Zionists.

The 'Bund': a socialist secular Yiddish organisation in Melbourne

The origins of the Bund can be traced to its inaugural meeting in the home of a Vilna blacksmith in 1897. Fifteen Jewish socialists gathered

---

1 *Australian Jewish Herald*, 29 April 1921.

secretly to establish a new political movement, Der Algemeyner Yiddisher Arbeter Bund in Rusland un Poyln (General Jewish Workers Union in Russia and Poland), to be known as the Bund, meaning union. At a time when nationalist movements were sweeping across Europe, the Bund became a galvanising cultural and political force amongst the Jewish workers in Eastern Europe. The Jewish working class was attracted to the initial aims of the Bund, which supported, in the words of one of its founders, Arkady Kremer, the 'specific interests of Jewish workers' and fought 'discriminatory anti-Jewish laws'. The Bund worked towards the political, social and cultural advancement of impoverished Jews across Europe.[2]

Within a short period, the Bund became engaged in political agitation, the formation of unions, strike action and Jewish defence groups. Its leaders and members became known for their audacity, their daring and their confrontational tactics. The early successes of their campaigns for better working conditions, with fewer hours and better pay, increased membership and support. In the interwar period the Bund was the largest Jewish political party in Poland.[3]

But the Bund was more than a workingman's party. Its mandate went beyond economic improvement; its social reach was extensive, cultural and nationalist.[4] Its ideology was underpinned by three key principles: socialism, *doykeit* and yiddishism. In opposition to capitalism, socialism advocated the democratic control and social ownership of the means of production, with the aim of establishing greater social equity for all citizens. *Doykeit* (the 'here and now') centred on strengthening Jewish cultural life wherever Jews lived, in

---

2 Wasserstein, *On The Eve*, pp.68–72.
3 Wasserstein, *On The Eve*, p.71.
4 Wasserstein, *On The Eve*, p.71.

opposition to the notion that Jews had to emigrate to other lands in order to survive. This was sorely tested in the 1930s when it became increasingly clear that survival would inevitably depend on Jews emigrating to the New World. Yiddishism emphasised the centrality of Yiddish language and culture to Jewish identity. As Yiddish was the language of the Jews of Eastern Europe and the language of the Bund, it was a marriage that blossomed during the Yiddish cultural renaissance of the early 20th century in Eastern Europe. The influence of the Bund spread. A number of Bundist schools were established in which a comprehensive secular education for children and adults was conducted in Yiddish, schooling them in history, science, philosophy and literature.[5]

The first official Bundist group in Melbourne was founded in late 1928.[6] Of the 12 men and women of the core group, Sender Burstin, later to become president of the Kadimah, was a galvanising force. From his earliest years, Burstin was committed to the socialist ideals of the Bund. In pre-war Poland he held a paid position for a period of time for Tsukunft, a Bund youth organisation founded in 1919 that organised summer camps, drama clubs and various cultural activities. For Bundists like Burstin, the principle of *doykeit* became untenable in exceedingly hostile environments such as Poland. As has been discussed, unable to secure more regular employment and convinced that Jews had no future in Poland, he went in search of better opportunities. He found them in Australia, the new *goldene medinah* (golden land), a free country with an open society that would enable the fullest expression of *doykeit*.

---

5   Wasserstein, *On The Eve*, p.323.
6   Moshe Ajzenbud, *60 Years of 'Bund' in Melbourne 1928–1988*, Melbourne: Jewish Labour Bund, 1996, p.9.

Burstin's experience in running election campaigns in Poland proved invaluable in the establishment of the Melbourne Bund and the growth of the Yiddishist movement. As well as Burstin, others present at the inaugural meeting were immigrants for whom the ideals of the Bund were paramount: Haskiel Davis, Myer Silman, Yides Silman, Lazer Bloustein, Yankev Ginter, Bela Wiener, Abraham Hildebrand, Manye Hildebrand, Moishe Oliver and Wolf Grodzenski.[7]

The first public function organised by the Melbourne Bund, held at the Kadimah, was a commemoration of the death of the important Bund leader, Beynish Mikhalevich. It drew a large crowd, some 150 people. As Burstin recalled, 'This initial public function of the Bund group was a success and it showed the Yiddish community that the Bundists had arrived.' A choir sang several Bundist and worker songs, Yankev Ginter recited poetry, including David Einhorn's *Tsen Milion* (Ten Million), which was about the tragic loss of lives during the Great War, and Aron Patkin, the Australian Zionist leader, spoke of the Bund and its aims.[8]

The Bund itself was not devoid of controversy and factionalism. One of the first activities of the Bund was its participation in the GEZERD, established in 1931. Sender Burstin was also a key figure in this movement. The GEZERD (Society for the Establishment of a Rural Jewish Community) raised funds to support the creation of a Jewish autonomous settlement in Birobidjan in the USSR. Its membership combined Socialists, Communists and Zionists; from

---

7   Ajzenbud, *60 Years of 'Bund' in Melbourne*.
8   Sender Burstin, *Yiddish Melbourne Observed*, translated by Ben and David Burstin, Melbourne: Australian Centre for Jewish Civilisation, Monash University, 2013, pp.144–5.

the outset the organisation was plagued by controversy and hindered by the disparate aims of its members. After a few years, the Communist faction won control of the GEZERD and the organisation was criticised in *Di Yiddishe Nayes* by Aron Patkin for being a 'minor branch of Russian Bolshevism.' Burstin and the Bund were fierce opponents of Soviet Communism and, in his efforts to steer the GEZERD's orientation back to its original aims, Burstin was labelled a 'wrecker' (the vernacular used in Soviet purges at the time) and expelled. The organisation collapsed as a consequence of the Nazi–Soviet non-aggression pact in 1939.[9]

In the lead-up to the outbreak of war, the Bund initiated the visits of emissaries from the CYSHO in Poland, notably Melech Ravitch and Joseph Giligich, who worked to strengthen the role of Yiddish language in the community. In addition, the Bund was supportive of Yiddish theatre and helped organise and sponsor the visits of Yankev Waislitz and Rachel Holzer, both of whom were also sympathetic to the Bund's ideals.[10]

Initially, the Melbourne Bund was a satellite of European political activity, primarily involved in raising money for Bundist and socialist causes in Poland, most notably Yiddish schools and the *Folks Tsaytung* (People's Newspaper), the official daily Yiddish newspaper of the Bund in Poland published in Warsaw between 1921 and 1939. Once established in Melbourne, however, the Bund had to adapt to different circumstances. Australia didn't need a revolutionary Jewish party. Australian workers were not excluded from the main fields of economic activity. Agitation against discriminatory legislation and

---

9   Burstin, *Yiddish Melbourne Observed*, pp.41–5.
10 Burstin, *Yiddish Melbourne Observed*, p.155.

anti-Jewish work practices were not called for. Self-defence associations to defend Jews in their homes, on the streets and in factories were not required. In Melbourne all were protected under the law.

The Bund reinvented itself, up to a point. The Bund was a political machine, unafraid to immerse itself in the politics of government and was particularly adept at forming alliances with mainstream socialist political parties. It was only a matter of time before the Bund became involved in the Australian Labor Party.

By the time political agitator and firebrand Jacob Waks arrived in Melbourne in early 1940, the Melbourne branch of the Bund was well established. But Waks brought new energy and political nous to its operations. He had been leader of the Bund in Bialystok and his exploits were legendary.[11] No stranger to political struggle or the inside of a prison cell, Waks had been arrested several times in Poland for his role in organising unions and strike action. An article in *Di Yiddishe Nayes* lauded his activism:

> He was engaged in the revolutionary political campaigns in general, and in particular for the basic rights of the Jewish masses in Poland. To these people the name Jacob Waks is well known. To the toiling masses, Jews, Poles, White Russians of Bialystok, and the Bialystok area as a whole, Waks is a revered figure. He would always support every important Socialist statement, and was at the forefront of all significant Socialist revolutionary rallies where he fearlessly and energetically called for and stimulated radical action.[12]

When war broke out Waks, together with thousands of other refugees, made his way to Vilna and on to Kovna in Lithuania. With

---

11   J.S. Hertz, *Doyres Bundistn 3*, New York: Unzer Tsayt, 1968.
12   Binem Warszarski, *Di Yiddishe Nayes*, 29 March 1940, quoted in Ajzenbud, *60 Years of 'Bund' in Melbourne*.

the assistance of his niece, Mina Fink (nee Waks), who had arrived in Melbourne in 1932, Waks and his wife obtained visas for Australia and they arrived in Melbourne in the beginning of 1940. In Australia he would make his mark as a fierce opponent of Communism and the Soviet Union, forge ties with the Australian Labor Party and cut through red tape to hasten post-war Jewish immigration. While Waks was a fierce advocate of the Bund, his niece's husband, Leo Fink, was a staunch Zionist. Both Waks and Fink were committed Yiddishists with different, often opposing, political views who coexisted in the one family, which mirrored the community to which they belonged.

The growth of Zionism

While all Bundists were Yiddishists, not all Yiddishists were Bundists. A range of competing political allegiances characterised this community, including support for Zionism. In opposition to the Bund's concept of *doykeit*, Zionism saw salvation through emigration to a new Jewish state in the historic Jewish homeland.

Secular Zionism had its origins in the late 19th century when the word 'Zionism' was adopted to describe the Jewish nationalist movement in which Eretz Yisrael (the land of Israel) becomes a Jewish homeland. The father of political Zionism was Theodor Herzl, whose experience and observations of the growth and acceptance of anti-semitism in Western Europe, in countries that had been beacons of liberalism and democracy, convinced him that Jews could never be fully integrated into European life. Jewish emancipation was a myth. For Herzl the only solution to the 'Jewish Question' was a Jewish homeland. Herzl convened the first Zionist Congress in Basel in Switzerland in 1897 at which the World Zionist Organization was created, formulating the Basel Program, which declared that 'Zionism seeks to establish a home for the Jewish people in Palestine secured under public law'.[13] Although Herzl died at a young age in 1904, he succeeded in forging a strong political identity for Zionism, which, in the face of growing antisemitism, struck a chord with many Jews worldwide. Zionism became a major political force.

Unlike the Bund, Zionism was not an immigrant movement brought to Melbourne by Eastern European Yiddish-speaking Jews. Zionism, a political ideal, an aspiration that spread throughout the Jewish world, garnered greater appeal within the established Australian Jewish community following the Balfour Declaration of 1917, which pledged British support for 'the establishment in Palestine of a national home for the Jewish people'.[14] Britain's support gave Zionism greater legitimacy, which appealed to a broad base of Australian Jews, including Major Isidor Isaacson, a Boer War and First World War veteran, Sir John Monash, and Yiddishists such as Samuel Wynn and Leo Fink.

In Australia, the Zionist movement gathered momentum with the establishment of Zionist groups in the interwar period, consolidated in the formation of the state bodies and, in 1927, a national federation. Throughout the 1920s a number of emissaries who came to raise funds for the Jewish homeland brought the Zionist message to Australia. Some were attracted to make *aliyah*, to migrate to Palestine, where they encountered a difficult and dangerous life, rather than the hoped-for land of milk and honey. By the late 1930s,

---

13 Walter Laqueur, *History of Zionism*, New York: Schocken Books, 1989.
14 Jonathan Schneer, *The Balfour Declaration: The Origins of the Arab-Israeli Conflict*, New York: Random House, 2010.

only two per cent of the world's Jewish population had made their home in Palestine.[15]

The failed settlement experience brought an additional small number of Yiddish-speaking immigrants to Melbourne from Palestine in the 1920s. One of these, Yehuda Honig, who arrived in 1926, taught at the Ivriah Hebrew school supported by the Ivriah Society of Hebrew speakers from Palestine, and was a co-editor of *Dos Australier Leben* in 1931, later becoming a regular contributor to *Di Yiddishe Nayes*. Honig served as president of the Kadimah, president of the Revisionist Zionist Organisation, which followed Ze'ev Jabotinsky's non-religious right-wing ideology, and was later one of the founders of the part-time Bialik Hebrew School, a secular Zionist school in North Carlton in 1942.

Yiddish was the language of the Bund and its followers, modern Hebrew the language of Zionists, although many Polish Jews knew both languages, or at least knew Hebrew as a language of prayer, in addition to Polish, Russian and German. Yiddish and modern Hebrew were two different Jewish languages, but also represented two different ideologies and spoke to different world outlooks.

Herzl had infamously characterised Yiddish as a 'stunted, shrivelled-up jargon . . . the furtive tongue of prisoners',[16] reflecting the view of many German-speaking Jews who viewed Yiddish as a primitive language, an obstruction to an enlightened way of life. Yiddish was seen as the language of the old Jew, powerless and stateless. Modern Hebrew would be the language of empowerment, of the new state, of a new people far removed from the impoverished *shtetlekh*

---

15   Wasserstein, *On The Eve*, p.57.
16   Quoted in Wasserstein, *On The Eve*, p.222.

and ghettos of Europe. For Zionists, Hebrew, which transformed the language of prayer to the modern language of a reborn people, could be the only legitimate language of Zionism.[17] This stance, an affront to the sensibilities of many Yiddishists, received British recognition in the 1922 constitution of the Palestine Mandate, which declared English, Arabic and Hebrew as the official languages of Palestine.

The battle over what should be the legitimate national Jewish language, Yiddish or Hebrew, would continue for decades. While Melbourne became one of its fiercest battlegrounds after the Second World War, there were earlier signs that Yiddishists would fight tooth and nail against claims for Hebrew supremacy. In 1936, at a celebration of the centenary of the birth of Yiddish writer Mendele Moykher Sforim at the Kadimah, one speech was delivered in Hebrew. The 300-strong audience of Yiddishists was in uproar. There were walkouts, foot-stampings and shouting. Sender Burstin vividly recalled the event: 'To speak Hebrew to this audience of everyday Carlton Jews was like talking to the wall . . . Having a Hebrew speech at a Mendele function is just playing the Zionist Hebraist tune . . . There is no room for Hebrew in Australia.'[18]

So how could some Yiddishists be Zionists, support the ideal of a Jewish homeland with Hebrew as its national language, and still retain Yiddish at the core of their cultural identity? Perhaps this can be summed up by one of Mendele Moykher Sforim's expressions: 'A Jew breathes with two nostrils, one for Yiddish and one for Hebrew'. Within this characterisation, the two languages are

---

17 Wasserstein, *On The Eve*, p.223.
18 Burstin, *Yiddish Melbourne Observed*, pp.100–2.

not in opposition but are two complementary entities that coexist in the one body. Both Samuel Wynn and Leo Fink were Eastern European Yiddishists, both had been Kadimah presidents and both were leaders of the Zionist movement in Melbourne. Yiddish was the language they lived. Hebrew was the ideal they supported.

Throughout the 1930s the Melbourne Jewish community continued to sustain a number of Zionist organisations whose reach spanned communities living north and south of the Yarra. The women's group, Women's International Zionist Organisation (WIZO), founded in 1920 in London, held its inaugural Melbourne meeting at Herzl Hall in Carlton in 1935. The Melbourne Friends of Jerusalem's Hebrew University was formally established in 1936 with I.D. Oderberg as chairman. In 1939 a new political Zionist entity emerged with the establishment of the Revisionist Zionist Organisation, with Samuel Rothkopf as its first president.[19]

By the end of the 1930s, a number of new immigrants enhanced the Zionist movement both as followers and as leaders. The national Zionist Federation located its headquarters in Melbourne in 1939, with Dr Leon Jona, a member of the local Jewish establishment, as president. In the same year over 700 people from all walks of life attended the public session of its conference held at the Kadimah and New Zealand was added to the Federation. It was, however, the tragic events of the Holocaust that had the most profound effect on the Zionist movement and cemented its place as the leading political movement of Australian Jewry.[20]

---

19 Bernard Hyams, *The History of the Australian Zionist Movement*, Melbourne: Zionist Federation of Australia, 1998, pp.48–9.
20 Hyams, *The History of the Australian Zionist Movement*, p.62.

The struggle for community leadership

An ongoing struggle for community leadership emerged in the 1920s. It centred on the issue of authority to represent the community. At first it was a battle between an exclusive synagogue-based hegemony of established Jews and an inclusive, broad-based secular authority. It was a battle that would last over 20 years in which the Yiddishists played a significant role. It took on a new dimension with the growing significance of two rival secular movements, Zionism and the Bund.

Before 1920 there was neither an umbrella community body to provide a united Jewish voice in dealings with government nor a forum for debate among organisations serving the established community. Among the organisations were four orthodox synagogues, three small Zionist organisations for adults and one for young people, seven organisations active in Jewish welfare and social services, three social and cultural clubs for youth and one for adults. Sports clubs were still in their infancy. There was one old-age home and a Jewish burial society. Issues of *kashrut* (regulation of kosher food) were controlled by the synagogues, which provided the main focal point for the organisation of community life.[21]

On the initiative of St Kilda Synagogue's Rabbi Danglow, the Melbourne Jewish Advisory Board was established in May 1921, following the visit to Australia of the chief rabbi of the British Empire. The Board was formed by a joint committee of the Melbourne, East Melbourne, and St Kilda congregations, which sought to bring unity and a collective voice to the community and 'to deal with matters

---

21 Peter Medding, *From Assimilation to Group Survival: A Political and Sociological Study of an Australian Jewish Community*, Melbourne: F.W. Cheshire, 1968, pp.28–9.

of importance to the Jewish community'.[22] Its presidency was to be rotated every six months. The Melbourne Jewish Advisory Board purported to represent all Melbourne Jewry.

The Carlton *shul*, whose congregants were Eastern European Yiddish speakers and which had been in existence since 1912, was excluded from the ruling elite. The elite limited representation to men deemed to be 'stable, trustworthy, tactful and dignified . . . [and] able to speak the King's English'.[23] The three 'main' congregational rabbis together formed the Beth Din (religious court of law). Social groups were also aligned with these synagogues, as were many of the charitable organisations. Even though there were secular organisations, such as the growing Zionist movement and the increasing number of cultural activities offered by the Kadimah, the three major synagogues were in control. In reality the Advisory Board's members were a self-appointed orthodox synagogue clique that represented only themselves. It did not reflect the fast-growing, diverse and increasingly secular Jewish community.

The first challenge to the Advisory Board's mandate did not come from the Yiddish newcomers but from others within the established community who protested the limited representation and lack of transparency. The formation of the Judean League in 1923 was in direct response to the restrictive religious hegemony of the three synagogues and signalled a growing shift towards Jewish identification that was secular rather than religious. Through the amalgamation of the Jewish Young People's Association, the Young Jewish Social Club, and the Young Judean Zionist Society, and led by the outspoken

---

22 *Australian Jewish Herald*, 10 June 1921.
23 *Australian Jewish News*, 17 June 1938.

and combative Maurice Ashkanasy, the League set itself up as a rival for community authority on matters other than religion. It wrested control of all matters other than religious education and observance; culture, social activities and, most significantly, the relatively new nationalist movement of Zionism came under its jurisdiction.[24]

The Judean League gained substantial support, claiming that within the first months of its formation it had nearly 1,000 members.[25] In turn, the Advisory Board became increasingly anachronistic and out of touch with the growing needs of a rapidly changing community, characterised by growing numbers of Eastern Europeans who rejected the Board's synagogue-based autocracy. The Kadimah, which became the collective representative of Eastern European Jews, also pressed for democratisation and broader communal affiliation. Broader representation would bring it more in line with the *kehile* model of governance, in keeping with the Yiddishists' sensibilities. The Advisory Board did not relinquish its authority easily or quickly, but over the years succumbed to pressure from a growing number of like-minded social and political groups wanting democratic representation.

Hitler's rise to power in 1933 provoked immediate condemnation from the community but not all were in agreement on the best way to respond. In 1934, a community meeting held at the Kadimah, sponsored by the Bund, chaired by Simche (Samuel) Brilliant, and adjudicated by E. Gorman, KC, debated the viability of an economic boycott of Nazi Germany.[26] English speakers from the established Jewish community opposed the boycott, with St Kilda synagogue's

---

24 H. Rubinstein, *The Jews in Australia*, p.38.
25 *Australian Jewish Herald*, 23 November 1923.
26 Kadimah Annual Report 1934.

A SECOND CHANCE

Rabbi Danglow dominating the meeting. Danglow argued that it would serve no useful purpose. Indeed, it would be counterproductive, he asserted, as it would arouse hostility and sway Australian public opinion against the Jewish community. Best not to rock the boat – 'If we raise our heads now and it is broadcast that the Jews have forced an official boycott movement, it will excite very unfavourable criticism, not only from the general public but from government circles'.[27] Yiddishists at the meeting were incensed. Sender Burstin complained that the Yiddish speakers in favour of the boycott 'were prevented from voicing their opinion and . . . thereby completely ignored'.[28] They were, according to Burstin, prevented from 'expressing their pain and grief'.[29]

In 1936 some limited concessions were made to try to stem the tide of discontent. The Board renamed itself the Victorian Jewish Advisory Board and drew up a constitution in which non-synagogue organisations were granted limited representation. The Kadimah, the Judean League and the Zionist organisation were allowed to nominate one delegate each on the Advisory Board, alongside the Carlton synagogue and the liberal reform synagogue, Beth Israel, established in 1930, which were also granted representation.[30] In 1938, following further controversy over immigration policy, discussed in the following chapter, the Board drafted a new constitution and came under the presidency of reformist lawyer, Zionist and son of

---

27 Quoted in John S. Levi, *Rabbi Jacob Danglow*, Melbourne: Melbourne University Press, 1995, p.195.
28 Andrew Markus and Danielle Charak, eds, *Yiddish Melbourne: Towards a History*, Melbourne: Monash University, 2008, pp.64–6.
29 Burstin, *Yiddish Melbourne Observed*, p.105.
30 Medding, *From Assimilation to Group Survival*, pp.34–6.

Russian immigrants, Alec Masel. It had made its first step towards democratisation.[31]

However, the push towards a more democratic, secular umbrella body was only crystallised during the war years when the Kadimah, the Zionists and the Judean League forced changes that would allow any organisation in the Jewish community to affiliate with the Advisory Board. At the heart of this decades-long conflict was the issue of identity – of what it meant to be a Jew in the Melbourne Jewish community of the 1920s and 1930s. The outcome of the struggle signalled a move towards a pluralist, secular identity, rather than a narrow religious definition of Jewishness from an earlier era. Eastern European Jews played a significant part in forging this new identity, which best suited the rapidly changing Jewish community.

---

31 H. Rubinstein, *The Jews in Australia*, p.43.

Chapter 6

ESCAPE

Yiddish writer and journalist Shmuel Bennett arrived in Melbourne on 11 April 1939 on board the P&O liner *Otranto*. He remembered the journey from Radom, Poland, via London as long, lasting more than six weeks, but uneventful. The story of how he got to Australia was anything but. The first part of the Bennett family migration story began 10 years earlier. In the face of rising antisemitism and worsening conditions in Poland, Shmuel's father, Moshe, a scholarly and pious man, made the momentous decision to leave the family home in search of a better life for his wife and children. In doing so, he had to leave Shmuel's mother, Rachel, to look after their two young boys. Moshe first travelled to Palestine in 1929, where he found work and was able to send back enough money to support his young family. But times were exceedingly tough in the Biblical land of milk and honey and prospects for a peaceful, secure life were slim. He returned to Radom after two years, despondent and fearful about the future.

In 1932 Moshe decided to make one more attempt at a new life and he set out 'just like the dove sent from Noah's ark to find a resting place for himself, his wife and sons,' Shmuel recalled. Leaving his family alone once more, in an act of desperation, he stowed away on a steamer bound for Britain. He survived the journey on dry rations supplied by a sympathetic sailor who kept him hidden and helped him jump ship in London unnoticed. With no money, travel documents or English, the only thing he had managed to understand from the sailor was that he would find Jews in an area called Whitechapel. Wandering the streets of London on a Friday evening, Moshe came upon a familiar scene. Here were Yidn filling a local synagogue in preparation for the approaching Sabbath. On entering the *shul* he heard the comforting sound of Yiddish, his *mame loshen* (mother tongue). The congregants soon recognised a stranger in their midst. On hearing of Moshe's plight, they offered advice and support.

Moshe was offered clandestine work in a kosher restaurant as a supervisor of *kashrut* (kosher observance). He earned a reasonable wage and for three years sent money to his wife in Radom. By early 1936 he could still see no clear way out of his predicament – how would he get his family out of Poland and where could they go?[1] As fate would have it, the Bennett family ended up in Australia; but before we tell the remarkable story of Rachel Bennett's intervention, we must first consider Australian immigration policy in the 1930s.

Jewish immigration

In response to the very high level of unemployment with the onset of the Great Depression, in 1930 the Australian government barred the entry of all aliens, except those with close family or with very substantial financial assets of at least £500, which was more than the annual salary of a factory manager and, consequently, far beyond the reach of workers.[2] Visa requirements were strictly enforced, as Rabbi Danglow found in 1933 when he travelled to Canberra to seek

---

1   Shmuel Bennett, *Chronicles of a Life*, Melbourne: S. Bennett, 1999, pp.41–44.
2   'Wages in Victoria', State Library of Victoria, http://guides.slv.vic.gov.au/whatitcost/earnings, accessed 6 April 2018.

compassionate treatment for a German Jewish refugee threatened with deportation. He was informed that the 'federal government is determined that its immigration laws must be obeyed'.[3] As economic conditions began to improve, the stringent monetary requirements were eased, first in 1936 when the Conservative Lyons government reduced the required amount to £200. The government also permitted residents to sponsor those in possession of £50 and qualified for work in occupations where there were vacancies.[4]

These changes came at a time when the position of European Jews was deteriorating significantly. In Poland, the growth of the radical right-wing political party Endecja led to increased boycotts of Jewish businesses and outbreaks of violence. A report to the Polish parliament in 1936 recorded 21 pogroms and 348 anti-Jewish outbreaks in the Bialystok region alone in the preceding 12 months. The British Board of Deputies Annual Report for 1936 observed that 'physical attacks on Jews [in Poland] have been an almost daily occurrence and on occasion [have] taken the form of organised pogroms.'[5] The Przytyk pogrom of 9 March 1936 was one of many. Peasants initially massed around the Jewish market, smashing stalls and shops, beating Jews and destroying property. A Jewish couple, Chaja and Josek Minkowski, were murdered in their home and their children viciously assaulted. Twenty-four Jews were seriously injured.[6] The

---

3   *Australian Jewish Herald*, 13 December 1933, quoted in John S. Levi, *Rabbi Jacob Danglow*, Melbourne: Melbourne University Press, 1995, p.184.
4   Charles A. Price, 'Jewish Settlers in Australia', p.402.
5   Rodney Benjamin, *'A Serious Influx of Jews': A History of Jewish Welfare in Victoria*, St Leonards, NSW: 1998, p.65.
6   Emanuel Melzer, *No Way Out: The Politics of Polish Jewry 1935–1939*, Cincinnati: Hebrew Union College Press, 1997; Yisrael Gutman, 'Polish Antisemitism Between the Wars: An Overview', in *The Jews of Poland Between Two World Wars*, edited by Yisrael Gutman et al., Hanover, NH: University of New England, 1989, pp.97–108.

pogrom attracted worldwide attention and inspired the Yiddish poet and songwriter Mordechai Gebirtig to write 'S'brent' (It is burning) in 1938. The song 'Undzer Shtetl Brent' (Our little town is burning) later became a rallying cry for Jewish resistance during the Holocaust.[7] Perpetrators of violence were rarely convicted and, when they were, their sentences were light. The Catholic Church in Poland, while often denouncing violence in general terms, would remind Poles at any opportunity that Jews were the Christ killers.

In Germany and Austria the position of Jews took a dramatic turn for the worse in 1938, with the annexation of Austria by Germany on 12 March and the Kristallnacht pogrom on 9–10 November. During the pogrom carried out by Nazi paramilitary forces and civilians, it is estimated that 91 Jews were beaten to death, 30,000 men were arrested, of whom hundreds died from maltreatment, women and children were terrorised, 267 synagogues were destroyed, over 7500 businesses were damaged, and homes and institutions were looted. The night of violence, carried out without any police intervention, was covered extensively in the international press. In Melbourne it was reported in an article on the front page of *The Argus*, which described

> a campaign against the Jews almost unparalleled in its violence. Synagogues have been burnt, Jewish shops have been smashed and set on fire and looted, and several thousand Jews have been arrested... Much of the damage has been done... by bands of Nazis, armed with crowbars, who paraded the streets in cars.[8]

Western powers were alarmed by the growing Jewish refugee problem that now engulfed Central and Eastern Europe. Attempts

---

7 'Our Town is Burning', *Holocaust Encyclopedia*, https://www.ushmm.org/wlc/en/media_so.php?ModuleId=10005213&MediaId=2621, accessed 6 April 2018.
8 *The Argus*, 11 November 1938, p.1.

to escape Europe to any country willing to take them saw a flood of Jewish applications to Australia House in London. By August 1938 Australia House was receiving 500 applications a week, an annual rate of over 25,000 people, and this was before panic engulfed German Jews later in the year.[9] Australia was under pressure to do more. Publicly Australia did not want to be seen as a major player in resolving the growing Jewish refugee problem – an approach that was typical of Western nations. At the American-sponsored Evian conference in July 1938, the Australian delegate, T.W. White, Minister for Trade and Customs, stated that 'undue privileges cannot be given to one particular class of non-British subjects without injustice to others . . . as we have no racial problem we are not desirous of importing one by encouraging any scheme of large-scale foreign migration.'[10] On the international stage Australia seemed determined to permit no increase of Jewish immigrants beyond its existing policy.

But a month before the Evian Conference, Australia had begun to further ease its restrictions. On 9 June 1938 the government put in place a numerical quota that set an upper limit of 3,600 places for Jewish people who could meet the landing money requirements and 1,500 places for nominated migrants. A total of 5,100 could gain entry, a relatively large number given that confidential government correspondence reveals that only an estimated 500 Jews had gained entry in 1937.[11] In the aftermath of Kristallnacht, Lord Bruce, former Australian Prime Minister and the High Commissioner in London, urged his government to take immediate action. In

---

9   Andrew Markus, 'Jewish Migration to Australia 1938–1949', *Journal of Australian Studies*, Vol. 7, No. 13 (1983): pp.18–31.
10 Quoted in Markus, 'Jewish Migration to Australia', p.21.
11 Markus, 'Jewish Migration to Australia', p.19.

response, in December 1938, Cabinet agreed to change its quota; it was announced that 15,000 would be admitted over three years, which in reality was no different in terms of numbers, but it indicated a three-year timespan for the quota. It covertly included the 5,100 already agreed to as its first year's commitment.

Very few of the Jews who arrived in 1938 and 1939 were Polish or others from Eastern European countries. The government stipulated that the 5,000 per annum were to be refugees, defined narrowly as nationals or former nationals of Germany, Austria and Czechoslovakia. Of these 5,000 places, 4,000 were for Jewish refugees and the other 1,000 for 'non-Aryan Christian' refugees – the classification for Jews who had converted to Christianity yet continued to be treated as a separate Jewish category.[12]

In response to mounting community appeals and the 'present disturbed conditions', on 27 April 1939 the government specified that an additional 1,000 places were to be provided for 'non-refugee' Eastern European Jews, on the proviso that they were sponsored by a relative.[13] In effect, Eastern Europeans, most of them Yiddish speakers, had to compete for less than 20 per cent of the available places in 1939. Little wonder that of the 5,080 Jews who arrived in 1939, close to 4,000 were German-speaking.[14] This was the largest intake of Jewish immigrants in any one year in the interwar period. Jewish arrivals for the entire period from 1935 to 1939 were estimated to total 7,300. With the outbreak of war, immigration to Australia came to an abrupt end.

---

12   Department of the Interior, Memorandum: Refugees, 27 April 1939 (National Archives of Australia (NAA), Series A433, 1949/2/46).

13   Department of the Interior, Memorandum: Refugees, 27 April 1939.

14   John Foster, *Community of Fate: Memoirs of German Jews in Melbourne*, Sydney: Allen & Unwin, 1986, p.xiii.

Compared with policies adopted elsewhere, Australia's quota was generous. Quotas were imposed on Jewish immigration throughout the New World, severely curtailing the number who were able to escape the perils of life in central and eastern Europe. Within the British Commonwealth, New Zealand admitted only a handful of Jewish refugees; South Africa, with a large Jewish population of 90,645 in 1936, admitted approximately 5,500 between 1933 and 1940; Canada admitted 6,955 over the same period.[15] The United States combined quota for Germany and Austria was 27,300 – less than a third of Australia's on a per capita (or population) basis.

In order to administer and regulate Australia's quota, the question 'Are You Jewish?' was inserted in application Form 40 (for family sponsorship) and Form 47 (for immigrants with capital). The government did not make public the decision to include this question, although Jewish community leaders were informed. In October 1938 the responsible minister, John McEwen, falsely stated that 'there is no specific discrimination against Jews in the policy of the Australian government.'[16] In 1938 unemployment in Australia had fallen to eight per cent, from a peak of 32 per cent in mid-1932.[17] It was believed both within Australia and overseas that the country was significantly underpopulated. So why the strict controls on Jewish immigration?

Internal government memoranda listed four reasons, the first of which was that Jews were supposedly not assimilable:

> [The Jews] are highly intelligent as a class and usually make a success at whatever occupation or business they follow; but in

---

15　Mark Wischnitzer, *To Dwell In Safety: The Story of Jewish Migration Since 1800*, Philadelphia: The Jewish Publication Society, 1949, Table IV p.292.
16　Quoted in Markus, 'Jewish Migration to Australia', p.19.
17　'Great Depression', National Museum of Australia, http://www.nma.gov.au/online _features/defining_moments/featured/great-depression, accessed 6 April 2018.

view of their religious beliefs and strict rules as regards marriage, they remain a separate race and this failure to become properly assimilated in the country of adoption appears to create difficulties in any country where they form a considerable proportion of the population.[18]

Other reasons included an alleged disregard for working and living conditions, by Polish Jews in particular, and the perceived risk that a large Jewish intake would lead to 'antisemitic disturbances'.[19] The underlying motivation was racial bigotry. Indicative of antisemitic attitudes of the time, in May 1939 Sir Frank Clarke, president of the Victorian Legislative Council, made a vitriolic assessment of Jews from Eastern Europe, calling them

> Weedy Eastern Europeans... slinking, rat-faced men under five feet in height and with a chest development of twenty inches... [who] worked in backyard factories in Carlton and other localities in the North of Melbourne for two or three shillings a week pocket money and their keep... One group tendered the supply of 100,000 articles of women's silk underclothing at seven and a halfpenny each. No Australian factory could compete with such prices and pay awards.[20]

Even within the Australian Jewish community opinion remained divided over large-scale immigration of European Jews, as it had in earlier years. In 1925 the chief rabbi of the Great Synagogue in Sydney, Rabbi F.L. Cohen, had cautioned against unrestricted Jewish immigration. 'We must guide and control our own immigration,' he warned; otherwise 'the present amicable relations between gentile and

---

18 Quoted in Markus, 'Jewish Migration to Australia', p.20.
19 Quoted in Markus, 'Jewish Migration to Australia', p.20.
20 *Daily Telegraph*, 9 May 1939; cited in Colin Golvan, *The Distant Exodus*, Crows Nest, NSW: ABC Enterprises, 1990, p.12.

Jew' would be 'undermined'.[21] In contrast, Dr Fanny Reading, the Russian-born founder of the New South Wales and then National Council of Jewish Women, championed the cause of the immigrants: 'who are we to say that we are pleased that certain immigration restrictions will be placed on the admittance of our brethren into our country? That we are glad that our task will be made lighter while our brethren languish for freedom and the right to live?'[22]

Such contrasting views were again in evidence in the late 1930s. In 1938, members of the Jewish establishment echoed government concerns, fearful of creating a Jewish 'problem', of upsetting the communal equilibrium and endangering their standing in Australian society. On 19 April 1938, the President of the Victorian Jewish Advisory Board, Isaac H. Boas, was quoted in *The Herald* in an article with the provocative headline 'Migration of Jews – Influx Opposed':

> The Jewish community of Australia was opposed to anything in the nature of mass migration from Austria or anywhere else ... Australian Jews were subscribing to funds for the relief of persecuted Jews in Europe, but immigration was only possible on a mutual benefit basis, there must be a definite opportunity in Australia before immigration was practical.[23]

In other words, money was being sent to alleviate problems confronting Jews 'over there' without having to bring them 'over here'. Additionally, Boas endorsed immigration only for those for whom there was guaranteed employment.

---

21 *Australian Jewish Chronicle*, 8 January 1925; cited in Golvan, *The Distant Exodus*, p.13.
22 Fanny Reading, *Council Bulletin*, Vol. 3, no 4 (November 1928), cited in Golvan, *The Distant Exodus*, p.13.
23 Quoted in Benzion Patkin, 'From Advisory Board to Board of Deputies in Victoria', *Australian Jewish Historical Society Journal*, Vol. IX, Part 1 (1981): pp.39–50.

Also voicing concern was Sir Samuel Cohen of Sydney, President of the Australian Jewish Welfare Society, who sought to prevent damage to the standing of Australian Jewry. In his words, the prospect of large-scale migration was

> awful, not only for the Jews, but for this country... Jews should only enter "in small lots". The present Jewish communities of Australia prize above all things the respect and goodwill of their fellow citizens. The Australian Jewish Welfare Society is determined to do nothing that might even remotely injure that goodwill.[24]

Certainly in 1938, if not in 1939, the Welfare Society urged that the paramount consideration was assimilability, not the desperate plight of European Jewry.[25] For some Australian Jews, the thought of large numbers of foreign Jews, with their strange mannerisms and different language, was abhorrent. As one remarked,

> I do not want this place overrun with foreigners, no matter where they come from. I can't stand them, their outlook or their method of living. I live Australian, think Australian and play Australian. My kids are Australian and won't have a bar of foreign kids. Maybe that seems intolerant, but I want to make it clear that I am an Aussie of the Jewish religion.[26]

Such views held by established Jews were not shared by Yiddish speakers, who knew firsthand the desperate plight facing their relatives and friends, nor by those who had recently arrived from Germany and other countries. In contrast to those fearful for their own positions, the Kadimah extended a warm welcome to immigrants who had recently settled in Melbourne.

---

24 Sydney *Sun*, 2 November 1938; Sydney *Truth*, 6 November 1938.
25 Markus, 'Jewish Migration to Australia', pp.22–23.
26 *Sunday Truth* 4 October 1938, cited in Golvan, *The Distant Exodus*, p.13.

> With the darkening clouds mercilessly enveloping our people in Central and Eastern Europe, numbers of our brothers and sisters have turned to these shores for life and hope. We note with pleasure the fine type of these newcomers. Many are already fitting themselves into the life of the community, and we have no doubt that they will be actively engaged contributing to our cultural life in the near future. We take this opportunity in extending them a hearty welcome.[27]

In response to worsening conditions in Poland and a sense that urgent action had to be taken, the Polish Jewish Relief Fund (PJRF) was formed in Melbourne in 1935, under the chairmanship of J. Lederman, with A.S. Rose as its treasurer. Rose, who was born in Poland in 1880, migrated to Melbourne in 1905 and was a successful manufacturer who was to remain an influential welfare advocate until his death in 1948. The PJRF continued to operate until 1942 when it transformed itself into the United Jewish Overseas Relief Fund although it remained composed entirely of Yiddish speakers from Eastern Europe, with a significant proportion of Bundists among its founders and committed workers. Indicative of the mood of the time of the PJRF's formation, Sender Burstin wrote in *Di Yiddishe Nayes*: 'We are receiving alarming reports from both the international press and from private sources about the catastrophic and hopeless situation of the Jewish masses in Poland. These reports are shocking to everyone regardless of whether or not one has family in *'der alter heym'*.[28]

One of the achievements of the PJRF was the rescue of 20 Polish Jewish male orphans aged 15 and 16, arranging their landing permits

---

27   Kadimah Annual Report, December 1937.
28   Sender Burstin, *Yiddish Nayes*, 6 June 1935; see also Sender Burstin, 'Rising Anti-Semitism Facing Polish Jewry in the 1930s', in *Yiddish Melbourne Observed*, translated by Ben and David Burstin, Melbourne: Australian Centre for Jewish Civilisation, Monash University, 2013, p.110

and welfare guarantees. They arrived on 28 May 1939, less than four months before the outbreak of war. Their guarantors included Samuel Wynn, Leo Fink, Moishe Plotkin, Israel Sher and Jonas Pushett. Each boy had a formal guardian, while Jonas Pushett acted as group guardian with oversight of all the group's undertakings.[29]

Warsaw-born Jonas Pushett had arrived in Melbourne in 1927 with only £50, a strong sense of community involvement, of *Yiddishkeit*, and of the importance of looking after one's own. In addition to being a founder of the PJRF, he became an active Kadimah committee member, a worker for Jewish Welfare for more than three decades, a treasurer of Carlton synagogue and a notable philanthropist, giving financial assistance and in kind support for Yiddish writers such as Pinchas Goldhar, Yehoshua Rapaport and Herz Bergner.[30] Pushett was typical of this generation of Yiddishists – prepared to roll up their sleeves, do the work that needed to be done and stand up and be counted.

The PJRF had a fractious relationship with the mainstream Australian Jewish Welfare Society over costs incurred and subsidies paid to the orphans for their maintenance. The PJRF seemed to be a law unto itself, in the eyes of the Welfare Society. Disputes centred on accountability and transparency, rather than on any belief in the 20 orphans, 16 of whom went on to serve in the Australian armed forces during the Second World War. They remembered fondly their weekly visits to the Pushett family home, where they were greeted with warmth, kindness, tea and biscuits with homemade jam.

It was not just Yiddish speakers in need of assistance. In 1936 the German Jewish Relief Fund was established to assist German and

---

29 Burstin, 'Rising Anti-Semitism Facing Polish Jewry in the 1930s'.
30 'Jonas Pushett (1898–1994)', *Yiddish Melbourne*, http://future.arts.monash.edu/yiddish-melbourne/biographies-jonas-pushett/, accessed 6 April 2018.

Austrian refugees arriving in Melbourne.[31] In the same year the Welcome Society was revived. Its office-bearers reflected a growing diversity and a wider brief. In 1938 its President was A.S. Rose, Louis Morris was Vice-President, and Jonas Pushett Treasurer. The expanded committee included St Kilda Rabbi Jacob Danglow, Rabbi Herman Sanger of the Liberal Reform congregation and Rabbi Joseph Gurewicz of the Carlton Synagogue.[32]

By 1939, the Australian Jewish Welfare Society offered an extensive range of welfare services: a children's home, Larino; a fulltime employment officer; regular English classes; land at Shepparton purchased for migrants wishing to be farmers; start-up loans to migrants wishing to go into business; student loans for those immigrants wishing to go to university; relocation loans for transportation and furniture; regular upkeep of the Polish Jewish orphans; and a women's auxiliary who met new arrivals and offered a wide range of support services.[33]

Viennese-born Shmuel Rosenkranz who arrived in Melbourne on 20 March 1939 summed up how the different welfare organisations co-existed:

> There were two or three societies covering different areas. There was the Polish Relief Society and the Pushett family was well connected to that... And there was already in existence the Jewish Welfare Society. These virtually competed. The only difference, and I'm speaking 1939, was the Jewish Welfare Society did not make great efforts to bring people. But the Polish Relief Society, Mr Pushett, tried to get people out. Jewish Welfare helped once they were already here. They helped with accommodation, interest free loans and a stipend.[34]

---

31 Benjamin, *A Serious Influx of Jews*, p.51.
32 Benjamin, *A Serious Influx of Jews*, p.52.
33 Benjamin, *A Serious Influx of Jews*, pp.79–80.
34 Shmuel Rosenkranz, interview with Jewish Museum of Australia, 4 August 1992.

ESCAPE

Mina Fink (nee Waks) came to Melbourne from Bialystok in 1932 as the young bride of Leo Fink who had arrived four years earlier. In 1938 the Finks returned to Bialystok on a family visit. They were shocked by the deterioration of Jewish life in Poland and the looming Nazi threat. On returning to Melbourne, Mina tried desperately to help family members escape Poland, but to no avail.

> In 1938, I managed to go for a trip to Poland to see the family. It was terrible there. You used to turn on the radio and the blurring voice of Hitler came through and a cold shudder went through my body. Members of the family were asking me to obtain permits for their 14 and 15 year olds. I only stayed three weeks and when I returned home there was not enough time to process the permits.[35]

Jews who succeeded in securing a landing permit often did so through personal contacts, or had sufficient capital to start new businesses and entrepreneurial skills, preferably both.[36] All faced obstacles. In a context in which only a very small proportion of applications could be granted, government policy, however, favoured German and Austrian Jews. A case in point is that of the Lippmann family. Hamburg-born Walter Lippmann, who was to become a leading community figure, arrived in November 1938 following a series of interventions by the family's close business associates in Melbourne. When the Lippmann family decided that they had no future in Nazi Germany, Walter's father, Franz Lippmann, contacted three business associates in Australia, Robert Bain, William McPherson and Walter Berry – men of considerable influence and stature – to act as sponsors for their landing permits. Prestigious connections were

---

35 Golvan, *The Distant Exodus*, p.11.
36 Janis Wilton, 'Refugees', in *Australians 1938*, edited by Bill Gammage and Peter Spearritt, Sydney: Fairfax, Syme & Weldon Associates, 1987, pp.409–415.

rightly thought to be advantageous at a time of great urgency and imminent danger.[37]

Walter Berry used personal contacts with the secretary of the Department of the Interior to expedite the applications, advising Franz Lippmann that 'as I addressed the Secretary of the Department of the Interior through a personal friend, your application will be received very much sooner than those who were not so fortunate in being able to take this unofficial action.'[38] McPherson not only attested that 'all members of the family would be most suitable immigrants to Australia' but also assured the authorities that 'Lippmann had the capital to commence and carry on his proposed trade'. Walter's landing permit arrived in time for him to leave in September 1938, aged 19, aboard the *Niagara*, arriving in Australia in November of that year. The events of Kristallnacht, during which Franz Lippmann was briefly imprisoned, hastened the departure of the rest of the family, who managed to arrive in Australia in January 1939. The Lippmann family, leading citizens of Hamburg, had financial resources and a proven record in business. It all added up to the ideal combination of factors needed to expedite a visa – together with the right Australian contacts and a substantial measure of luck.[39]

Yiddish speakers of Eastern Europe were rarely so advantaged. Desperation did not get you a visa. Among the few who did manage to escape was Shmuel Bennett and his immediate family. It was during the mid-1930s that the second stage of the Bennett family migration story unfolded in Poland. The bloody Przytyk pogrom of

---

37   Andrew Markus and Margaret Taft, eds, *Walter Lippmann, Ethnic Communities Leader*, Melbourne: Australian Centre for Jewish Civilisation, Monash University, 2016, pp.2–6.

38   Markus and Taft, *Walter Lippmann*, pp.2–6.

39   Markus and Taft, *Walter Lippmann*, pp.2–6.

ESCAPE

9 March 1936, so close to Shmuel Bennett's family home in Radom, was the last straw for the family. The Bennetts decided to leave Poland by any means possible. In an audacious move and out of sheer desperation, Rachel Bennett took matters into her own hands. In 1936 she engaged an English translator to write an appeal to the new king, His Majesty King Edward VIII, to provide the Bennett family with a visa to one of his dominions as a coronation gift. The letter, simply addressed to 'Buckingham Palace, London', concluded with profuse blessings and best wishes for his royal future, which was to prove extremely short.

While her family and friends derided Rachel Bennett for what seemed a foolhardy undertaking, within two weeks she received, as if by miracle, a response from the British Home Office in Whitehall. Rachel Bennett was advised to present herself to the British embassy in Warsaw where she was provided with an immigration permit to Australia. But there was a condition – she had to be in possession of £200 landing money in addition to travel expenses. This was a sum well beyond her means.

Two American Jewish welfare organisations, the American Jewish Joint Distribution Committee (known as the Joint), founded in 1914 for the rescue and relief of Jews in crisis, and the Hebrew Immigrant Aid Society (known as HIAS), founded in 1881 in New York to assist Jews fleeing pogroms in Russia and Eastern Europe, came to Rachel Bennett's aid. Although it is not clear how she came to approach these organisations or why they decided to help, they provided the full cost of the journey for the entire family. This all took time and considerable effort and it was another two years before the family was reunited in London, in early 1939. Using his Polish identity papers, Moshe was able to join his family on the trip to Australia. The family left the *shtetlekh* of Europe and the teeming streets and alleyways of London's East End just months before the outbreak of war.[40]

The unusual case of the Bennetts reveals the extraordinary ingenuity and tenacity and support and luck that were required, over a number of years, to escape the perils of Poland. The Bennett migration story entailed family separation that spanned a decade, hazardous journeys and direct appeals to high authorities and Jewish agencies. In most other cases, Polish Jews had to reach out to the small number of family and friends already living in Melbourne, and to other parts of the world where they had connections.

For the overwhelming majority of Eastern European Yiddish-speaking Jews who gained entry to Australia in the interwar years, sponsorship provided the pathway to a new life. It was usually provided by family members already domiciled in Australia or by others who came from their town – *landsman*. This was the pattern of chain migration, a universal pattern among immigrant populations. In the case of Jewish migration, it all came down to a small number of Jews helping other Jews. For most, the pathway to a life in Australia was to prove elusive. The thought that so many of her family were unable to escape Poland haunted Mina Fink for the rest of her life: 'The news that war had broken out left me devastated. I had a terrible guilt complex as to why I didn't hurry with the permits. I could have saved a few more lives.'[41]

---

40   Bennett, *Chronicles of a Life*, pp.44–6.
41   Golvan, *The Distant Exodus*, p.11.

Part Two

Redefinitions: The Holocaust and Israel

Chapter 7

'IN A MOMENT OF CRISIS . . . DIVISIONS DISAPPEARED'

Jewish refugee Shmuel Rosenkranz remembered the lonely, grief-stricken men who came in search of safety, but who soon found themselves cut off from their loved ones: 'There were lots of married men who left their families and said, "We are coming to Australia, we'll make a few bob, we'll send for our wife. We'll send for our children."'[1] But for many, this ambition never materialised as the outbreak of war brought to an abrupt end any hope of escape. If migration to Australia had been difficult in the pre-war years, now it was impossible. Instead of much hoped-for family reunions, now came the horrendous news of the murderous campaign waged against Europe's Jews.

Press reports of the fate of Europe's Jews

The mainstream and Jewish press reported the progress of the war, often documenting atrocities committed by the Nazis. In contrast to the daily press, for which the plight of Jews was but one of many issues reported, for the Jewish press the slaughter in Europe was

---

1   Shmuel Rosenkranz, interview with Jewish Museum of Australia, 4 August 1992.

paramount. As early as October and November 1939 the *Australian Jewish Herald* began employing terms such as 'annihilation' and 'extermination' to describe the Nazi campaign in Poland.

In an article airmailed to Australia by the Jewish Telegraphic Agency and published on 26 October, it was revealed that 'short-wave broadcasts by Polish secret stations in Nazi-occupied territory picked up here [Paris] give a graphic picture of the annihilation of the Jewish population in all the towns occupied by the Nazis'. On 23 November, the lead story on the front page of the *Jewish Herald*, headlined 'Polish Jews Facing Extinction', described how 'one and half million Jews are threatened with starvation and extinction'. The *Hebrew Standard of Australasia* ran a front-page story on 21 December 1939: 'Nazis Massacre Jews in Polish Towns', in which gruesome facts of 'mass murders' were detailed.

News reports were received via a number of information channels, with the Jewish press relying heavily on the Jewish Telegraphic Agency, which had been founded in 1917 as an international news and wire service for Jewish communities and media outlets. Among other sources were a range of international newspapers: *Jewish Frontier, Jewish Chronicle, Jerusalem Post, Daily Telegraph, Lithuanian Newspaper* and German newspapers. Underground reports were often smuggled out of occupied territories and made public through the BBC, the Polish Government in Exile in London and war correspondents, in particular those of *The New York Times* and *New York Post*. Messages from clandestine radio stations operating in Poland were monitored and published. Eyewitness accounts were recorded and sent to different newsagencies for public release. One of the most famous was the report written by the Jewish secular socialist Bund in early May 1942, smuggled out of Poland to London and broadcast by the BBC on 2 June. It began with the declaration, 'From the day the Russo-German war broke out, the Germans embarked on the physical extermination of the Jewish population on Polish soil, using the Ukrainian and the Lithuanian Fascists for this job'.[2]

From the outset there was an understanding in the Jewish press that what was occurring to Europe's Jews was without precedent, even if the full implications were unclear. It was 'difficult to find in the world's history another instance of annihilation that can match in ruthlessness and cruelty that being conducted by the Nazi conquerors of Poland' reported noted Zionist leader of the Poale Zion movement, author and journalist Abraham Revusky in 1940.[3]

An understanding of the Jewish genocide was still developing, but as mass murders continued, readers were given graphic descriptions of Nazi actions. Reports emerged from all occupied countries and cities, often citing numbers executed and sites of mass killings. On 23 October 1941, the *Australian Jewish Herald* ran a report from the *Jewish Herald* Special Service, which gave an overview of the situation in France, Hungary, Poland, Croatia and Rumania. It listed numbers executed: 'nearly 9000 Jews have been executed under German direction in Rumania'; numbers deported: 'over 6000 Croatian Jews have been deported from the cities to the salt mines where they are forced to work under conditions that must mean their virtual extermination'; and ghettos to be established in Poland: 'it is expected that ghettos will be established shortly in the towns of the incorporated territory'.

---

2   Quoted in Walter Laqueur, *The Terrible Secret: An Investigation into the Suppression of Information about Hitler's 'Final Solution'*, London: Weidenfeld and Nicolson, 1980, p.137.
3   *Australian Jewish Herald*, 1 February 1940.

A SECOND CHANCE

In 1942, the year in which the killings of the Final Solution reached their peak, the Jewish press was unequivocal that 'the Jews of Europe are no longer being persecuted, but systematically exterminated'. Mention was made of Treblinka, Belzec and Sobibor, and methods of execution that included 'gassings'.[4]

The mainstream press also carried stories about Nazi atrocities, but not with the same force or urgency. It wasn't their main concern and was rarely given prominence; nor were the full implications understood at the time. On 30 November 1939 *The Argus* ran a story entitled 'Terror and Plunder: Nazi Rule in Poland'. Rather than pinpoint the Jews as the main victims of Nazi aggression, it emphasised the transgressions against all Poles, with the Jews as one of the targets. The universalisation of the victim was common when publicising atrocities against Jews. The American press frequently identified Jewish victims as 'Poles', 'Russians' or innocent civilians.[5]

Information did not easily translate into knowledge and understanding. Sometimes the truth lay buried beneath a mass of information, or it was positioned away from headline coverage as it was deemed a relatively low priority. When *The Sydney Morning Herald* reported on 26 June 1942 the 'vast slaying of Jews: Nazis kill 700,000 in Poland', it did so on page six, in a small indistinguishable column under a large photo of damage done to Darwin by Japanese bombardment. Two columns to the right, an article extolled the virtues of allowing 'liquor concession to war workers', giving equal space to both stories on the same page. Australia's own interests were understandably paramount. Immediately to the left of the report on

---

4   *Australian Jewish Herald*, 26 November 1942.
5   Deborah E. Lipstadt, *Beyond Belief*, New York: The Free Press, 1986, p. 250.

the mass killings were two international reports, 'Attack on Hawaii: How First News Came to USA' and 'German Raids on Britain: Five Planes Down'. In the larger scheme of things, Jewish deaths were seen as just another story from the war front that was no more or less important than the others.

In December 1942 the Allied powers issued a joint statement condemning the Nazi actions. The mainstream press treated this as a major story about the Allied response to Jewish victimisation rather than about Jewish suffering. On 18 December 1942 *The Argus* ran a front-page story, 'Annihilation of Jews, Allied Declaration', in which it reported that 'The Allied Governments condemned in the strongest terms these brutalities'. Other Australian newspapers, such as the Tasmanian *Advocate* and *The West Australian* also reported on the Declaration and the state of European Jewry, headlined 'Inhumanity to Jews One of World's Greatest Calamities'[6] and 'Jewish Horror: The Allied Declaration'.[7] The story was not, however, always given prominence. On the same day, *The Sydney Morning Herald* ran the story on page four, 'Massacre of Jews: Joint Declaration by Allies', and reported that Jews from all occupied countries were being transported to Poland which had 'been made the principal Nazi slaughterhouse'.[8]

What was known about the war and relayed publicly through the media was not always understood. When the Adelaide *Mail* reported on 4 September 1943 that 'Nazis Steamed Jews To Death' it revealed a partial truth. The Nazis were indeed using a 'new', more efficient way of committing mass murder in the form of gassing. It was not

---

6 *The Advocate*, 19 December 1942.
7 *The West Australian*, 19 December 1942.
8 *The Sydney Morning Herald*, 19 December 1942.

steam but a far more deadly vapour that was used. Still, the truth lay in the method if not in the means; clarity and understanding of this nature was to come later.

In late 1943 the mainstream press featured an estimate that four million Jews had been murdered. A Nazi newspaper was quoted on 11 March 1943, boasting that most towns under occupation had been rendered *judenrein* (free of Jews). In March 1944 Auschwitz was named as the largest death camp and the mass round-up and extermination of Hungarian Jewry was duly reported, although the devastating ramifications of these reports were not understood until the end of the war.

News of individuals

While there was much information to feed the anxiety of those with family in the countries occupied by the Nazis, there was little news of the fate of particular individuals. Letters from family and friends trapped in hostile territory rarely reached Australia. As a child, Sarah Wein, whose family arrived from Warsaw in January 1939, witnessed the toll that lack of information about family had on her parents: 'My parents, especially my mother, were very depressed and worried about the absolute silence from the family in Poland. No matter how many letters were sent, there were no replies'.[9]

The fate of individuals trapped in Europe was rarely known to those in Melbourne until 1945 or later. Julie Meadows was a young child growing up in a Yiddish-speaking family in Carlton during the war. She also had family trapped in Poland. Julie recalled that,

---

9   Sarah Wein in *A Shtetl in Ek Velt: 54 Stories of Growing up in Jewish Carlton*, edited by Julie Meadows, Australian Centre for Jewish Civilisation, Monash University, 2011, p.253.

'Anxiety must have gnawed at everyone, but nothing was ever said in front of the children. Pola was to lose Shia and also her parents and youngest sister, Yocheved, my mother's loss as well. My father lost everyone except two nephews, but none of this was known till after the war'.[10] Sam Lipski, whose formative years were spent within Carlton's Yiddish-speaking community, recalled that, 'People did not know what had happened to their families . . . during the war, news was not specific. Everyone knew something terrible had happened. This was made worse by the sheer length of the war'.[11]

With few exceptions, most Jews in Melbourne were left in the dark. Erwin Rado, an assimilated Hungarian Jew who had arrived in Melbourne in August 1939, recalled that 'there was no correspondence [during the war]. I knew nothing [of] what went on in Hungary, I didn't know what happened to my folk, [my] parents [and] aunt and the rest of the relatives',[12] even though Hungary was not occupied until 1944. And when information was available it defied belief. As Malcha Brown, who had arrived in Melbourne in March 1939 to join her husband Chaim, recalled, 'We listened to the radio for news of the war. One night we heard that Shmuel Zygielbaum [Bund leader] had suicided in front of 10 Downing Street, London [in 1943]. We couldn't believe what was happening in Europe'.[13]

The systematic and total extermination of an entire people was beyond human experience, beyond comprehension. There was no point of reference. A famous encounter in Washington in 1943 between Polish emissary Jan Karski and US Supreme Court Justice

---

10 Julie Meadows in *A Shtetl in Ek Velt*, p.201.
11 Sam Lipski interview with Jewish Museum of Australia, 10 August 1992.
12 Erwin Rado, interview with Andrew Markus, 25 January 1991.
13 Malcha Brown in *A Shtetl in Ek Velt*, p.207.

Felix Frankfurter exemplifies the chasm between knowledge and understanding. When Karski told Frankfurter about the slaughter of Jews that he had witnessed, Frankfurter responded that he did not believe him. When Karski protested, Frankfurter explained that he was not implying that Karski was lying, just that it was beyond his understanding.[14]

When personal information did arrive, the consequences were often devastating. Leon Mann, whose father migrated to Australia from Poland via Palestine in the 1920s, remembers the effect of such news: 'One day in spring 1942, one of the young religious men snapped mentally when he received terrible news about the fate of family in Europe. For hours he wailed inconsolably and then had to be forcibly restrained . . . I was frightened by the outpouring of such profound grief'.[15]

Yiddish actor Yasha Sher recalled the workings of informal networks and information-sharing when a letter arrived: 'The theatre [at the Kadimah] was a meeting place for *landsleit* (people from the same town). One got a letter, another got a letter and they tried to put together what happened'.[16]

Melbourne Jewry unites

Hitler's war against the Jews gave Melbourne Jewry a common purpose and an understanding of their shared destiny. While the Jewish community still had many factions – orthodox, reform, secular, Bundist, Zionist, established Jews, German and Yiddish-speaking newcomers – it nevertheless demonstrated an ability to pull

---

14 Walter Laqueur, *The Terrible Secret*, p.3.
15 Leon Mann in *A Shtetl in Ek Velt*, p.256.
16 Yasha Sher, interview with Jewish Museum of Australia, 30 July 1992.

together in the face of extreme adversity. The community directed its collective energy to supporting the war effort. Internal divisions did not disappear, but some could be put aside, for the time being anyway. As Shmuel Rosenkranz recalled:

> I would say that there were a number of communities. There was a community that centred around religious institutions ... And then there was a community which centred around the Kadimah – no question the Kadimah was the home of the secular Jew. But let me put it this way, in a moment of crisis these divisions disappeared.[17]

The community's response to the war was a gritty determination to do all it could to support an Allied victory and its activities were on a number of fronts.

Public meetings, rallies, days of mourning

Public meetings and rallies were a way of demonstrating communal solidarity, to bolster both fundraising initiatives and recruitment for the armed forces; but they could also be occasions for sharing precious information. The Bund organised a regular *lebedike tsaytung* (living newspaper, delivered verbally) at the Kadimah. Sender Burstin recalled how this worked:

> The editorial was presented by *chaveyrim* Yankev Waks, Binem Warszawski, Yitzhak Kahn, Chaim Rosenstein and me. Also the well-known journalist from Bialystok, A. Zbar, would often contribute a literary essay. The 'live newspapers' would attract an audience of between 300 and 400 because the information that we provided was not to be found in the Jewish press.[18]

---

17 Shmuel Rosenkranz, interview with Jewish Museum of Australia, 4 August 1992.
18 Sender Burstin, *Yiddish Melbourne Observed*, p.129.

A SECOND CHANCE

As news of the escalating death toll in Europe spread, public days of mourning and fast days were proclaimed. These were a public means of dealing with private loss and grief, in accordance with Jewish custom. On 16 February 1942, a public fast day was declared by the Beth Din, the Jewish religious court. Special prayers and *slichot* (penitential prayers) appropriate to the occasion were held at the *mincha* service at the Carlton United Hebrew Congregation in Palmerston Street. Rabbi Gurewicz officiated and delivered a special sermon to a full synagogue.

On 11 July 1942, a mass meeting was held under the auspices of the new Zionist organisation to protest the mass murder of European Jewry. The Carlton hall was filled to capacity and many were turned away. The meeting passed a number of resolutions. They demanded that all Nazi criminals be prosecuted after the war in accordance with the rule of law, that compensation be paid to all victims, that international conventions be put in place to stop these acts of murder ever happening again, that the British government and the Allied forces arm every man and woman in Palestine so that they could defend themselves and fight the enemy threatening their existence, and called upon all Australians to give unconditional support to the war effort. These resolutions were forwarded to the leaders of the allied powers, Curtin, Churchill, Roosevelt and Stalin.

On 13 December 1942, a day of mourning for the Jewish community was declared. This time the event was organised by the established Jewish community, the Melbourne Advisory Board and supported by the Beth Din. The function was held at the Melbourne Hebrew Congregation synagogue. Rabbi Danglow gave the public address. In publicising the day of fasting, the announcement in the *Jewish Herald* began with a statement of Nazi intent: 'Himmler's decree that half the Jews of Poland must be exterminated by the end of the year has shocked the world and plunged Jewry into deepest grief'.

Welfare and fundraising

The Jewish press was in full support of the community's patriotic efforts. The front page of the *Australian Jewish Herald* was often emblazoned with advertisements calling for its readers to 'give until it hurts' and to dig deep, 'No money – no victory. We must back the attack!'

On 22 February 1940, a major appeal was launched in Melbourne to provide aid to Jewish refugees able to escape Nazi-occupied countries and flee into Hungary and Rumania. In a demonstration of communal unity, the president of the appeal committee was Mr Archie Michaelis, a member of the established Jewish community, and the chairman was Mr Samuel Wynn, a well-known Yiddishist.[19] The extent of fundraising activity during the war years was far-reaching. It seemed that every group, every synagogue, every organisation had a hand in raising money, both for an Allied victory and for Jewish relief. One minor news item in the *Australian Jewish Herald* on 18 March 1943 lists activities of 13 different organisations – the Kadimah, Ezra Association, North Judean League, WIZO Younger Set, Judean Red Cross, Jewish Youth Council, Youth Aliya Committee, Ladies' Auxiliary, Melbourne Hebrew Congregation, Jewish Philanthropic Society, War Effort Circle, Council of Jewish Women and the Junior Auxiliary of the Jewish Women's Guild.

The Victorian branch of the Sydney-based United Emergency Committee (UEC) was formed at a meeting in Melbourne on

---

19   'Polish Jewish Relief', *Australian Jewish Herald*, 22 February 1940.

28 January 1943. The *Australian Jewish Herald* noted that the meeting 'embraced all shades of opinion within the Melbourne Jewish community'.[20] Rabbi Dr Freedman was elected chairman and a committee, comprising Rabbi Dr Hermann Sanger, Alec Masel, Dr Aron Patkin, Alec Mushin, Sam Yaffe, Leslie Abrahams and Paul Morawetz, was appointed. Walter Lippmann was co-opted as honorary secretary. It claimed 62 different organisations as its members.[21] In June 1943 the UEC launched the Jewish People's Relief Fund, which quickly became an autonomous entity, with its own constitution and a 25-member board. Most of those who seized control of this initiative were Yiddishists: Leo Fink, Wolf Fink, B. Frydman, Joseph Giligich, Jacob Ginter, B. Harrison, Maurice Hiller, Yehuda Honig, M. Isaacson, H. Lederman, Jewel Okno, S. Oshlack, Jonas Pushett, Isaac Ripps, Arthur Rose, Israel Sher, R. Shulman, Myer Silman, A. Sokol, S. Stock, Yankev Waks, Binem Warszawski, Rabbi Warszawski and Myer Zeltner.

Within a month the Fund took over the running of the UEC. In a letter published in the *Australian Jewish News* on 23 July 1943, signed jointly by Rabbi Freedman as chairman of the UEC and Leo Fink as chairman of the People's Relief Fund, it declared that 'there will henceforth be one fund only to be known as the United Jewish Relief Fund.' By November 1943 it had been reconstituted as the United Jewish Overseas Relief Fund (UJORF). It strove to represent all sections of the Jewish community but was predominantly run and led by Eastern European Yiddishists, with Leo Fink as its first elected

---

20   *Australian Jewish Herald*, 4 February 1943.
21   Rodney Benjamin, 'A Serious Influx of Jews', p.142.

president. It was the start of a Yiddishist revolution in Jewish welfare that would reach its peak in the post-war years.

The UJORF's charter was to 'render moral and financial support to European Jews wherever they may be'. By 1944 its chief focus had changed to rescuing survivors. In June 1944 the annual report of the UJORF claimed a membership of 1,794, with an additional ladies' group of 771 members. In its first year £40,000 (equivalent to nearly $3 million in today's currency) had been sent overseas. During the twelve months to the end of June 1945, another £42,000 in cash was sent to relief organisations overseas: £26,000 to the American Joint Distribution Committee, £13,250 to the Jewish Agency for Palestine, and £750 to each of the World Jewish Congress, OT-OZE (Union of Jewish Health Organisations), the New Zionist Organization, and Agudas Israel.[22]

The community didn't just send money; an abundance of goods was also shipped to relief centres overseas: 22 tons of soap, 18 tons of honey, over 26,000 woollen blankets, 1,500 tons of kosher meat, second-hand clothing (20,000 items of clothing, 6,800 pairs of shoes), tinned food, jams and sheep skins. Given that Australia was still operating under a wartime economy, this was a monumental achievement.[23] While all this was going on, the Bund was making its own commitment to Jewish relief through its links with the Australian Labor Party. Close connections with a prominent member of the Labor government, Arthur Calwell, bore fruit. As Sender Burstin recalled:

---

22 Benjamin, *A Serious Influx of Jews*, p.157.
23 Benjamin, *A Serious Influx of Jews*, p.158.

Calwell helped us in another matter. We wanted to send funds to Poland to help Jews suffering in the ghettos. This was not an easy thing to put into effect. What government would permit sending money to a country occupied by the enemy? But we did get permission ... The path to Poland was via the channels of the Jewish Labor Committee in America.[24]

While fundraising to support Jews caught in catastrophic circumstances overseas was the community's immediate concern, the need to support local Jews continued. The Australian Jewish Welfare Society continued to focus on a diverse range of local welfare services to the migrant community – the Larino children's home, agricultural resettlement, subsistence loans for those experiencing hardships, and the Polish Youth Migrant Fund. During the war years, the Welfare Society board members were, with the exception of Archie Michaelis, either migrants or the children of migrants; none were descended from English Jews.[25]

'Young men started appearing in uniform'

Just as they had done during the Great War, Australian Jewry answered the call to enlist. Leaders from the established Jewish community were at the forefront of the Jewish recruitment drive. Even before war was officially declared, Rabbi Falk, acting chief minister of Sydney's Great Synagogue, told his radio listeners that 'should the hour strike when the Empire calls its sons to defend its flag, Israel will respond with a mighty "Here I am"'.[26] Four days after Australia declared war with Germany, the Victorian Jewish Advisory

---

24 Burstin, *Yiddish Melbourne Observed*, p.128.
25 Benjamin, *A Serious Influx of Jews*, p.83–4.
26 Radio address, 30 August 1939, cited in Mark Dapin, *Jewish Anzacs: Jews in the Australian Military*, Sydney: NewSouth Publishing, 2017, p.159.

'IN A MOMENT OF CRISIS...'

Board proclaimed that 'we stand united' and that 'the community places all its resources behind those who fight for civilisation and human rights'.[27] In a letter to the Director General of recruiting, the President of the Victorian Jewish Advisory Board, Archie Michaelis, pledged the Jewish community to 'energetic support of the campaign for recruits'.[28]

The call to arms was echoed by the Kadimah, which reiterated at one of its general meetings that 'we must be ready for duty and service to our country and to our people in whatever capacity we are called upon to serve'.[29] But their readiness wasn't only in support of the British Commonwealth or the urging of Prime Minister Menzies to contribute 'to the last man and the last shilling'. It was based on the expectation that a speedy Allied victory would halt the extermination of Europe's Jews.

Some 4,200 Jewish men and women served in the Australian Imperial Force, with a further 940 in the Royal Australian Air Force and 120 in the Royal Australian Navy, representing an enlistment rate that was significantly higher than the national enlistment rate.[30] They came from all walks of life: European-born Yiddish speakers, Australian-born children of immigrants, and those whose ancestry dated back to the earliest arrivals in the Australian colonies. Australian Jewish servicemen and women received 120 wartime awards for bravery and conspicuous service.[31] The most senior ranking Jewish soldier in the Second World War was Major-General

---

27 *Australian Jewish Herald*, 7 September 1939.
28 *Australian Jewish Herald*, 6 June 1940.
29 *Australian Jewish Herald*, 6 June 1940.
30 Dapin, *Jewish Anzacs*, p.259.
31 Walter Jona, 'The VAJEX Story: Achievements in War and Peace', *Australian Jewish Historical Society Journal*, Vol. XII, part 1 (1993): p.171.

Paul Alfred Cullen, while the senior Hebrew Chaplain was Colonel Rabbi Jacob Danglow whose service as chaplain spanned two world wars.[32]

The high rate of enlistment had an impact on Jewish community life. Of the 72 male members of the youth group of the Liberal synagogue in Melbourne, 59 enlisted. One hundred and twenty-nine, or 25 per cent, of the 3rd St Kilda Scout Group (known as Danglow's Own) enlisted; ten were killed in action. Almost 100 per cent of male members of Jewish sporting clubs joined the services.[33]

Of the personal toll on individuals, Julie Meadows recalled:

> In Melbourne, young men started appearing in uniform. My cousin Joe joined the air force. He was sent to England and survived many sorties but was shot down over France in 1944. Soon after, his youngest brother Charlie died of a ruptured appendix in an army training camp in northern Victoria. My auntie Tsesha became ill and was never well again.[34]

Initially, Jews who had not been naturalised and were thus still legally 'aliens' were unable to join the army. The Australian government modified its policy and enabled unnaturalised subjects to join, but initially they could only serve in the army's Labour Corps, established in February 1942.

Jews from the Melbourne community were mostly concentrated in Fourth, Sixth and Eighth companies, later commonly known as Employment Companies. They were unarmed units that, although uniformed and subject to army discipline, had labour rather than combat as their line of duty. With few exceptions, all served locally

---

32   Dapin, *Jewish Anzacs*, p.153 and Jona, 'The VAJEX Story', p.172.
33   Jona, 'The VAJEX Story', p.171.
34   Julie Meadows in *A Shtetl in Ek Velt*, p.201.

and were not deployed overseas. Erwin Rado commented that it was a bitter blow: 'We were all fairly disgruntled. Those who joined wanted to fight. They explained that under international law they couldn't give us a gun, we couldn't fight, so we had to work.'[35] Painter and artist Yosl Bergner also hoped to fight the Germans, but was similarly conscripted to the Labour Corps.

The exact number of volunteers to serve in the ranks of the Labour Corps is unclear. One report indicates that the Eighth Company eventually reached a maximum strength of 600, with some serving well into 1946.[36] The age range of the Eighth Company was considerable; a father and son are known to have served together. Unit members initially picked fruit, but were later used to sort decaying rubber goods, load and unload trucks, ships, and railway wagons, handle crates of tinned food, potato sacks, even coffins, and American supplies of clothing for its forces. Eventually one detachment was stationed at Albury and another at Tocumwal to work in the railway goods yards.[37] The work in all the employment companies was menial and army discipline was tedious, as Rado recalled:

> We were trained how to march and about turn and wheel and what not and we sneered at this because we said we didn't need it, and if occasionally there was no work they took us on a route march. We had to sing Australian songs which we didn't know.[38]

It wasn't only Jews who made up the Labour Corps. Yosl Bergner recalled the different nationalities in his unit:

---

35 Erwin Rado, interview with Andrew Markus, 25 January 1987.
36 Klaus Loewald, 'The Eighth Australian Employment Company', *Australian Journal of Politics and History*, Vol. 31, issue 1 (1985): p.80.
37 Loewald, 'The Eighth Australian Employment Company', p.85.
38 Erwin Rado, interview with Andrew Markus, 25 January 1987.

> We were Division 6, which had Italians, Greeks, Albanians, Yugoslavs and even an Estonian – there must have been twenty different nationalities. Yossel Birstein [the Yiddish poet] joined up too and we were in the same platoon – four and a half years in the same tent. The officers were Australians and they felt very superior to us.[39]

The Jews who made up the Labour Corps were from many different political factions and backgrounds – German Jews, Polish Jews, Russian Jews, Bundists, Zionists, orthodox, secular – and thus representative of the community they came from.

Work on the home front

As part of the government's manpower management, many individuals within the Jewish community were also called upon to work in jobs directed by the government. Carlton resident Hymie Kolt, whose parents arrived from Russia in the mid-1920s, recalled his father's role on the domestic front during the war years: 'those who worked in non-essential industries, among them my father, were organised by Manpower Australia to work for the war effort. My father never told us what work he was assigned to, and when asked, he would whisper, "Top Secret"'.[40]

The son of Polish immigrants, Bernie Zerman remembers his family's contribution to the war effort: 'It was 1942 and my parents' factory was flat out manufacturing clothing and camouflage netting for the war'.[41] Julie Meadows' father became a clicker in a factory making boots for the army until 1944,[42] while Theo Weisberg recalls

---

39 Yosl Bergner in *A Shtetl in Ek Velt*, p.167.
40 Hymie Kolt in *A Shtetl in Ek Velt*, p.44.
41 Bernie Zerman in *A Shtetl in Ek Velt*, p.88.
42 Julie Meadows in *A Shtetl in Ek Velt*, p.210.

that 'during the war my father made braces for the armed services, and my mother had a dress shop in Sydney Road, Brunswick'.[43] Shirley Freedman's immigrant father 'worked at the Ellinson Brothers' factory as a tailor, making uniforms for the soldiers'.[44] Leon Mann's family were relocated from Broken Hill in New South Wales to Melbourne in 1942 so that his father could contribute to the war effort; 'Before long, he was working as a riveter in the Commonwealth Munitions factory at Fishermans Bend, Port Melbourne'.[45]

Some businesses were designated as particularly important to maintaining the home front. Harry Pose's family emigrated from Russia in the 1920s. They were grocers. Harry Pose recalled, 'During World War Two, grocery stores were declared "required businesses" so Sol was exempt from military service. He and Rae [Sol's mother] kept the business running, mixing chicory with the rarely available coffee and receiving payment in ration stamps as well as money'.[46]

In other ways individuals made their own small contribution to the welfare of the community. Mary Goffin's father, Yacov Bogatin, ran a cut-price tobacco shop in Lygon Street. She remembers how he tried to be fair and reasonable when luxury goods were in short supply:

> During the war it was hard to get cigarettes to meet the demand, so what my father did was to remove the cellophane from the packets, take half the cigarettes out and sell half-packs, so no customer would miss out altogether. Unlike other retailers who profited from shortages he never charged a penny more.[47]

---

43   Theo Weisberg in *A Shtetl in Ek Velt*, p.229.
44   Shirley Freedman in *A Shtetl in Ek Velt*, p.236.
45   Leon Mann in *A Shtetl in Ek Velt*, p.255.
46   Harry Pose in *A Shtetl in Ek Velt*, p.53.
47   Mary Goffin in *A Shtetl in Ek Velt*, p.191.

Life must go on

Social life in Melbourne didn't stop during the war years; life went on. Maybe it was because of people's attempt to enjoy life while they could that community activities thrived. This was a time for solidarity. Jews from all of walks of life supported the war effort, fundraising and each other. In this the Yiddishists stood shoulder to shoulder with their Australian Jewish counterparts, but differences within the community did not disappear or go away. The differences were most pronounced in the way they lived their lives and went about their daily business.

Australian Jews continued to enjoy the bachelors' balls they held at the Palais de Danse in St Kilda, gala music nights that guaranteed 'a passport for real fun and gaiety' under music maestro Jay Whiddon and his boys, Purim masked balls and card parties. These events often doubled as fundraisers, supporting local and Jewish causes. A new *matzah* factory opened in Ripponlea in early 1940. Although the Jewish population did not increase during the war years, Yiddish theatre and the activities of the Kadimah increased. Kadimah membership grew from 360 in 1938 to 681 in 1945. Ben Burstin recalled, 'During the 1940s the Kadimah was a hive of activity. There were many lectures, meetings and theatre productions and most of it was in Yiddish. As a family, we were always going to the Kadimah'.[48]

Yiddish theatre thrived. Classical Yiddish plays were staged, audiences saw what they had seen before. This was not a time for innovation. Plays that replicated what they had seen in *der alter heym* appealed. At a time of great turmoil, theatre provided a point of

---

48 Ben Burstin in *A Shtetl in Ek Velt*, p.136.

cultural stability.[49] The number of productions peaked in 1940 and 1941 when eight different plays were produced in each year. As the war intensified, causing more absences for military duty and bring more news of mass murder, the number of productions halved between 1942 and 1945.

The Kadimah served many purposes during the war years. As already discussed, for Jews with family trapped in Europe, the Kadimah provided a common space that offered solace through community support. Membership of the Kadimah gave individuals experiencing hardship and loss a sense of belonging at a time when their family in Europe were being dispossessed and murdered. 'There were a lot of people who left their dearest behind – wives, parents and so on. So the Kadimah was partly their second home,' recalled Yasha Sher. 'They didn't have their own homes yet . . . and they were very, very lonely. So they flocked to the Kadimah performances . . . .they came to the plays for comradeship, for company, for community'.[50]

In 1942 the Kadimah hosted an exhibition of Yosl Bergner's paintings, together with some by his other radical artist friends. Bergner's paintings depicted dislocated and dispossessed Aborigines with whom he empathised, seeing parallels between their treatment and the persecution and disenfranchisement of Polish ghetto Jews. In 1942 the Kadimah also published its second Yiddish book, the *Australian Jewish Almanac*. It included articles written by prominent Yiddish writers B Warshawski, Isaac Horowitz, Hirsh Munz, Dr Steinberg, Herz Bergner, Pinchas Goldhar, Chaim Rosenstein and Joseph Giligich.

---

49 Arnold Zable, *Wanderers and Dreamers: Tales of the David Herman Theatre*, Melbourne: Hyland House, 1998, p.81.
50 Yasha Sher, interview with Jewish Museum of Australia, 30 July 1992.

As well as the Kadimah, social activities were hosted by a variety of other Jewish organisations, such as synagogue congregations, WIZO, Zionist groups and the Bund. They included lectures, debates, concerts, and art exhibitions. Sam Lipski recalled that much of the Jewish community's social activity revolved around informal 'talk', in and around the synagogue; 'Talk was all about the family, the parents, the brother, the sister'.[51] Malcha Brown also recalled the role 'talk' played and its ability to heal and cross the emotional divide:

> The friends and *shiff shvester* [ship sisters who had arrived on the same ship] and *shiff brieders* [ship brothers] gathered and socialised in each other's homes, talking about the day's or week's happenings, reminiscing about the old country, discussing news of the war in Europe and sharing concerns about family and loved ones left behind.[52]

The Kadimah Younger Set was a mainstay of the youth of Carlton. In 1939 they commenced a series of Sunday night lectures, mostly in Yiddish. Often upwards of 100 young people attended the functions. Regular meetings were held on Thursday nights, the clubrooms were kept open on Wednesday evenings for social gatherings, while balls and socials were organised on many Saturday nights.[53] For Lou Jedwab, his involvement with the Kadimah Youth Organisation during the war years and the formation of a new network called the Open Forum Group in 1942 was an important part of his adolescence.

> They felt they needed more information, more discussions, particularly when the facts about the mass killing of Jews in Europe started to filter through in the early 1940s. The group met in the Culture House in North Carlton and some joined the Eureka

---

51 Sam Lipski, interview with Jewish Museum of Australia, 10 August 1992.
52 Malcha Brown in *A Shtetl in Ek Velt*, pp.207–8.
53 Susan Ivany, *Melbourne Chronicle*, June-July 1981.

Youth League when it was formed. Many young Jews joined the military forces or were conscripted; those still at school participated in campaigns to collect aluminium scrap and sheepskins for Russia, and collected signatures for a petition calling on the Allies to open a second front in Western Europe to relieve the beleaguered Russian armies slogging it out with the Germans in Stalingrad and other Russian cities.[54]

Jedwab talked of those who became his heroes when he was a teenager in war-time Australia: 'The Warsaw ghetto fighters were revered. The British fighter pilots who defended England against the Nazi bombers were cheered whenever they appeared on the newsreels; likewise the partisans in occupied Europe and of course the Red Army, which was delivering death blows to the Nazi invaders'.[55]

In May 1945 the war in Europe ended. Ticker-tape parades welcomed home the victorious Allied armies. The leaders of the free world promised a new era and a new world order; but the end of hostilities did not bring an end to suffering and grief for European Jews directly touched by the horrors of the Holocaust, nor for those living in its shadow in Melbourne. The war was over for some; it would never be over for others.

---

54 Lou Jedwab, 'The Kadimah Youth Organisation in Melbourne: Reminiscences 1942-53', *Australian Jewish Historical Society Journal*, Vol. XII, Part 1 (1993): p.180.
55 Jedwab, 'The Kadimah Youth Organisation', p.181.

Chapter 8

WORST FEARS CONFIRMED

'My first sense was of the sound of a lot of women crying', recalled Sam Lipski. 'You would hear this communal weeping. My father told me that's what it was all about – they were mourning. It was non-specific. Who knew?'[1] Leon Mann witnessed one personal response to the news that war was over:

> I began to comprehend the war a little better and the emotional pain suffered by the Jews of Carlton who came from Eastern Europe. Around the corner on Fenwick Street, our neighbours, the Dyskins, also listened to news of the war. Mr Dyskin was a tailor working at home. It was early in 1945 when news of the Allies' liberation of the extermination camps of Poland and what they found was broadcast to the world. Mrs Dyskin closed the curtains, put on a headscarf, lit two memorial candles and mourned for days.[2]

The full extent of the horrors of the Holocaust immediately began filtering through, as the camps were liberated by the Allies. On 21 April 1945, two weeks before the official surrender of the Nazi regime, the Melbourne *Argus* ran a story on page three with the headline 'Ghastliness of Nazi Prison Camp – How Able-Bodied

---

1 Sam Lipski, interview with Jewish Museum of Australia, 10 August 1992.
2 Leon Mann in *A Shtetl in Ek Velt*, p.257.

SS Brutes Wreaked the Fuhrer's Will'. Australian special correspondent Ronald Monson had entered British-liberated Bergen Belsen with the Royal Army Medical Corps and a team of international journalists. His four-hour visit filled him with horror as he 'saw the unbelievable'. His description of the camp was filled with graphic details of the dead and the dying, the starving and the helpless. He concluded his lengthy report: 'You might not like to believe this, but I do. Come to Belsen and you will believe anything.'[3]

Liberation of the concentration camps brought a plethora of reports, newsreels and photographs exposing Nazi brutality, in which 'the atrocities at these camps are beyond words or pictures'.[4] The Jewish press ran its own stories. On 2 March 1945, the *Australian Jewish News* article 'Death Camp – Oswiecim [Auschwitz]' reviewed transcripts from a Yugoslav War Crimes Committee as well as the 1944 clandestine report by the Jewish Labour Movement of Poland, which detailed the extent of murders carried out at Auschwitz.

The Jewish press, however, was more concerned with publishing eyewitness accounts by victims of Nazi brutality and not just those by observers. On 4 May 1945, it began a series of extracts from Yankel Wiernik's personal account of the Treblinka death camp. Titled 'The Hell of Treblinka', it gave graphic depictions of the horrors of the extermination camp. The paper provided a disclaimer, warning that it was 'no reading matter for people with weak nerves but for everyone who wants to see the naked truth'.

Throughout the early post-war years, more and more damning evidence emerged of the Nazis' proficiency in mass murder and its grim outcome. Australians may have been geographically isolated from the

---

3   *The Argus*, 21 April 1945.
4   'Pictures of German Camp Horrors', *The Argus*, 20 April 1945.

devastation of Europe, but they were not immune from information about its extent or its horror. For the Jews of Australia there was an added dimension – the bitter realisation that this had been a deeply personal war. Even though it was conducted in faraway Europe, it was a war waged against and aimed at *all* Jews, irrespective of where they lived.

In its editorial on 1 June 1945, in response to what appeared to be the Australian public's surprise, horror and disbelief at the news-reels of Buchenwald and Bergen Belsen in the local cinemas, the *Australian Jewish News* told its readers:

> We Jews were more intimately conversant with the Nazi perse-cution policy in Europe . . . we react somewhat differently. We are upset, disgusted, raving with anger, but not surprised. The film means to us another evidence rather than an unexpected revelation . . . We don't experience the same shock effect as the unprepared Australian.

Given that many of them had only recently left Europe, many Australian Jews were deeply connected to events in Europe. With the arrival of the survivors, that connection was intensified.

Surviving survival

After their liberation, survivors found themselves in an unsympa-thetic, hostile post-war world. Antisemitism had not disappeared with the defeat of Hitler. Because of antisemitic attacks in Poland in 1946, including the Kielce pogrom of 4 July in which 42 Jews were mur-dered and over 40 injured, some 62,000 Polish Jews fled the country in July, August and September of that year.[5] Even in a defeated and

---

5   Margaret Taft, *From Victim to Survivor: The Emergence and Development of the Holocaust Witness 1941–49*, London: Vallentine Mitchell, 2013, p.83.

subdued Germany, there were many reports of antisemitic attacks. In April 1946, German police entered a displaced persons' camp, shooting dead one displaced Jewish person and wounding four others. The Jewish press claimed that the matter was 'under investigation', amidst allegations of Jews dealing with contraband, and reinstated the status of German perpetrator and Jewish victim.[6]

The *Australian Jewish News* carried reports detailing antisemitic incidents all over Europe.[7] To confound matters, the source of some of the hostility was also the occupying forces, supposedly the 'liberators'. On 21 December 1945, *The New York Times* reported on Britain's handling of survivors, 'Britain Denies Abuse of Jews', and on 3 May 1946, it ran another damning story, 'US Soldiers Accused of Anti-Semitism'. Clearly, encounters between Jewish survivors, their liberators and neighbours continued to be unresolved, fractious affairs.

For many survivors the road to recovery was arduous and difficult. Physically weak and psychologically traumatised, many simply could not recover. One estimate calculated that 40 per cent of the Jewish displaced persons liberated in Germany perished within a few weeks of the arrival of the Allies.[8] International relief organisations were ill prepared for the scale of human catastrophe and the military were often called upon to assist with the physical rehabilitation and organisation of displaced persons' camps, a task they were often reluctant to take on and for which they were also ill equipped.[9] One

---

6   *Undzer Vort*, 5 April 1946.
7   'Anti-Semitic Demonstration in Germany', *Australian Jewish News*, 7 November 1947.
8   Michael Marrus, *The Unwanted: European Refugees in the Twentieth Century*, New York: Oxford University Press, 1985, p.332.
9   Taft, *From Victim to Survivor*, p.81.

survivor recalled, 'My last brother died in my bed eight days after the war ended. He was ten years older than me and I was left alone'.[10] Another survivor buried his best friend two days after liberation and remembered his last words to him: 'We did survive them, didn't we'. He had the dignity of a being given a grave.

Conditions in the displaced persons' camps were often appalling. Many Holocaust survivors were housed in former concentration camps and confined yet again behind barbed wire, alongside hostile non-Jewish inmates and guarded by unsympathetic liberators. While Jews were liberated, they certainly were not free. The Harrison Report, commissioned by President Truman to investigate claims of antisemitism and mistreatment of Jewish survivors in the camps, made an explosive claim when it was tabled on 1 August 1945:

> As matters now stand, we appear to be treating the Jews as the Nazis treated them except that we do not exterminate them. They are in concentration camps in large numbers under military guard, instead of the SS troops. One is led to wonder whether the German people, seeing this, are not supposing that we are following or at least condoning Nazi policy.[11]

On 30 November 1945, the *Australian Jewish News* published its own report, 'Horrible Conditions Reported in Displaced Persons Camps'. The Harrison Report did result in some improvements – most significantly, by late 1945 Jewish displaced persons were placed in separate camps. But survivors, though publicly depicted as helpless and passive, in some camps took matters into their own hands. They argued for autonomy – to run the camps themselves, to determine their own

---

10 Margaret Taft, 'From Displaced Person to New Australian: A Journey Towards Self Determination', MA thesis, Monash University, 2004, Interview 7.
11 Taft, *From Victim to Survivor*, p.82.

lives. In the Bergen Belsen displaced persons' camp, 34-year-old Auschwitz survivor and camp leader Josef Rosensaft courageously defied British authorities by refusing to send displaced persons from Belsen to another camp (Lingen) which lacked basic amenities. One report claims that he placed himself in front of the trucks to stop them leaving. He was brought before a British military tribunal, but was acquitted and resumed his unofficial leadership position.[12]

Not all survivors found themselves in displaced persons' camps; approximately 20 per cent chose to be 'free living'. Some had the strength and personal agency to seek their own safety. One woman explained, 'I had had enough of camps . . . when the Russians came they were full of vodka and victory. Women were not very safe'. With assistance from the Jewish Agency, she travelled to Switzerland to be reunited with her brother, a Buchenwald and Auschwitz survivor. 'This was 1945', she explained, 'and we were nobody's property and nobody claimed us'.[13] Together they arrived in Melbourne in 1948. Another managed to meet up with members of the Jewish Brigade who took her to safety to Italy.[14]

European countries offering temporary refuge to survivors either as displaced persons or as free-living transients did not provide the long-term security that many survivors craved. While they were able to establish some form of community life, citizenship in many European countries was difficult to obtain, as was permanent residency. Jews returning to some countries of birth in Western Europe, especially France, Italy and the Netherlands, and in Central Europe

---

12 Joanne Reilly, *Belsen: The Liberation of a Concentration Camp*, London: Routledge, 1998, p.84.
13 Taft, 'From Displaced Person to New Australian', Interview 11.
14 Taft, 'From Displaced Person to New Australian', Interview 9.

(Czechoslovakia, Romania and Hungary) often did resettle, either temporarily or more permanently; but most of those who came from the East (the Baltic states and Poland) did not.

In Poland, the loss of property that could not and would not be repatriated and a population hostile to the return of Jewish settlers hastened the exit of the remaining Jewish survivors. Poland, the site of six extermination camps and the murder of three million (92 per cent) of its Jewish population, was perceived by its survivors to be a huge cemetery, an inhospitable wasteland now devoid of Jewish life and full of painful memories. 'There was only death and desecration . . . there was nothing there and no reason to go back. Go Back? How could I? Why? With what?' exclaimed one survivor who came to Melbourne in 1949.[15]

For survivors from Eastern Europe, long-term renewal and revival was dependent upon escape and permanent resettlement far from the turmoil and instability of Europe. Finding countries in which Jewish survival and continuity were possible became the prime objective for Eastern European Jewish survivors in the years immediately after the war.

Why Australia?

Survivors were desperate to leave the devastation of Europe behind them. For some, Australia was their first choice because they had relatives here or they had heard that there were opportunities for work. For others, Australia was the first to grant them a visa.

> I didn't choose Melbourne, it chose me . . . I wanted to get out of Europe . . . My husband had a sister-in-law already in

---

15   Taft, 'From Displaced Person to New Australian', Interview 1.

Melbourne. She came in 1948 and was helped by the Bialystoker. She said there were plenty of jobs and very importantly, it was safe.[16]

Opportunism and expedience played a big part in the survivors' choice. One survivor rationalised it this way: 'Coming to Australia was the quickest way to get out'.[17] Another explained that 'I tried to get out of Europe for four years. The Joint had lists for migration and I put my name down on many lists. When I was accepted as a migrant for Australia, I took it. Jewish Welfare sponsored me as a refugee'.[18] For another immigrant, Australia seemed the best option available: 'The HIAS near the Rome immigration office said that Australia was willing to take refugees. The USA had long waiting lists and small quotas. I loved Italy but I could not get permanent residency there. Jewish Welfare sponsored me and I came to Australia'.[19]

Equally important, Australia was viewed as a sanctuary, a corner of the world far removed from the trauma of Europe and the tensions of the 'old world'. Australia promised greater opportunities with a fresh start in a 'new world'.

Post-war antisemitism

In relative terms, Australia did provide a safe haven. Its Jewish population was not subjected to pogroms or government-sanctioned discrimination. But countries that were beacons of democracy and were not occupied by the Nazis remained, nevertheless, infected with antisemitism. In Britain, George Orwell, writing for the *Contemporary*

---

16   Taft, 'From Displaced Person to New Australian', Interview 2.
17   Taft, 'From Displaced Person to New Australian', Interview 2.
18   Taft, 'From Displaced Person to New Australian', Interview 9.
19   Taft, 'From Displaced Person to New Australian', Interview 1.

Jewish Record in April 1945, claimed that 'antisemitism is on the increase and it has been greatly exacerbated by the war'.[20] This trend was also evident in polling of the American public in the same period. One such poll 'characterized 5–10 per cent of Americans as rabidly antisemitic and 45 per cent as mildly so'.[21]

In Australia, while Jews were protected by the rule of law and there was no imminent threat to life, stereotypical attitudes prevailed. As in England and America, Australian public opinion was not sympathetic towards Jewish immigration. In one survey conducted in 1948, 60 per cent wanted to keep Jews out, while 25 per cent wanted to only let a few in.[22] Jews were seen as unscrupulous and untrustworthy. Outcries against Jewish refugees were fuelled by the media. Sections of the press, notably *Smith's Weekly* and the *Bulletin*, kept up a smear campaign against Jews. Cartoons and articles defamed Jews both as capitalists controlling the financial centres of the world and as communists. The *Bulletin* in December 1946 published a notorious cartoon in which stereotypically ugly Jews, complete with hooked nose and swarthy complexion, were enticed to enter the country at the expense of white Australians who were seen as leaving. Other newspaper articles added to the hysteria, making outrageous claims that Jewish refugees were opium dealers, jewellery smugglers and unscrupulous businessmen. In one such article, 'Refugees Tricks Foiled', the *Melbourne Herald* alleged that refugees tried to smuggle

---

20 George Orwell, 'Anti-Semitism in Britain', *Contemporary Jewish Record*, Vol. 8, No. 2 (1945): p.163; 'Gentiles Only! Anti-Jewish Discrimination in England', *Australian Jewish News*, 1 August 1947.

21 Leonard Dinnerstein, 'Anti-Semitism Exposed and Attacked', *American Jewish History*, Vol. 71, No. 1 (1981): p.134.

22 O.A. Oeser and S.B. Hammond, *Social Structure and Personality in a City*, London: Routledge, 1954.

in 'jewellery and diamonds'.[23] Furthermore, they would be taking jobs and housing from hardworking, trusting Australians, 'men who enlisted, leaving homes and shops returned to find them occupied by refugees'.[24]

Parliament was not immune from extreme antisemitic rhetoric. Federal Liberal member for Henty, H.B. Gullet, argued that Australia 'was not compelled to accept the unwanted of the world' nor should it be 'the dumping ground for people whom Europe itself . . . has not been able to absorb for 2000 years'.[25] He described 'the arrival of additional Jews . . . [as] nothing less than the beginning of a national tragedy and a piece of the grossest deception of Parliament and the people by the Minister for Immigration'.[26] Gullet's views were supported by several public figures, including a former premier of New South Wales, then member of the House of Representatives, J.T. Lang, who spoke of 'German and Austrian aliens' occupying scarce housing and taking employment opportunities away from returned servicemen.[27] At the annual conference of the Australian Natives' Association in March 1947, the President, P.J. Lynch, stressed that Australia should not be a 'tip for the refuse of Europe'.[28] Leslie Haylen, Labor MHR and first chairman of the Immigration Advisory Council who in 1948 visited Shanghai to assess the situation of Jewish refugees, was told by a confidant that a 'big percentage . . . are in the black market, money riggers, brothel owners and drug runners'. He found the generalisation

---

23 *Melbourne Herald*, 31 January 1947.
24 *Sydney Morning Herald*, 19 August 1948.
25 *Sydney Jewish News*, 20 December 1946.
26 *The Argus*, 12 February 1947.
27 *Sydney Jewish News*, 10 January 1947.
28 Quoted in Suzanne D. Rutland, 'Postwar Anti-Jewish Refugee Hysteria: A Case of Racial or Religious Bigotry?' *Journal of Australian Studies*, Vol. 27, Issue 77 (2003): p.75.

to be 'convincing' and concluded that 'Australia has very little to gain from Shanghai migration'.[29]

The image of Jews as part of a criminal class that would not assimilate persisted for many years after the war and manifested in public and political circles. It was against this backdrop of populist and mainstream anti-Jewish feeling that a small yet significant number of the *she'erit hapletach*, this 'surviving remnant', arrived in Melbourne.

---

29   'Report of Mr. Leslie Haylen, M.H.R., Leader of the Parliamentary Delegation to Japan on his Visit to Shanghai', 24 August 1948, National Archives of Australia (NAA), Series A434, 1947/3/21.

Chapter 9

SHE'ERIT HAPLETACH, THE SURVIVING REMNANT

The Treblinka extermination camp, located in a forest some 50 miles north-east of Warsaw, was the second largest Nazi death camp in occupied Poland. Between July 1942 and October 1943 over 900,000 Jews were murdered in its gas chambers.[1] Chaim Sztajer, born within the Yiddish heartland of Poland in a town called Czestochower, was one of Treblinka's few survivors. He migrated to Melbourne in 1956 after being sponsored by his brother Laibl (Leon) Sztajer. Late in life Chaim recorded an interview with the Shoah Foundation. He gave a chilling eyewitness account of his arrival at Treblinka and the camp's murderous operations.

> SZTAJER: We still knew nothing, we still did not believe . . . they told us to leave everything on the platform, they led us to a barrack . . .
>
> INTERVIEWER: You had a child with you? How old was the child?
>
> SZTAJER: The child [daughter Blima] was two and a half years old . . . [he breaks the interview and pauses for several

---

1   'Treblinka', *Holocaust Encyclopedia*, https://www.ushmm.org/wlc/en/article.php?ModuleId=10005193, accessed 7 April 2018.

seconds, unable to speak] There is a lot to say here . . . [but he is still unable to speak]

INTERVIEWER: What happened next?

SZTAJER: We undressed and they asked us to go into the barrack, naked all naked, men, women and children, all completely naked . . . and we still didn't know.

INTERVIEWER: What did you think?

SZTAJER: That we were going to bathe and get fresh clothes, we thought the women would be sent to the kitchens, the children to schools and we would be sent to work . . . we still did not know. As my wife [Hela] went into the gas chambers, as she was in front of me, it was deemed that the gas chambers were full so I was stopped from entering and I was left standing in the yard naked like others, with my child in my arms for about 25 minutes. [As Chaim held his daughter, a notorious camp guard 'Ivan the Terrible' tore Blima from his arms, bent her in two and threw her on top of the others already in the gas chambers. Chaim's last memory of his daughter was her cries to him as the doors of the chamber were closed.]

SZTAJER: There was a Ukrainian guard – he pulled a girl from the group, I don't know how old she was, maybe fourteen or fifteen, beautiful as gold, and he attempted to rape her. She resisted, she screamed, she was so strong, she tried to resist but he took out his bayonet and he slit her open from top to bottom. A German came up and asked what happened and he said that she threw herself at him. The German said, 'You did well . . .'

SZTAJER: By then we were maybe 30–50 men left. There was a Jew standing who refused to undress. An Orthodox Jew, very Orthodox – he didn't want to undress – so they attacked him and severely beat him. They saw he was an Orthodox Jew – with a beard and a Jewish hat – they asked to bring him a *tallit*, *tefillim*, a *sefer torah* and a garter to tie it all around him. They burnt him alive. I only heard him say one thing 'Oh my God' – nothing else. Others would say *Shemah Yisrael* but he only looked to the heavens and said, 'Oh my God' as if to say to God, 'Look down!!'

I saw an ex-neighbour of mine walk past with a German guard. He saw me and told the German, 'He is a good worker.' . . . It's pure luck. I still didn't know – maybe I wasn't so smart, I don't know – or confused. The same German guard hit me on the back and ordered me to run to where a group of prisoners were sorting clothes. As I was still naked, the prisoners thought I was trying to escape so they made a 'well' amongst the clothes and pushed me into it. The prisoners then whispered to me to quickly put on a pair of trousers and a jacket so I could join them in their work . . . I still asked, 'When do the people come out from the baths? When are they coming out?'

Later I looked through a crack in the wooden fence and I could see them pulling corpses from the gas chamber . . . They shot people too. Sometime later, while I was still sorting clothes, the Nazis began a shooting rampage. We fell to the ground terrified. The shooting went on for about half an hour. The Nazis murdered over 500 men because two men had tried to escape, killing two Nazis and a 'Kapo' in the process. When the shooting stopped we were told to stand up and clean up the 'vermin'. While doing this an acquaintance of my family ran past carrying one of the dead and said, 'Your oldest brother is lying there'. So I ran and dragged him out, saying *Kaddish* [prayer for the dead] while I carried him . . . Three weeks later I was forced to enter the extermination compound with 30 other men to take the dead out of the gas chambers. I worked with the dead, from day till night, and sometimes through the night for eleven months.[2]

---

2   Interview in Yiddish given on 29 October 1995 to the Shoah Foundation Visual History Archive, translated by M Taft. For purposes of accuracy and clarity, additional information was provided by Chaim Sztajer's daughter, Malka Blima Zylbersztajn on 29 July 2015 and is included in brackets.

A SECOND CHANCE

Chaim survived the hell of Treblinka, the murder of his wife and child, and the uprising in August 1943, of which only some 100 managed to survive. Chaim Sztajer and others like him were part of what came to be called the 'surviving remnant' – *she'erit hapletach*. These were the ones who, against all odds, through luck and circumstance, managed to cheat death. These survivors brought with them to Australia not only the cultural trappings of life in the Yiddish-speaking *shtetlekh* and towns of Central and Eastern Europe, but the experiential baggage of an unimaginable, brutal past. They came to Australia after enduring the murder of their entire families – siblings, parents, husbands, wives and children – after the total destruction of their communities and way of life.

Lusia Haberfeld who arrived in Melbourne in 1949 survived deportation from the Warsaw ghetto to the death camp Majdanek where her father and brother were murdered, then Auschwitz and finally a death march to concentration camp Bergen Belsen.[3] Saba Feniger, another 1949 arrival, survived four years in the Lodz ghetto and a forced evacuation to Stutthof concentration camp.[4] Leon Berk, who emigrated from Israel in 1956, was witness to the mass shootings by the mobile death squads, the Einsatzgruppen, in his home town of Baranovichi.[5] Others endured horrific conditions in numerous concentration camps. Kitia Altman survived Annaberg labour camp, Auschwitz, Ravensbruck and Beendorf, before arriving in Melbourne in 1947. In Auschwitz she became Katzetnik A 25441, the number branded on her forearm, an enduring reminder

---

3   Lusia Haberfeld, *Lauferin: The Runner of Birkenau*, Melbourne: Makor Jewish Community Library, 2002.
4   Saba Feniger, *Short Stories: Long Memories*, Melbourne: Vista, 1999.
5   Leon Berk, *Destined to Live*, Melbourne: Paragon Press, 1992.

SHE'ERIT HAPLETACH, THE SURVIVING REMNANT

of life in that 'other world'.[6] Shmuel Migdalek was deported to Auschwitz in July 1944, and was then sent to Vajhingen concentration camp and finally Dachau where he remained until liberation, arriving in Melbourne in 1947.[7] Bono Wiener's parents both died in the Lodz ghetto, from where he was deported, together with his maiden aunt, to Auschwitz. After surviving the 'selections', he was sent to Mauthausen and Güssen concentration camps. He came to Melbourne with his sole surviving relative, his brother Pintche in 1950.[8] Aron Sokolowicz survived Auschwitz, while his wife and son were murdered, coming to Melbourne from Israel with his second family in 1956.[9]

Some survived in hiding; others assumed a false identity, as did child survivor Hania Ajzner.[10] She lived in constant fear of being found out. Child survivor Danielle Charak was taken away from her family and placed in the care of a Christian family in Brussels who protected her until liberation when she rejoined her parents and sister Floris who had also survived in hiding. Danielle and her family arrived in 1949.[11] David Landau took part in the resistance and was a combatant in the Warsaw ghetto uprising who witnessed the final, brutal destruction of the ghetto. He and his young wife Luba arrived

---

6 Kitia Altman, *Memories of Ordinary People: For Those Who Have No One to Remember Them*, Melbourne: Makor Jewish Community Library, 2003.
7 'Shmuel Migdalek (1924–2003)', *Yiddish Melbourne*, http://future.arts.monash.edu/yiddish-melbourne/biographies-shmuel-migdalek/, accessed 8 April 2018.
8 'Bono Wiener (1920–1995)', *Yiddish Melbourne*, http://future.arts.monash.edu/yiddish-melbourne/biographies-bono-wiener/, accessed 8 April 2018.
9 'Aron Sokolowicz (1911–1991)', *Yiddish Melbourne*, http://future.arts.monash.edu/yiddish-melbourne/biographies-aron-sokolowicz/, accessed 8 April 2018.
10 Hania Ajzner, *Hania's War*, Melbourne: Makor Jewish Community Library, 2003.
11 'Danielle Charak (1939–)', *Yiddish Melbourne*, http://future.arts.monash.edu/yiddish-melbourne/biographies-danielle-charak/, accessed 8 April 2018.

in 1947.¹² Following his incarceration in the Vilna ghetto, Avram Zeleznikow made his perilous escape through the sewers in 1943 to join the partisans in the Rudicki forest. He fought with them until his liberation in 1944, arriving in Melbourne in 1951.¹³

Many came to Australia alone or in newly formed relationships, often forged in the displaced persons' camps or in newly constituted survivor communities. Yiddish writer and poet Jacob Rosenberg, a Lodz ghetto, Auschwitz and Mauthausen survivor, met his wife, fellow survivor Esther Laufer, in Italy in a displaced persons' camp at Santa Maria di Bagna. They married in 1946 and departed for Melbourne in 1948.¹⁴ Some had children born in the displaced persons' camps or in transit. Others were children themselves who had survived in hiding, with false Aryan papers, in Catholic convents or were part of the pre-war Kindertransport, a rescue mission instigated by British Jewry between 1938 and 1939 that gave 10,000 unaccompanied children from Germany, Austria and Czechoslovakia sanctuary in England. They left behind parents and siblings who, in most cases, did not survive.

Some Jews who arrived in Australia in the post-war period had been able to escape Nazi-occupied territories during the conflict. Some survived in the free port of Shanghai, which didn't require a visa for entry. An established community of 4,000 Russian Jews in Shanghai was joined in the 1930s by some 17,000 German/Austrian Jews and then by 2,100 Polish Jews who made the same journey in 1940. In December 1941, the Japanese occupied Shanghai, and in 1943 a ghetto

---

12   David Landau, *Caged: A Story of Jewish Resistance*, Sydney: Pan Macmillan, 2000.
13   'Avram Zeleznikow (1924–)', *Yiddish Melbourne*, http://future.arts.monash.edu/yiddish-melbourne/biographies-avram-zeleznikow/, accessed 8 April 2018.
14   'Jacob Rosenberg (1922–2008)', *Yiddish Melbourne*, http://future.arts.monash.edu/yiddish-melbourne/biographies-jacob-rosenberg/, accessed 8 April 2018.

was established for stateless refugees. Although no specific mention was made of Jews, those stateless refugees were indeed Jews. In the ghetto, food was scarce and living conditions impoverished and overcrowded. People starved and died of disease, but there were no death camps and no executions. In his memoir, *Chinese Exile*, Berlin-born Horst Eisfelder described the hazardous life in the ghetto.

> It was difficult to provide even the very minimum of food to keep everyone alive. If people who were completely dependent on handouts wanted to supplement their meagre diet, they had to use their own resources. Those who had brought a few family heirlooms with them to Shanghai managed to sell them. Others, who had already disposed of their very last possessions, including their only overcoat, did so in the hope that by winter the war would be over. As the summer of 1943 drew to a close and their last suits had been worn to shreds, empty calico bags that once held flour – supplied by the Red Cross – were the only alternative left for clothing. These flimsy white garments marked with large red crosses did little more than hide the nakedness of their wearers as winter approached.[15]

As well as Horst Eisfelder, who arrived in Australia in 1947, among those who subsequently migrated to Melbourne from Shanghai were Yiddishist and community activist Jacob Kronhill,[16] renowned Yiddish teacher and I.L. Peretz School kindergarten director Cluwa Krystal,[17] and staunch Zionist and Bialik College supporter Israel Kipen.[18]

---

15 Horst Eisfelder, *Chinese Exile: My Years in Shanghai and Nanking*, Melbourne: Makor Jewish Community Library, 2003.
16 'Jacob Kronhill (1907–2000)', *Yiddish Melbourne*, http://future.arts.monash.edu/yiddish-melbourne/biographies-jacob-kronhill/, accessed 8 April 2018.
17 'Cluwa Krystal (1893–1981)', *Yiddish Melbourne*, http://future.arts.monash.edu/yiddish-melbourne/biographies-cluwa-krystal/, accessed 8 April 2018.
18 Israel Kipen, *A Life to Live*, Melbourne: Chandos Publishing, 1989.

A SECOND CHANCE

A comparatively large number of Eastern European Jews survived the war by fleeing to the relative safety of the Soviet Union. These survivors experienced the brutalities of the gulags, imprisonment in labour camps, starvation and disease, but not the Nazi concentration camps. While conditions were harsh and life was perilous, survival rates in the Soviet Union were higher than in Nazi-occupied territories. Of the pre-war Jewish population of Poland, estimated at 3,200,000, only 350,000 Polish Jews survived the Holocaust, of which some 230,000 survived in the Soviet Union.[19]

Viennese-born Eva Marks's family tried to escape to the United States via Riga. When Germany invaded the Soviet Union in June 1941, Eva's family were declared enemy aliens and sent to a work camp in Siberia. Conditions were unbearable: the weather was freezing, lice rampant and food scarce. Every day was a struggle to survive. 'Each day was the same, eating horrible food, itching from lice and everything dirty and smelly.'[20]

Yiddish teacher and community figure Symche Burstin fled Warsaw to Bialystok in 1939, then in 1940 was arrested by the Soviet occupiers and sent to a Siberian labour camp. Following his release in 1941, he lived the rest of the war in Buchara and Uzbekistan.[21] Yiddish writer and teacher Moshe Ajzenbud made his escape deep into central Asia in the summer of 1941. From there he was sent to a labour camp in Siberia where he remained until 1945.[22] Renowned

---

19 Laura Jockusch and Tamar Lewinsky, 'Paradise Lost? Postwar Memory of Polish Jewish Survival in the Soviet Union', *Holocaust and Genocide Studies*, Vol. 24, No. 3 (2010): pp. 373–399.
20 Eva Marks, *A Patchwork Life*, Melbourne: Makor Jewish Community Library, 2002.
21 'Symche Burstin (1924–)', *Yiddish Melbourne*, http://future.arts.monash.edu/yiddish-melbourne/biographies-symche-burstin/, accessed 8 April 2018.
22 'Moshe Ajzenbud (1920–)', *Yiddish Melbourne*, http://future.arts.monash.edu/yiddish-melbourne/biographies-moshe-ajzenbud/, accessed 8 April 2018.

musician, conductor and music teacher Boruch Kaluszyner escaped from Lodz in late 1939 with his wife and daughter to the Ural Mountains where he and his wife were sent to work in a munitions factory. From there Boruch was sent in mid-1941 to a labour camp in Kazakhstan, while the women and children were sent to a *kolhoz* (a working collective).[23] Yiddish teacher Genia Wasserman and her daughter were exiled to Kazakhstan in Siberia on 13 April 1940 following the arrest of her husband, Bund leader Heniek Storch. They remained there until 1946.[24] Founder of Sotsyalistisher Kinder Farband (SKIF, the Bund youth movement) in Australia and Yiddish radio, Yiddish teacher Pinye Ringelblum made his escape to Russia after the Nazis occupied his native Warsaw. He remained there for the duration of the war, returning to Poland in 1945 to find that his entire family had been murdered.[25]

---

23 'Boruch Kaluszyner (1911–1974)', *Yiddish Melbourne*, http://future.arts.monash.edu/yiddish-melbourne/biographies-boruch-kaluszyner/, accessed 8 April 2018..

24 'Genia Wasserman (1906–1986)', *Yiddish Melbourne*, http://future.arts.monash.edu/yiddish-melbourne/biographies-genia-wasserman/, accessed 8 April 2018.

25 'Pinchas (Pinye) Ringelblum (1922–1999)', *Yiddish Melbourne*, http://future.arts.monash.edu/yiddish-melbourne/biographies-pinchas-pinye-ringelblum/, accessed 8 April 2018.

Chapter 10

AUSTRALIAN RESPONSES

On a Saturday morning in August 1945, Alec Masel, inaugural President of the newly formed Executive Council of Australian Jewry (ECAJ) and Paul Morawetz, the ECAJ honorary secretary, met with Arthur Calwell, Minister for Immigration in the Chifley Labor government. They came with an urgent request for assistance: 'What can we do?' they asked, concerning the rescue of Holocaust survivors desperate for resettlement. Calwell's immediate response was, 'Well, I'll do anything that can possibly be done to help.'[1] Following this meeting, Calwell announced that 2,000 close relatives of Jewish residents in Australia would be granted landing permits on a humanitarian basis. In order to speed up the process, he accepted the offer of typists from the Jewish Welfare Society.

Four years later, during the last months of his term as Minister for Immigration, Calwell's approach was very different. In 1949 he directed a deliberate slowdown in the processing of Jewish applications and banned applicants without close family in Australia from the then largest source countries of Jewish immigrants, on the pretext that these countries were under Soviet control and presented a security risk. Calwell's actions over the five years of his ministry are puzzling. On the one hand, he responded generously and immediately to facilitate

---

1   Golvan, *The Distant Exodus*, p.35.

the entry of Holocaust survivors in 1945; on the other, he developed an increasingly restrictive policy designed to stem the flow of survivors desperate to leave a devastated Europe. In this chapter, we will try to unravel what appears to be a contradictory policy, which has led historians and the Jewish community to subscribe to different, often opposing views of immigration policy in the post-war years.

In the decade following the Second World War, Australia did provide opportunities for Jewish settlement, resulting in a very substantial increase in the country's Jewish population, from an estimated 32,019 in 1947 to 59,343 in 1961, with large numbers coming from Eastern Europe. During the period of greatest immigration, 1946–54, by one estimate, close to 70 per cent of these immigrants spoke Yiddish, the highest proportion in any period.[2] But we must see this total increase in the context of a record intake of immigrants, of which Jews formed a very small part.

Calwell announced a radical shift in immigration policy, which was the result of years of planning, on 2 August 1945, justifying it in a speech to the House of Representatives on the grounds that 'our first requirement is additional population. We need it for reasons of defence and for the fullest expansion of our economy'. The Second World War had exposed Australia's vulnerability; it was a large, resource-rich, yet underdeveloped continent with a small population, without the capacity to defend itself in time of war. Consequently, Calwell made the case for an urgent, extensive post-war immigration program on a scale unprecedented in the nation's history. In a break with the past, Australia would sponsor migration from continental Europe, not just from the United Kingdom and Ireland: 'Australia wants, and will welcome, new

---

2   John Goldlust, *The Melbourne Jewish Community: A Needs Assessment Study*, Canberra: Australian Government Publishing, 1993, p.30.

healthy citizens who are determined to become good Australians by adoption'. The stage was set for a massive influx of people who would be termed 'New Australians' and who were expected to assimilate into the 'Australian Way of Life'.[3]

Calwell's plans did not, however, provide a place for Jewish immigrants. Following his 1945 humanitarian gesture, Australian policy never actively encouraged Jewish immigration. Instead, allowances were made for a limited intake. In the decade 1945–55, Australia admitted 970,850 'New Australians'. Of these, 17,300, or 1.8 per cent, were Jews and their passage and settlement costs were borne by the Jewish community. Under the Displaced Persons Program, which brought more than 170,000 immigrants to Australia between 1947 and 1952, there was provision for free passage, employment on arrival and housing, albeit under conditions of tight government regulation and short-term separation of some families. By contrast, Jewish arrivals received no government support for travel, settlement and employment, and their sponsors were required to furnish a guarantee of support for their first five years.

In 1945 Calwell justified the 2,000 humanitarian places as part of the 15,000 quota established in 1938, which remained unfilled. Calwell was not bound to follow the 1938 offer, but arguably sought an excuse to facilitate Jewish immigration. Nevertheless, as before, any Jewish immigration still required the community's support, so the vast majority of Jewish survivors who entered Australia did so through 'sponsorship', either by individuals or Jewish Welfare.

At the time, Calwell's action was applauded within the community. The *Australian Jewish News* editorial on 31 August 1945 observed

---

3 Commonwealth Parliamentary Debate, House of Representatives, 2 August 1945, Hansard, Vol. 31, pp.4911 and 4912.

that, 'The announcement does not merely represent a gesture of goodwill and co-operation. It is the result of Mr Calwell's long-standing interest both in the problem of migration and in the people who have come to Australia in recent years'. Calwell was, and continues to be, seen as the great champion of Jewish immigration. It was a view propagated by many, including his close friend Paul Morawetz, who viewed Calwell as 'a true Christian' for whom 'the Holocaust went very close to his heart'.[4] According to Alec Masel, if not for Calwell, 'many Jews would not have found their way to the safety of Australia. In the face of hostility from his own colleagues . . . Calwell stretched the "close relatives scheme" of immigration to its utmost limit'.[5] The truth is more complicated. While Calwell moved comfortably in Jewish circles and had many Jewish friends, including Yiddishists Leo Fink and Jacob Waks, he only offered assistance when it did not come at a significant political cost.

In October 1945, following further negotiations between the ECAJ and Calwell, the humanitarian intake was extended to include Jewish refugees from Shanghai, Manila and other far-eastern countries who had either found refuge there after the Bolshevik revolution of 1917 or after fleeing Nazi Europe.[6] In November 1945, the classification was widened to include all relatives, and in 1946 some 700 Jewish refugees arrived from Shanghai. The first ship to arrive from Europe with Jewish refugees was the *Ville d'Amiens* in November 1946. The *Hwa Lien* arrived from Shanghai in January 1947 and the *Johan de Witt* from Europe in March 1947.

---

4   Golvan, *The Distant Exodus*, p.38.
5   Danny Masel and Debbie Masel, 'Alec Masel', *Australian Jewish Historical Society Journal*, Vol. XIX, Part 2 (2008): pp.269–278.
6   Andrew Markus, 'Jewish Migration to Australia 1938–49', *Journal of Australian Studies*, Vol. 7, Issue 13 (1983): p.25; Rutland, *Edge of the Diaspora*, p.229.

When the *Johan de Witt* berthed, the young reporter Eugene Kamenka, later a prominent Australian academic, recorded the emotional, heartfelt scenes as families were reunited after years of separation.

> Many had been in concentration camps and still bore the tattoos that marked their bodies as indelibly as many of their minds were marked ... a woman becoming hysterical when a relative persuades her to leave her baggage. A man with tears in his eyes, staring unbelievably at a grown girl running by the side of the boat crying, 'Daddy, daddy it's me. Don't you recognise me?' Everywhere relatives in each other's arms, for the first time in many years. The remnants of shattered families at last reunited with the few survivors whom they can call their own.[7]

But these early arrivals were not presented in a positive light by sections of the media and Calwell came under fierce criticism from some parliamentarians and organisational leaders, as discussed in chapter 8.

Political backlash – further restrictions

At a time when antisemitism in Australia was evident in public life to some degree and there was a perception that immigrants from Europe would monopolise scarce shipping berths from the United Kingdom desperately needed to repatriate Australian servicemen, there was a limit to what Calwell would or could do without incurring public criticism and the risk of a voter backlash. Fearing a political storm raised by the arrival of Jewish immigrants, Calwell the political pragmatist pulled in the reins. He was, above all, a political survivor, adept at managing often opposing interests. In 1947 he introduced a

---

7   *Sydney Jewish News*, 21 March 1947, quoted in Golvan, *The Distant Exodus*, p.52.

number of stringent measures to limit Jewish arrivals, in an attempt to lessen criticism while still providing scope for a restricted and less visible flow of Jewish immigration.

On 23 January 1947, Calwell announced the end of the humanitarian intake and introduced a restrictive quota on Jews entering under general immigration requirements. In future, no more than 25 per cent of the passengers on any one boat could be Jewish. This presented a major problem. To obtain shipping places for those granted Australian landing permits, the Hebrew Immigrant Aid Society (HIAS) chartered boats. As they were not a travel agency and not in a position to fill the remaining 75 per cent with non-Jewish fee-paying immigrants, their approach to providing passage had to change. They also faced obstructive immigration officials. Noel Lamidey, Chief Migration Officer at Australia House in London, with support of Australian government officials in Canberra, took the view that Jews were defined by race and not religion, which meant that any Jews who had converted to Christianity were to be included in the 25 per cent passenger quota.[8]

When the government entered an agreement in July 1947 with the International Refugee Organisation for the entry of displaced persons, secret instructions to the Australian selection teams directed that Jews were not to be recruited, with first preference to people from the Baltic States, who came to be known as Calwell's 'blonde Balts'. One year later, when the government was finding it more difficult to recruit enough people in the preferred categories, Calwell approved the recruitment of Jews who agreed to work in remote areas, were young and deemed fit and suitable

---

8   Suzanne D. Rutland, 'Postwar Anti-Jewish Refugee Hysteria: A Case of Racial or Religious Bigotry?', *Journal of Australian Studies*, Vol. 27, Issue 77 (2003): pp.69–79.

for hard physical labour.[9] Only a small number of Jews, less than 500 of 170,000, came to Australia under the International Refugee Organisation agreement.[10]

When Calwell was notified in late 1948 that Jews with landing permits who were unable to secure berths on ships would arrive in chartered airplanes, he ordered that the 25 per cent ruling apply to all forms of transportation. Following negotiations with Maurice Ashkanasy, ECAJ President, who gave assurances that the flow of Jewish arrivals would never exceed 3,000 in any one year, Calwell agreed in February 1949 to lift the quota to 50 per cent.[11]

In 1949 Calwell enforced a calculated slowdown in the processing of Jewish applications, described as 'pinpricking', so that applications 'were to be delayed as far as possible by requiring every detail of an application to be completed'. Department of Immigration correspondence noted that 'all officers are carrying out their instructions loyally but . . . their morale is not being improved by what appears to them departmental subterfuge . . . The Sydney office is becoming besieged by angry and distressed applicants'. Further, Calwell directed that applications from countries that most Jewish immigrants were coming from – Poland, Hungary and Czechoslovakia – were to be disallowed except for immediate family members nominated by Australian residents, on the excuse that all nationals of countries behind the Iron Curtain posed security risks.[12]

---

9   Markus, 'Jewish Migration to Australia 1938–49', p.29.
10 Rutland, *Edge of the Diaspora*, p.240.
11 Rutland, *Edge of the Diaspora*, p.240.
12 'Immigration of Jews', 20 Oct 1949 (National Archives of Australia (NAA) Series A445, 235/5/4; see also Rutland, *Edge of the Diaspora*, p.241.

AUSTRALIAN RESPONSES

Different government – same policies

In 1949 the Chifley government was defeated and Calwell's tenure as immigration minister came to an end. In the Menzies government Harold Holt first served as Minister for Immigration. To a large degree, the new government followed Calwell's earlier direction for immigration policy and practice, including the controls on Jewish immigration. They continued the Iron Curtain embargo until 1956. Over the decade of high migration to Australia, 1945–55, an average of 2,000 Jewish people arrived each year.

Jewish community leadership never remained idle in the face of blatant discrimination. The ECAJ made strong representations to the government which did result in a liberalisation of the Iron Curtain policy during the Menzies era, firstly by accepting applications from those who had left countries behind the Iron Curtain before the establishment of communist regimes and had family to sponsor them, and then those with friends ready to sponsor them. Government policy was not consistent, however, after 1952, with variations to sponsorship policy occurring several times. Nevertheless, by 1957 Jews from Hungary, Poland and Rumania were able to come to Australia. Many thousands arrived on landing permits, again sponsored by other Jews, the Welfare Society, family and friends.[13]

The ECAJ worked tirelessly, through personal representations to members of Parliament, to remove anti-Jewish discriminatory features of immigration policy designed to control the Jewish intake. In February 1949, ECAJ President Maurice Ashkanasy objected to the question: 'Are You Jewish?' on departmental application forms for landing permits, which had been in place since

---

13   Peter Medding, *From Assimilation to Group Survival*, p.157.

December 1938.[14] His objection was rejected. The matter was again raised with the Immigration Department by an ECAJ delegation in July 1949. Again the matter was quashed with a stern warning to the ECAJ delegates to desist from exerting pressure and risk jeopardising further Jewish immigration. The matter was not raised again until 1951, first by Ben Chifley, then Leader of the Opposition who felt that the question could be deleted and that there were other ways to ascertain if an applicant was Jewish. But the matter was left unresolved until the Dutch parliament, which had entered into a migration agreement with the Australian government, probed the inclusion of such a racially charged question as being in violation of Dutch law and contrary to the United Nations Declaration of Human Rights. The matter received press coverage both here and in Holland.[15] Further discussions were held with Immigration Minister Harold Holt, but it was again decided to leave the wording in place. Assurances were given that the inclusion of such a question was to assist in a 'balanced immigration program where non-British Europeans were concerned and from a racial and statistical point of view the retention of the wording in the forms would continue to serve a useful purpose'.[16]

Finally, in November 1952, when post-war Jewish immigration had passed its peak, the question was removed from Form 40, with Sir Tasman Heyes, Secretary of the Department of Immigration from 1946–61, concluding that 'the number of Jewish admissions has

---

14 'Alleged Discrimination vs Admission of Jews. Question Jewish or not on Departmental forms', NAA Series A445, 235/5/9; see also Medding, *From Assimilation to Group Survival*, p.158; Suzanne D. Rutland, 'Are You Jewish?' *Australian Journal of Jewish Studies*, Vol. V, Part 2 (1991).
15 Question asked by Mr de Loor, 19 July 1951, NAA Series A445, 235/5/4.
16 Rutland, 'Are You Jewish?', p.45.

dropped from some thousands to some hundreds annually, the need to keep so closely in touch with this particular intake into Australia is not so important as it was'.[17] By the early 1950s, Jewish immigration, small in relative numbers but significant for a community the size of Melbourne's, was reshaping the Jewish community. Melbourne, the city that in the interwar period had attracted two-thirds of the Polish and other Eastern European immigrants, continued to draw the lion's share of Yiddish-speaking Eastern European Holocaust survivors. For these new immigrants, an existing community of Yiddish speakers confirmed their hopes that Yiddish life could and would continue. The 1954 census reveals that more than double the number of Eastern Europeans settling in Sydney had settled in Melbourne – some 7,600 compared to Sydney's 2,876. Of these Eastern Europeans, most were born in Poland – 6,603 of Melbourne's Jewish population and 2,030 of Sydney's.

The Jewish community's response – rescue and resettlement

The Jewish community in Melbourne reacted to the new emergency confronting Jewish survivors with resolve and determination. It quickly shifted its focus from wartime relief to post-war rescue and resettlement. Yiddishists who had arrived from Eastern European countries before the war and had established a new life in Melbourne stood ready to assist Jews stranded in Europe. Nowhere was this more evident than in the workings of Jewish Welfare. It was here that the Yiddishists caused their greatest disruption to the prevailing practice.

---

17   Rutland, 'Are You Jewish?', p.45.

A SECOND CHANCE

By 1947, the United Jewish Overseas Relief Fund had 'merged' with Jewish Welfare. In reality, it was a takeover by the Yiddishists. As a consequence, the newly constituted Australian Jewish Welfare and Relief Society (AJWRS) had the authority to take control of all welfare issues in Melbourne. It quickly led to a fundamental cultural shift from an 'establishment' organisation run on charitable lines to a dynamic proactive association that worked in the best interests of Jewish immigration and the integration of survivor Jews in Melbourne. Its executive members were almost all pre-war Yiddish speakers and annual reports were published in Yiddish and English. Its leadership was taken over by dynamic, reformist Eastern European Jews (Leo Fink in particular) who were not Holocaust survivors but who had lost families in Europe and were willing to challenge rather than accept the letter of the law, and aimed to influence government policy on immigration. This also signalled a break with the style of Jewish Welfare leadership in Sydney, which was more conservative, risk-averse and sought to avoid confrontation with the authorities.[18]

Perhaps the most significant issue concerning cultural change was the way in which sponsorship was interpreted by some individuals, including Leo Fink, Jonas Pushett and Sender Burstin. They did not hesitate to act as 'family' sponsors for numerous Jewish immigrants with whom they may have had no direct familial connection but who were desperate to leave Europe and had no family to act on their behalf. Yankel Pushett recounted that his father, Jonas Pushett, 'wrote up permits for people – he acted as guarantor. Once we got a letter saying, according to our records, you have 50 people staying in

---

18   Rutland, *Edge of the Diaspora*, p.254.

your house and we feel that this is as much as your house can handle. You cannot sponsor any more immigrants'.[19]

Bialystok Yiddishists Leo Fink and his wife Mina personally sponsored a large number of immigrants, prompting Calwell to remark, 'I never knew a man who had so many cousins'. This implied an understanding on the part of some government officials towards the handling of sponsored immigrants, either by individuals or through 'collective' sponsorship guaranteed by recognised community organisations, such as the Federation of Australian Jewish Welfare Societies, which in turn was guaranteed by the state bodies.[20] As long as the burden of responsibility remained with the community, the sponsorship practice could be tolerated. The willingness for some local community members to assume family connections, to act as 'cousins' in order to secure landing permits for total strangers desperate for resettlement did, nevertheless, cause some consternation amongst immigration officials, but their reservations were easily dismissed. When one immigration officer challenged Jacob Waks for arranging to have blank immigration forms for 'cousins' who were unrelated filled in by Carlton residents, Waks replied with an indifferent shrug, 'All Jews were cousins or brothers'.[21]

Mina Fink explained the imperative to assist Jewish survivors in Europe and the unspoken bond that existed between them:

> Those who came before the war felt very close to those who suffered in Europe. Those people who didn't have close relatives who survived felt a special bond with the survivors and many permits were signed using the description that they were

---

19 Yankel Pushett, interview 20 March 2009.
20 Benjamin, *A Serious Influx of Jews*, p.226.
21 Golvan, *The Distant Exodus*, p.55.

brothers, though by relationship they were not really brothers, but we felt that all Jews were brothers.[22]

While local fundraising initiatives were undertaken to support Jewish immigration, the successful reception and absorption of post-war Jewish immigrants could not have been achieved without the substantial assistance of overseas Jewish organisations. Leo Fink made an impassioned plea in a meeting with representatives of overseas organisations: 'We have turned to overseas organisations for assistance . . . we as a community need no money but we must have money to help the immigrants'.[23] In particular, the role of the leading Jewish organisations in the United States, the Hebrew Immigrant Aid Society (HIAS), the American Joint Distribution Committee (JDC) and the Refugee Economic Corporation (REC) were of major importance in the years leading up to 1954. After 1954 a key source of funding was the Claims Conference, an organisation founded in 1951 to represent world Jewry in its negotiations with Germany over compensation and restitution for victims of Nazi persecution. Other organisations, such as the Jewish Colonisation Association (ICA) in England, also played a part in financially supporting Jewish resettlement in Australia, but nothing matched the contribution from the American organisations.

Following requests for financial assistance from Australian Jewish leaders in 1948 and 1949, the three relief organisations JDC, HIAS and REC agreed in January 1950 to provide $200,000 to Australian Jewry to establish hostels and provide loans to individual refugees. The JDC committed $120,000, HIAS $40,000 and REC $40,000.

---

22 Golvan, *The Distant Exodus*, p.55.
23 Meeting with representatives from JOINT, HIAS and REC, 8 September1949, in Fink Archives.

This marked a significant shift from Europe to the USA for Jewish welfare support in Australia. There is no doubt that without this financial assistance the AJWRS would not have been able to meet its obligations towards Jewish immigration.[24] As a consequence of government policy, which directed the Jewish community to take responsibility for its own immigrants and the response of Jewish Welfare to this mandate, survivors came to rely on and benefit from the cultural and directional change brought to Jewish Welfare by Eastern European Yiddish-speaking reformers and the manner in which they operated. Symche Burstin recalled, 'The new immigrants got help with work, with housing – not from the government, but from the Yiddishe Hilfsfund (Jewish Welfare). We could borrow money and pay back later. Whenever there were difficulties they helped'.[25]

Meeting arrivals

Many survivors who came to Australia had no relatives to meet them on arrival and did not know what to expect in this strange and distant land. Jacob Rosenberg recalled his wife's plaintive questions as they stood on the deck of their ship as it approached the Australian coastline in 1948: "And what about us, whom are we going to see? Who will be there to welcome us?" No one, I admitted to myself. No one, not here, and not back there'.[26] But Jews here,

---

24 Suzanne D. Rutland, 'I Am My Brother's Keeper: The Central Role Played by Overseas Jewry in the Reception and Integration of Post-war Jewish Immigration to Australia', *Australian Jewish Historical Society Journal*, Vol. XI, Part 4 (1992): pp.687–701; Suzanne D. Rutland and Sol Encel, 'Three Rich Uncles in America', *American Jewish History*, Vol. 95, No. 1 (2009), p.79.
25 Symche Burstin, interview 9 July 2008.
26 Jacob Rosenberg, *Sunrise West*, Sydney: Brandl & Schlesinger, 2007, p.121.

once strangers in a strange land themselves, were prepared to do all they could to meet and welcome the next wave of newcomers. Jacob and Esther Rosenberg's fears were soon allayed. When their boat docked in Fremantle, David Abzac 'brought on board a supply of *matza* and kosher wine and when evening fell our shipboard community, festively attired, sat down to celebrate our everlasting Exodus'.[27]

Pre-war Yiddishists, such as David Abzac, the Pushetts and Mina Fink, played a large part in the resettlement in Melbourne of post-war Holocaust survivors. Warsaw-born David Abzac, who had arrived in Melbourne in 1939, was Chairman of Jewish Welfare's immigration committee. He took personal responsibility for meeting new immigrants at their port of arrival. This meant that he travelled to Sydney in 1947 to meet the *Ville d'Amiens* and in 1948 travelled across the continent to Fremantle to meet the *Derna*, which carried some 60 Jewish orphans for resettlement in Melbourne. With Charles Slonim, he travelled with them on board the boat to Melbourne, offering guidance, reassurance and assistance. On many occasions, David, in the company of Hans Fischer, would meet those arriving in Melbourne at the entrance to Port Phillip Bay by going out in the pilot boat. In addition, he and Mina Fink initiated a program of entertainment and a formal reception for the new arrivals and, when appropriate, attendance at Shabbat services. His daughter recalls that 'his time was never his own, he spent countless hours counselling newcomers on jobs, filling in applications and finding schools and accommodation'.[28] Yankel Pushett remembered his family's involvement with the new arrivals: 'My mother and sister would go and meet

---

27 Rosenberg, *Sunrise West*, p.120.
28 'David Abzac (1901–1951)', *Yiddish Melbourne*, http://future.arts.monash.edu/yiddish-melbourne/biographies-david-abzac/, accessed 8 April 2018.

people at the ships and translate for them and help them through immigration'.[29]

Mina Fink 'adopted' a group of young war orphans, many of them concentration camp survivors, who came to be known as the Buchenwald boys, a tightknit group who had been liberated together from the camp in April 1945. She met them on arrival 'with a big smile on her face', one of them, Max Zilberman, recalled, helped them find accommodation, employment and opportunities for further training, and offered them Sunday outings and visits to her family's Frankston holiday home. An enduring friendship developed with many of them. Mina became President of the UJORF Ladies' Group (1945–47), co-ordinating fundraising and the despatch overseas of money, clothing, medicines and foodstuffs. The fund also established seven hostels in Melbourne to provide initial settlement for postwar immigrants. Mina's responsibilities included meeting ships at Port Melbourne, the day-to-day running of hostels, and regular visits to the Bialystoker Centre, St Kilda.[30]

Housing, hostels – finding a place to live

Following the Second World War, Australia was in the grip of an acute housing shortage. This was in part due to the lack of housing construction during the Depression and the war years, and the problem was exacerbated by the increase in post-war immigration. As larger numbers of Jewish immigrants began to arrive, the need for temporary housing grew. The establishment of privately owned and

---

29 Yankel Pushett, interview 20 March 2009.
30 Andrew Markus, 'Fink, Miriam (Mina) (1913–1990)', *Australian Dictionary of Biography*, National Centre of Biography, Australian National University, http://adb.anu.edu.au/biography/fink-miriam-mina-12493.

managed hostels in Melbourne greatly aided the absorption of newly arrived Jewish immigrants, even though living conditions were not always ideal.

The settlement of Jewish immigrants became the responsibility of the immigrants themselves or the Jewish community. Reisel Ceber recalled the assistance given by the Chelmer *landsmanshaft*, one of a number of such networks of Polish Yiddish speakers from the same towns and *shtetlekh*. 'There was a shortage of housing and getting roofs over the heads of these newcomers required a great deal of money'.[31] Accommodation was overcrowded and basic, with shared amenities. New arrival Ida Gurvis, who together with her family survived the Holocaust in Siberia and Kazakhstan and arrived in Melbourne aboard the *Ville d'Amiens* in 1949, recalled how her family found their first home in Carlton: 'There were fewer rental properties than the demand in post-war Melbourne, particularly in Carlton, so landlords were able to demand a large amount of key money. We felt lucky to have found this house and willingly handed over all our savings'.[32] Sonia Hornstein, who with her parents and brother survived hunger and disease in the forests of the Soviet Union, remembered the crowded conditions her family endured in their first Melbourne home: 'We were taken to a large house in Drummond Street, North Carlton. Three other families were already living there, each with one room. The kitchen was shared'.[33]

Jewish Welfare, by now a Yiddishist-led organisation, and the *landsmanshaftn* often worked hand in hand in the resettlement of new

---

[31] Julie Meadows ed., *Fun Himlen Blayene Tsu Bloye Teg (From Leaden Skies to Blue Days): 45 Stories growing up in Jewish Carlton*, Melbourne: Australian Centre for Jewish Civilisation, Monash University, 2014, p.59.
[32] Meadows, *Fun Himlen Blayene Tsu Bloye Teg*, p.196.
[33] Meadows, *Fun Himlen Blayene Tsu Bloye Teg*, p.227.

arrivals. Anush Friede, who was born in 1940 while his Polish-born parents were refugees in the Soviet Union, was met by members of Jewish Welfare and resettled immediately; 'The Welfare Society met us at Port Melbourne and took us to a house in Camberwell which we shared with other families. We stayed there for two or three weeks and then were transferred to Welfare House in Herbert Street, St Kilda'.[34]

The first Jewish hostel in Australia in the post-war period was established by the Bialystoker *landsmanshaft* in Robe Street, St Kilda in July 1947. It was established on property purchased in 1945 for £12,000.[35] The second hostel to be established was known as Camberwell House or HIAS House. It was a large, two-storey property with 17 rooms and was able to accommodate 70–80 people.[36] Two other hostels were provided by *landsmanshaftn* – the Radomer and the Warsaw Jewish Centre, although other *landsmanshaftn* also assisted their *landsleyt* in resettlement. Sonia Hornstein remembered her arrival and being met by representatives of the Chelmer community: 'We docked in Melbourne on 7 December 1949 and some members of the Chelmer *landsmanshaft* were there to greet us. They were Mr Gotlib, a grocer, and the Ceber brothers. We all climbed into Mr Gotlib's horse and cart and headed for Carlton'.[37]

Cyla Hartman, who with her parents survived the Soviet gulags before arriving in Melbourne on the *El Misr* in January 1951, remembered the crowded conditions that she encountered in her first accommodation.

---

34 Meadows, *Fun Himlen Blayene Tsu Bloye Teg*, p.244.
35 Suzanne D. Rutland, 'Resettling Survivors of the Holocaust in Australia', *Holocaust Studies: A Journal of Culture and History*, Vol. 16, No. 3 (2010): p.50.
36 Rutland, 'Resettling Survivors of the Holocaust'.
37 Meadows, *Fun Himlen Blayene Tsu Bloye Teg*, p.227.

> We went from the boat to Camberwell House for two or three weeks and then moved to another Hilfsfond house in Drummond Street. There were three or four families in this house. We had a room in the back yard that had probably been converted from a garage and we all shared the only kitchen. It was not the calmest of environments.[38]

Between 1947 and February 1951, eleven hostels were purchased and operated to temporarily house Jewish immigrants in Melbourne. The last of these to be sold was the Frances Barkman Home in Balwyn in 1958. Over 400 people were accommodated in 1949–50, over 1000 were housed in 1950–51 and 1400 in 1951–52.[39]

Shared housing, with its lack of privacy and communal facilities was a physical burden that had to be endured. But it also had an upside; it ensured that the community remained tight-knit and cohesive rather than individuals dispersed in lonely isolation, far removed from the cultural milieu they needed or desired. Through communal living, many friendships and networks were established that lasted for years. Theo Balberyszki and his sister, Deborah Zuben, children of Yiddish activist and bookshop owner Mendl Balberyszki, survived the Vilna ghetto, Estonian and Latvian labour camps and the Stutthoff concentration camp before arriving on 5 December 1949 on the *Cyrenia*. They remembered being greeted warmly by Mrs Pushett before moving to a Jewish immigrant hostel in Coburg. Theo and Deborah recalled the family friendships established in their first 'home':

> Our first residence was a new immigrant hostel at the Grove in Coburg. It was established and managed by the Jewish

---

38 Meadows, *Fun Himlen Blayene Tsu Bloye Teg*, p.251.
39 Suzanne D. Rutland, '"I Never Knew a Man Who Had So Many Cousins": Differing Attitudes to Postwar Survivor Migration: Melbourne and Sydney', *Australian Jewish Historical Society Journal*, Vol. XII, Part 2 (1994): p.102.

Welfare Society. Mr Abzac was in charge of working with the new immigrants. Several families that had been on our ship were brought to the same address and we were all allocated one or two rooms per family. Dr Jack Randa, his wife Dasha and their children Evichka and Tomik were already there, as well as Mr and Mrs Mokotow and their son Grisha. It was the beginning of a great friendship between our families, one which has endured over the years.[40]

In so many ways, the bonds formed by these new arrivals in the early resettlement years became the foundation for a new kind of community – a community of survivors – and Yiddish would remain at the heart of it.

---

40   Meadows, *Fun Himlen Blayene Tsu Bloye Teg*, p.220.

Chapter 11

NIGHTMARES

The Holocaust tore apart the lives of Europe's Jews. Their resettlement in this corner of the world gave them a second chance at life, but it did not diminish their suffering. They had survived, but into this new life they brought the horrors of the past – a past that insistently intruded on the present. The survivors were emotionally and psychologically traumatised by the pain and suffering inflicted upon them. The extreme nature of the continual actions of the Holocaust over a sustained period sets it apart from other traumatic events. Here was a chronic, prolonged experience of terror. Dehumanisation, humiliation and torture marked their daily existence. The survivors' various emotional responses were normal reactions to an extremely abnormal situation; they were survivors of an unprecedented genocidal campaign designed to exterminate an entire civilisation.[1]

The trauma expressed itself in different ways. For some, like newcomer Hania, intrusive thoughts and images exacerbated the pain and anguish that would never end.

> But the picture in my mind of Auschwitz and Treblinka is a picture I look into every day. I see it. And it keeps the pain alive. That's what I want. I don't forget and I can't forget what

---

1   Natan P.F. Kellermann , 'The Long-Term Psychological Effects and Treatment of Holocaust Trauma', *Journal of Loss and Trauma*, Vol. 6, No. 3 (2001): pp.197–218.

happened. It's a part of my life, something I went through ... You always remember. You always have the fear that it can happen again, and that your children and grandchildren might be subjected to these things. I have learned how bitter life can be and that one has to fight to survive.[2]

For Esther Rosenberg, recurring nightmares of impending death gripped her in the dark stillness of the night: 'Will they ever let me go?' she whispered. 'Will they or is this for life?'[3] For Kitia, the night brought images of executions: 'I dreamt that there were gallows standing in our backyard where the outside toilet used to be'. There she would stand, desperately trying to hide her swollen pregnant belly while awaiting the 'selections', ready to be led to her death. 'I felt such fear that I would wake every night sweating and shivering'.[4]

Fear and insecurity often surfaced in public spaces. Rozka knew many who 'wouldn't enter a synagogue [for years] because they were concerned about entering a place in which so many Jews were concentrated'.[5] Hiding one's identity was a method of survival. It, too, left an indelible mark. 'I know many people now active in Jewish organisations who, when they first arrived in Australia, would not admit to being Jewish. These were the initial consequences of living with constant anxiety and fear for four or five years of your life'.[6]

---

2 Naomi Rosh White, *From Darkness to Light: Surviving the Holocaust*, Melbourne: Collins Dove, 1988, p.197.
3 Jacob Rosenberg, *Sunrise West*, Sydney: Brandl & Schlesinger, 2007, pp.126–7.
4 Anna Rosner Blay, *Not Paradise: Four Women's Journeys Beyond Survival*, Melbourne: Hybrid Publishers, 2004, p.147.
5 Rosh White, *From Darkness to Light*, p.196.
6 Rosh White, *From Darkness to Light*, p.196.

Many survivors were overcome by a fear that 'another Hitler' would murder their children. As newborns began to arrive, so too came a heightened sense of imminent danger. When Erna's son was born, she kept dreaming of hiding places where she could be safe, an imaginary place 'beneath the stairs' where she could remain concealed with her baby until the danger had passed. Kitia was overcome with panic about the safety of her son who was born in Melbourne in 1949.

> I prepared a little suitcase for Eugene in case something would happen. It had holes in it so that he could breathe. I scrutinised the neighbours, wondering: can I trust them to leave my child with them? And then as Eugene grew bigger my fear grew – where would I get a bigger suitcase? How will I manage to hide him without being detected?[7]

Some survivors felt that the depth of their sorrow left them incapable of ever living a 'normal' life again. For Frania, the intense loss was irreconcilable with any sense of normality: 'I lost all my family because of the war – my parents, brother, sister, uncles, aunts and cousins. I have nobody left. Sometimes I look at myself from a distance and I think – How is it possible for someone so mutilated to live?'[8]

Nuritt Borsky remembered how her survivor parents, Aron and Cyla Sokolowicz, were unable to trust authority: 'Trust was a very big issue [for my parents]. You really only ever trusted your own – other Jews – they might cheat you out of money but on a profound level you only trusted the people with whom you shared a common fate'.[9]

---

7   Rosner Blay, *Not Paradise*, p.149.
8   Rosh White, *From Darkness to Light*, p.192.
9   Nuritt Borsky, interview 20 November 2014.

Arthur Calwell speaking at the 50th Anniversary celebration of the Bund at the Bialystoker Centre. Listening to Calwell are Jacob Waks, Sender Burstin and Fayge Burstin, October, 1947.

David Abzac sorting clothes to be sent overseas, 1940s.

David Abzac and Solomon Berenholtz, with donated clothing destined for the DP camps in Europe, 1949.

David Burstin and Danielle Gryfenberg-Charak at SKIF camp, Ocean Grove, 1952.

Jacob G. Rosenberg 'Shneii in Friling' (Snow in Spring) book launch, 1984.
Left to right: Ben Kamienicki, Shmuel Bennett, Jacob G. Rosenberg, Yasha Sher, Avram Cykiert.

Jacob Waislitz and Rochl Holcer, 1942.

Jacob Waislitz's production of 'The Dybbuk', 1957.

Jewish Writers' Union in Melbourne, 1950. Seated left to right: Yosef Sperling, Mendl Balberyski, Gedalia Shaiak, Yehoshua Rapoport, Jacob Waks, Abram Zbar. Standing from left to right: Yosef Orbach, Mr Borsky, Mr Wiencentovski, Lew Frydman, Yitzhak Kahn.

Leo Fink, 1930s.

Shmuel Bennett in army uniform, 1942.

Shmuel Bennett with Isaac Barshevis Singer, 1986.

Sender and Fayge Burstin on their wedding day, April 1928.

Shifsbrider (ship brothers) from the Eridan in Noumea, 1937.

A group of new arrivals with David Abzac (centre), Fremantle, Western Australia, late 1940s.

בעקאנטמאכונג

מיר גיבען צו וויסן דעם פובליק אז

דינסטאג אין דער פריה דעם 9 דעצעמבער 1930

האט זיך געעפונט די נארט–קארלטאנער

כשרה בוטשער שאפ

אין 797 רעטהדאון סטריט נארט קארלטאן וועלכע איז אונטער דער השגחה פון דעם בית–דין אויף מעלבורן.

מ"ר שלמה זילבערמאן שוחט ובודק אנערקענט פון פאלעסטינער טשיף ראבינאט אונד אויך פון מעלבורנער רבנים שעכט פאר אונז.

מיר אראנזשירן אויך א פעקטארי פון גוטע סארטן ווארשט געררייכערטע פליש וכדומה. פרישע פליש טעגליך, בעסטע קוואליטע, מעסיגע פרייזן, ארדערס ווערן צוגעשטעלט.

מיט אכטונג מאיר און יעקב פאלאנסקי

797 רעטהדאון סטריט נארט קארלטאן (2טע שאפ פון קינג און גאדפריי)

טעלעפאן F 8393

ANNOUNCEMENT

We beg to notify the Jewish Public, that The North Carlton

KOSHER BUTCHER SHOP

HAS BEEN OPENED

On Tuesday, December the 9th, 1930

The Shop is situated at

797 Rathdown St., Corner McPherson St., North Carlton.

and is under the supervision of the Beth Din of Melbourne.

Mr. S. SILVERMAN qualified from the Chief Rabbi of Palestine and the Beth Din of Melbourne is engaged as Shochet.

We are also arranging a Small Goods Factory. Complete Satisfaction to Customers is assured.

BEST QUALITY FRESH MEAT DAILY.   REASONABLE PRICES.

ORDERS CALLED FOR AND DELIVERED.

Soliciting Your Patronage, Yours Faithfully,

POLONSKY BROS.,

797 Rathdown Street, Corner McPherson Street (2 Doors from King and Godfree) North Carlton, N.4, Phone F 8393

DAVID ALTSHUL, Printer, 318 Drummond St., Carlton, N.3

Bilingual poster announcing the opening of Polonsky's Kosher Butcher shop, 1930.

Full house at the Kadimah, 1940.

Interior of Mendl Balberyszki's bookstore, 108 Rathdowne Street, Carlton, late 1950s.
Mr Balberyszki and daughter Devorah.

Kadimah Ball, 1936.

Kadimah Library, 1930s.

Pinchas Goldhar in Ludawigshafen Germany before his arrival in Australia in 1928

פאריין יידישע בינע מעלבאורן

רעזשיסער: יעקב גינטער

טעמפרענס האלל, ראסעל-סט., סיטי

מונטיק, דעם 14טן נאוועמבער, 1927

ווערט געשפילט צום ערשטן מאל אין מעלבארן

א מאמעס טרערן

לעבענס ביל אין 3 אקטן פון י. מארקאוויטש

די קונסט ר״א. פרומע.	פירט אייס.	מאדאם האניק
די מ-אני—קאמישע ר״א. משהלע.	פירט אייס.	י. גינטער
די דראמאטישע ר״א. שרהלע.	פירט אייס.	מיס סטנגאל

עס נעמט אנטייל אונזער גאנצער אנסאמבל

אנפאנג / אין אווענט

Tickets : 1s 6d, 2s 1½d, 3s 6d : בילעטן

TEMPERANCE HALL, RUSSELL STREET, CITY

MONDAY, 14th NOVEMBER, 1927
At 8p.m.

A MOTHER'S TEARS
In 3 Acts

Geo. J. Ford, 668 Smith-st., Clifton Hill. Ring N'cote 2/8.

Flyer advertising Yiddish performance, 1927.

Flyer and program for 'Freud's Theory of Dreams', April 1940.

Flyer for 'Breadmill', 1940.

Graduation from Yiddish teachers training course, 1959. Back row left to right: Ruszke Goldbloom, Leon Glazer. Centre row left to right: Doris Nusbaum-Burstin, Joseph Giligich, David Burstin, Maryla Buks-Ringelblum. Front row left to right: Danielle Gryfenberg-Charak, Symche Wolski, Leon Goldman, Chana Korman-Mrocki.

Children at the I.L. Peretz school annual breakup party and speech day, December 1960.

I.L.Peretz school summer camp, 1948-9.

Common suffering – a community of survivors

The horrific circumstances that brought these Jewish refugees to Australia defined them as a community of survivors. Their journey back to life was enhanced by the size of Melbourne's survivor community. Large numbers of survivors living in close proximity provided the basis for mutual support, helping them to find their own pathways and networks. Survivors developed their own coping mechanisms, drawing on the strength they garnered from each other. Jack Felman recalled how his survivor parents dealt with the enormity of their loss:

> They had their generation therapy – you know what that was? The Saturday nights when they got together with their own group ... the most effective means of healing is not from a doctor, not from a psychologist but simply from shared experiences. I think the bottom line is the shared experiences and that they were able to talk about it ... They had each other after the war ... they were all in communities.[10]

Talk amongst themselves of horrific experiences was accepted and encouraged. Large numbers of survivors would meet regularly in small social groups and talk compulsively about their experiences, at times competitively and obsessively. This is now recognised as a form of group therapy and, for some, was the key to a form of normalcy. The power of group interaction and support is explained by an expert in group dynamics:

> Groups blur the boundary between the self and other, for members retain their personal qualities – their motives, emotions and outlooks – but add to them a sense of self that is based on their group identity. Groups transform the *me* into the *we*.[11]

---

10 Jack Felman, interview 27 May 2011.
11 Donelson R. Forsyth, *Group Dynamics*, Belmont CA: Wadsworth Cengage Learning, 2014, p.62.

For some survivors, group acceptance led to empowerment. It did not diminish the trauma but enabled it to be absorbed, understood, accepted and validated by others in the group. 'For my parents,' Jack Felman observed, 'the trauma was shared amongst those who were alive. So they stuck to people who had gone through the same thing. And I think they found comfort because they didn't have to explain a lot'.[12]

Annie Gawenda, another child of this community, explained how important familial connections were formed out of new friendship groups. They created families where there were none: 'There weren't cousins, sisters, brothers. There were the memories of them. People without extended families – so they recreated families from friends – for a family atmosphere. Everyone felt like family. There were people in the group who had no family'.[13]

Holocaust survivor Jacob Rosenberg recalled how very little was said in his group, but so much was understood.

> Very few words were spent around the table, and yet there was so much said. The six of us, torn inside out, unable to return to the land of our birth, shared the knowledge that only four years ago we had been shortlisted to die – that our being here [in Melbourne] on this night was but a miscalculation in one of Hitler's equations.[14]

For survivors, the opportunity to find acquaintances and friends from the pre-war years was greater in a large survivor community such as Melbourne. For Jacob Rosenberg it provided a sense of continuity and reassurance that life is ongoing:

---

12   Jack Felman, interview 27 May 2011.
13   Annie and Michael Gawenda, interview 10 March 2011.
14   Rosenberg, *Sunrise West*, p.123.

The three of us were overjoyed to meet up like this – an emotion so common among survivors who had known each other before their world crumbled to pieces. It carried a confirmation of one's existence, dispelling for a while the sense of a too-fragile reality.[15]

The drive to recreate the security and vitality of the lost world often gave survivors the impetus to live life to the full. Annie Gawenda was struck by the joy her parents were still able to express.

My parents had an amazing circle of friends, so determined to live a joyful life. People who stuck together who mostly knew each other from before. In the early days they would meet every weekend, have parties and celebrate everything. They had secular celebrations for the *chagim* [festivals]. They had crazy celebrations – fancy dress, dancing. They went on holidays together. They were really close-knit, joyful people.[16]

Regardless of where or how they survived the Holocaust, for many, a commonality of suffering underpinned the shared experience. It provided the primary point of reference and identification. When Jack Felman got engaged, it was to another child of survivors. There was an instant bond between the families.

When Lottie and I got engaged . . . our parents came over and they sat down and said, 'Hello, how are you? And so where were you during the war?' That was the first question and Lottie and I just walked out because I knew what the rest of the evening would entail because my parents-in-law were in Auschwitz and Bergen Belsen – that's where Lottie was actually born and my parents had a different thing . . . but you know, I think that the commonality of suffering helped create a very tightly knit community and Yiddish was part of that. I mean Polish wasn't.[17]

---

15   Rosenberg, *Sunrise West*, p.149.
16   Annie Gawenda, interview 3 June, 2009.
17   Jack Felman, interview 27 May 2011.

These survivors also faced the same challenges that all migrants do when relocating and adapting to a new environment. Living in the suburbs, rebuilding and trying to reconnect to a new life was often a struggle, compounded by feelings of isolation and alienation. Frania explained the displacement she felt in Melbourne suburbia:

> It was very painful for me when I realised that people here live differently from how they live in Warsaw. Here everyone lives in his own house and garden and neighbours have very little contact with each other. In Warsaw we lived in apartments and we knew all the neighbours. We were constantly going into each other's homes to borrow something or to talk a little. We knew the neighbours' children and we all played together. There was very close contact between people. I knew practically everyone in the area. And here there were big spaces, empty streets and houses that I passed when I went for walks with my child. I longed for the crowded streets of my home.[18]

Serge Liberman's mother felt an acute sense of loss and dislocation, unable to reconcile herself to life in this new, seemingly sterile world:

> Of all the misfortunes available to the children of this earth, she moans, Melbourne was the one she had to choose. Melbourne, a tail torn from the rump of the world, where she is lost, amongst neighbours, generations, continents, galaxies apart from herself, a foreigner Jew in an Australian marsh. Like satin in tweed, perfume in tar, crystal in glass.[19]

In spite of the vibrant Yiddish world that now thrived in Melbourne, she perceived her new home as a cultural wasteland:

> Mother complained more than once, and with the barest provocation, about the barren wilderness into which, after Warsaw, after Tashkent, after Paris, she had been tossed. And wilderness

---

18 Rosh White, *From Darkness to Light*, p.174.
19 Serge Liberman, *On Firmer Shores*, Melbourne: Globe Press, 1981, p.5.

to her was any place where a Yiddish word was not spoken, where Sholem Aleichem and Leibush Peretz were not heard of, where one, so to speak, clung to the shadows lest a gentile finger be pointed or a sneer thrown or allusion be made, however subtly, to one's Jewishness ... The lighting of a memorial candle, the reading of a Yiddish newspaper, the humming of a Yiddish tune, the exchange of memories of times and places past – these were the *form* and *content* of our Jewishness on this remote shore.[20]

---

20 Liberman, *On Firmer Shores*, pp. 199–200.

Chapter 12

TIES THAT BIND

Landsmanshaftn

In spite of all the hardships they endured in Eastern Europe, Jews like pre-war arrival Shmuel Bennett retained a loyalty to their place of origin. Shmuel remained a proud Radomer until the day he died. It was a loyalty that transcended the bloody pogroms, the discrimination, and the Holocaust. It was loyalty to a distinct cultural heritage, to kinship, to a way of life. The centrality of regional identity therefore helped shape and frame the lives of Jewish immigrants like Shmuel Bennett in the New World. Eastern European Jews saw their identities bound to the cities and towns of their birth. This regionalism did not supplant but deeply influenced the way these immigrants recreated life as a new diaspora.

No matter how many years elapsed from the last time they ever stood on Polish soil, for the rest of their lives these Jews were Warsawer, Bialystoker, Lodzer, Kaliszer or Cracower. The place of their birth remained a crucial part of their identity. This was not loyalty to the Polish nation, but to the life they had once lived in these cities and towns.

The Yiddish language also had its regional differences. Dialects, different accents, specific vocabularies often highlighted different regions. Sometimes a word, an expression or a joke was all it took.

A person's town of origin could be easily pinpointed by the way that individual spoke Yiddish. A Litvak could never be confused with a Lodzer![1]

Rebuilding a community meant re-establishing networks and an organisational framework. Survivors fell back on pre-existing community models that had worked in the past. The self-help *kehile* structure that had flourished in the Yiddish centres of Eastern Europe provided representation and assistance. This took on a particular form in Melbourne. The desire to re-establish a sense of kinship and the need to help one another gave rise to the *landsmanshaftn*, a Yiddish word meaning an organisation of people from the same geographic region. In reality, it came to mean much more than just a geographic link.

Jews who had lived in poorly resourced Eastern European cities prior to the war were familiar with the type of self-help and welfare organisations that had thrived due to hardship and necessity. These survivors were well acquainted with the need for self-reliance. So, while cities and communities were destroyed during the Holocaust, the memory of how they operated was not. Their self-help organisations were effective means of establishing a cultural identity, with fraternal links and a common bond. They also filled the cultural and social void that existed in the early life of the first-generation Yiddish-speaking refugees, providing social activities and events. Most importantly, they offered practical help to survivors wanting to re-establish themselves. All of this was central to a way of life that held Yiddish close to its heart.

Landsmanshaftn were not, however, a new post-war phenomenon. The first known *landsmanshaft* to operate in Melbourne was

---

1   For a good introduction to Yiddish, see Miriam Weinstein, *Yiddish: A Nation of Words*, South Royalton, VT: Steerforth Press, 2001.

the Bialystok Lending Society founded in 1928. Its charter in its formative years was to provide financial assistance to those *landsman* experiencing hardship or starting up businesses. The organising committee, a group of enterprising Bialystokers who arrived on the same boat in 1927, also arranged to have new Bialystok arrivals met at the dock, to assist with housing and immediate financial support. Over the next 20 years, the Bialystoker *landsmanshaft* developed into an extensive organised formal network. The importance of the Bialystok *landsmanshaft* in Melbourne reflects the pattern of chain migration to Australia, which brought a disproportionate number of immigrants from certain towns and regions, while there were few from other areas.

By 1949 the Bialystoker Centre, as it was named at its annual general meeting on 3 March 1946, was a formally constituted organisation with its own property at 19 Robe Street, St Kilda, its own office, accommodation facility and an extensive welfare mandate. It comprised an executive committee with a president, two vice-presidents, two honorary treasurers and an honorary secretary. It had a working committee of ten members. A number of sub-committees had responsibility for housing, finance, functions and culture. In addition, the Centre hosted a ladies' committee with its own president, two vice-presidents, an honorary treasurer, honorary secretary and honorary member.

Over a 12-month period, the centre undertook an extraordinary number of initiatives. In its 1949 annual report, the centre recorded that 120 people had been housed at its premises in the past year, and it had opened the Peisach Kaplan Library in 1948, with its own librarian, in response to an increasing demand for Yiddish books. It set itself the target of matching the number of books held in the

Kadimah library. The centre also recorded opening its own kindergarten in response to an acute shortage of kindergarten places when some were closed because of a polio epidemic. The ladies' auxiliary raised funds for this initiative and purchased the necessary furniture and equipment. In addition, the centre recorded a host of cultural activities such as literary evenings, public lectures, other fundraising initiatives and the sending of 102 relief parcels to Israel and Europe.

The Bialystoker Centre, located in the emerging centre of Jewish life in St Kilda rather than in Carlton, also became a hub of activity for other organisations. Numerous functions were held at the centre by the broader Jewish community; organisations such as the orthodox Mizrahi, the Women's International Zionist Organisation (WIZO), the Welfare and Relief Fund, the Zionist group Poale Zion, the socialist secular Bundists, Keren Kayemeth which supports ecological development in Israel, and the National Council of Jewish Women all staged events at the premises. In addition, the I.L. Peretz and Sholem Aleichem Yiddish schools, Elwood Talmud Torah religious school, the association of ex-inmates of concentration camps and various *landsmanshaftn* were all offered the use of the centre's facilities.

In 1949 the centre passed a resolution pledging £2,000 towards the establishment of a village in Israel to be called Kiryat Bialystok. By the time the centre's finances closed for audit on 30 June of that year, £625/5/- had been collected.

The Bialystoker Centre also took on the role of community arbitrator, mostly of business disputes, on a fee-for-service basis. This committee was chaired by its President, Michael Pitt. This new income stream yielded £670 in its first year of operation. In its annual report, the President thanked all committee members for their efforts, noting that:

> Considering the scope and diversity of the centre's activities and the significant status to which it has attained in the community as a whole, its contribution to local cultural life, its efficient care for newly arrived compatriots, and its complicated organisation, one cannot but admire the maturity to which this institution has attained in a comparatively short span of time.[2]

The Bialystoker Centre provided a robust and engaging model for other *landsmanshaftn*, which was soon emulated. One of the most prominent and prodigious was the Lodzer *landsmanshaft*. Lodz was the second largest city in pre-war Poland with a population of 233,000 Jews in 1939, one-third of the city's population. The major difference between the two *landsmanshaftn* was that the organising committee of the Bialystoker Centre were pre-war Jewish immigrants, whereas the Lodzer *landmanshaft* committee was mostly composed of post-war Holocaust survivors. Numerous attempts had been made to form a Lodzer *landsmanshaft* after the war, but it was not until 1953 that an initiating committee was formed with the task of organising a general meeting of Lodzer. The first meeting was chaired by M. Bialkower and the secretary was Motl Nusbaum.

Some 400 attended an evening function in August 1953 at the Kadimah Hall to commemorate the anniversary of the liquidation of the ghetto. Of these, 110 enrolled as members of the Lodzer Centre. On 21 September 1953, the annual general meeting of the Lodzer *landsmanshaftn* took place in the Bialystoker Centre. The inaugural office-bearers were I. Einhorn (President), A. Eichenbaum (Vice-President), M. Nusbaum (Secretary), B. Horowicz (Treasurer) and

---

2   Bialystoker Annual General Report 1949.

S. Kalus was member of the executive. Soon after, sub-committees for finance and culture were formed and representatives were elected to the newly formed Federation of Landsmanshaftn. The centre's first venue was the Kinneret café, where Lodzer met every Sunday, and its first organised functions were held there too. An interest-free loan fund was established and £1,000 was raised for it, from which any needy Lodzer *landsman* could borrow up to £100 and pay it back without interest.

The Lodzer Centre carried out a variety of communal activities: cultural evenings, family evenings, functions celebrating specific events and fundraising for the United Israel Appeal (from 1955) and the Welfare Appeal (from 1956). As well as fulfilling their financial and cultural obligations, these functions were opportunities for Lodzer to get together. In addition, the Lodzer Centre became a financial supporter of Melbourne's post-war Jewish schools: Mount Scopus College, Bialik College, I.L. Peretz School and Sholem Aleichem College. The centre also became a financial member of the Board of Deputies, on which it had two representative delegates. A sub-committee was formed to visit sick Lodzer, a task initially undertaken by I. Weinberg, L. Zalbe and S. Gomplewicz.

Financial assistance was extended to *landsman* in Lodz and in other countries where Lodzer resided. Assistance was also sent in the form of medication and clothing. The Lodzer *landsmanshaft* in Israel were sent 9,000 Israeli pounds to help establish an interest-free loan fund. The Lodzer Centre also devoted time and effort in obtaining entry permits for Lodzer who wished to migrate to Melbourne. In the years 1956–60, when the communist government of Poland relaxed its closed emigration policy and allowed some Jews to leave the country, the centre appointed a full-time officer to work with authorities to expedite their immigration to Australia. As well as this, the centre ensured that all ship documents were completed and travel expenses covered. Through this undertaking, hundreds of *landsman* were able to leave Poland. In 1958 the centre organised a special reception for the new arrivals, who were welcomed by Bono Wiener, Shimon Rogozinski and Yehuda Kersh. The Lodzer Centre also organised two exhibitions comprising objects and books relating to the destruction of the Lodz ghetto. The first was staged in 1959, lasted for four days and was attended by 500 people; the second, marking the 20th anniversary of the destruction of the ghetto, was held in 1964 over two days and was visited by over 400.[3]

As post-war Holocaust survivors arrived during the 1940s and 1950s, there was a desperate need for common cultural and social connections that were not being met by traditional, formal communal organisations. Consequently, the number of *landsmanshaftn* increased rapidly. In 1945, the Lensziter *landsmanshaft* was formed, followed by the Kaliszer, Radomer, Zelichover, Biale Podliaske, Zaglembie, Cracower, and Warsawer. The Lodzer *landsmanshaft*, as already noted, was established in 1953, the Vilner *landsmandshaft* in 1958 and the Lomzer *landsmanshaft* as late as 1962. The *Victorian Jewish Year Book* of 1963 noted that there were 21 *landsmanshaftn* operating in Melbourne.[4] While still providing a cultural and social framework, during the 1950s their charter broadened to include temporary housing for new immigrants, philanthropic assistance and Holocaust commemoration. By 1954, with the main intake of Holocaust survivors coming to an end, the focus of these *landsmanshaftn* changed

---

3   Shimon Rogozinski, 'The Lodzer Centre in Melbourne 1953–1974', Melbourne: 1974.
4   Medding, *From Assimilation to Group Survival*, p.28.

from resettlement to welfare issues. Jewish Welfare's annual report of that year thanked the *landsmanshaftn* for collecting pledges from their members for their annual appeal.[5]

On an organisational level, *landsmanshaftn* formed a parallel communal structure to that of the pre-war established community, providing leadership, direction and social cohesion within their own communities. Meetings were commonly held in Yiddish and minutes were often taken in Yiddish. Most significantly, the *landsmanshaftn* became an authoritative and influential feature of the Melbourne post-war Yiddish-speaking community, continuing well into the 1980s.

Holocaust commemoration: 'The Republic of Memory'

With the arrival of large numbers of survivors in Melbourne, the Holocaust could not be perceived simply as a tragic event that occurred in Europe during the war years; it was a lived catastrophe that had devastated the lives of people living in Melbourne. The prominence of the Holocaust within the community shaped its identity, set priorities and influenced public events, particularly commemorative and memorial functions. On a communal level the survivor community developed a number of coping strategies to ameliorate the effects of individual trauma, including collective mourning, the sharing of grief at events such as the commemoration of the Warsaw ghetto uprising, and a number of smaller events organised by the *landsmanshaftn* to commemorate the destruction of individual towns and ghettos.

---

5   Markus and Charak, eds, *Yiddish Melbourne: Towards a History*, pp. 89–92.

Initially, survivors were the driving force behind Holocaust commemorations. These evenings came to occupy a central place in the community, taking on increased significance and patronage. By openly and visibly sharing their experiences through public events, survivors contributed to the shaping of a collective memory of the Holocaust within a thriving Yiddish culture. Jacob Rosenberg explained that 'it was within this expanding cultural hive that the Holocaust survivors established their Republic of Memory'.[6]

In the years following the war, the language of commemoration was Yiddish. It was not only the language most of these survivors spoke; it was the language on the lips of most Eastern Europeans who perished. This effectively sealed commemoration as an event by and for the survivors and it remained as such until the mid-1960s when a push for greater inclusiveness would see more English and Hebrew in public proceedings and a growing understanding that the commemorative event needed to attract a broader section of the community, especially its second generation.

Beginning in 1944, the Warsaw ghetto uprising became the enduring symbol for major commemorative and communal Holocaust memorial services. Even though these communal evenings were the expression of grief at the loss of six million victims, the service, importantly, venerated the heroes of the Warsaw ghetto uprising. After the war, this was a common way of thinking which sought to frame a tragic past in a positive, redemptive and heroic way. Resistance and heroism could then be linked with the establishment of the state of Israel in 1948 and, in many ways, gave birth to the concept of 'the new Jew' as someone with military prowess who valued a robust

---

6   Jacob Rosenberg, *Sunrise West*, p.143.

and muscular Jewish identity. The diaspora Jew – the ghetto Jew – was perceived to have been powerless, unable to defend himself and therefore to have failed. By 1964, all forms of active resistance in all the camps, ghettos, forests and towns were recognised at the Warsaw ghetto commemoration. All acts of defiance and active confrontation with the enemy were upheld as models of survival; they provided a pathway forward, a way to live life and to defy death.

In 1950, the Warsaw ghetto revolt was commemorated simultaneously at three venues. At the Kadimah Hall in Carlton 700 attended, at the Samuel Myers Hall in St Kilda there were 400 attendees, and 500 attended the commemoration at the Assembly Hall in Carlton.[7] Commemorations continued to grow in importance. Within a few years, when the population of post-war survivors reached its peak, these annual events attracted huge crowds of between 2,000 and 3,000 attendees each year. In 1955, two Warsaw ghetto commemorations were held, one in the Samuel Myers Hall and the other at the Kadimah. Both venues were overflowing, and there were calls for one single event to be held in a hall large enough to meet the demand.[8] The following year the event was moved to the Melbourne Town Hall and jointly organised by the Victorian Board of Deputies and the Kadimah, signalling a move towards broader acceptance and ownership of the event. In 1957, over 3,000 attended and many hundreds more still had to be turned away because the venue could not accommodate them. Although the organisation of the event was broadening, the audience were still predominantly survivors.

---

7   *Australian Jewish News*, 21 April 1950.
8   'Warsaw Ghetto Commemoration: Public Demand Single Service', *Australian Jewish News*, 22 April 1955.

Even though these annual commemorative events were by the late 1950s intended to engage the whole community, the matter of who attended and who did not became a sticking point. Many still considered Holocaust remembrance as the domain of the survivor and their compatriot Yiddish speakers, so it was not yet 'owned' by all sections of the community. Divisions between the Yiddishist community and the pre-war established Jewish community were exacerbated. In 1959 the Kadimah annual report noted tersely:

> It is a pity that, notwithstanding the big publicity in the Yiddish and English parts of the Jewish press, the memorial evenings attracted mostly the Yiddish-speaking Jews who originally came from Eastern Europe. The other sections of our community seemed to be indifferent to this function and do not consider it their duty to attend.[9]

In 1961, journalist Sam Lipski, referring to Australian-born Jews, asked, 'Where are they? Have they no need to remember? What will be said when those who come year after year are no longer with us?'[10] Additional efforts were made to spread the message of the Holocaust beyond the community that owned it. In 1961 a Warsaw ghetto exhibition was mounted at the Melbourne Town Hall from 10–14 April, organised by committee that was representative of the entire Jewish community – the Victorian Board of Deputies, the Kadimah, State Zionist Council of Victoria and Jewish Welfare. The exhibition was divided into three sections, the first of which commemorated the Warsaw ghetto revolt of 1943 and depicted some of the horrors perpetrated by the Nazis. The second section depicted the integration of survivors

---

9   Kadimah Annual General Report 1959.
10 *Australian Jewish Herald*, 7 April 1961, cited in Judith Berman, *Holocaust Remembrance in Australian Jewish Communities 1945–2000*, Perth: University of Western Australia Press, 2001, p.33.

in Israel, and the third highlighted the integration of survivors into Australia and the contribution of the Jewish community to Australia's progress.[11] Bernard Evans, Lord Mayor of Melbourne, opened the exhibition and extolled the contributions made by Melbourne Jewry: 'We in Australia are very mindful of the contributions of the Jewish community to art and music and the culture the Jewish people have brought here'. The Anglican Archbishop of Melbourne, Frank Woods, also spoke at the opening, calling on thousands to 'make a pilgrimage of penitence. We cannot cut ourselves off from this happening – the things done by European Christian civilisation.'[12]

Over 6,000 visitors viewed the exhibition, mostly non-Jews. It was photographed by the daily newspapers and received television coverage. It was then transferred to Mount Scopus Memorial College where it was seen by a further 1,600 people, including college students, trainee teachers, and teachers from the surrounding districts, as well as members of the public.[13]

By 1964 the Warsaw ghetto uprising commemoration had expanded its organisational base and its reach further. It was held at the St Kilda Town Hall, organised by a much broader range of community organisations: the Victorian Jewish Board of Deputies, the Kadimah, the Victorian State Zionist Council, Federation of the *Landsmanshaftn*, the Victorian Association of Ex-Servicemen, Association of Victorian Jewish Youth, former Concentration Camp Inmates, B'nai B'rith, Orthodox and Liberal congregations. The St Kilda location signalled a shift in demographics, with more survivors now living south of the river in suburbs away from the centrality of

---

11 *Australian Jewish News*, 14 April 1961.
12 *Australian Jewish News*, 14 April 1961.
13 *Australian Jewish News*, 28 April 1961.

Carlton. It also points to a growing general acceptance that Holocaust memorialisation belonged to all Jews, regardless of their background and experiences.

The growing success of temporary exhibitions, together with the broader appeal of community commemorations throughout the 1960s and 1970s gave impetus to the notion of a permanent museum to memorialise the Holocaust. The outstanding success of the 1980 Holocaust exhibition at the Royal Exhibition Building in Carlton, with some 7,500 attendees in addition to 2,500 school students, demonstrated once and for all the need for a more enduring exhibition. Those who were instrumental in the founding of the Holocaust Museum and Research Centre in Melbourne in 1984 had been key players in the exhibitions of 1953 and 1961, all were Holocaust survivors and Yiddish speakers: Aron Sokolowicz, who provided artefacts from his personal collection; Ursula Flicker, archivist and convener of the 1980 exhibition; Saba Feniger, who became the inaugural curator of the museum; and Bono Wiener whose live testimony accompanied the exhibition. As Chair of the Victorian Jewish Board of Deputies Jewish Heritage Committee, Avram Zeleznikow played a leading role in finding a suitable location for such a museum. Mina Fink, who had been a leading advocate for the resettlement of Holocaust survivors in the years after the war, as Chair of the Appeals committee, not only donated $50,000, which, together with funds from the Federation of Polish Jewry and the Kadimah secured the purchase of 13 Selwyn Street, Elsternwick, but also continued as a leading light of the museum. In 1984 the Holocaust museum, one of the first of its kind in the world, opened its doors to the public.[14]

---

14 Steven Cooke and Donna-Lee Frieze, *The Interior of Our Memories: A History of Melbourne's Jewish Holocaust Centre*, Melbourne: Hybrid Publishers, 2015, pp. 1–28.

Holocaust commemorations held by the various *landsmanshaftn* were more personal and exclusive and went some way in addressing the need for private mourning. These events, though still public affairs, were much smaller and more intimate. In this way, the survivors could link their own personal tragedy with those of the communities from which they came and with whom they shared common experiences. These commemorations were sombre affairs and took the form of Yizkor evenings, with prayers for the dead, recitations and songs sung, such as the Partisans' anthem and *Hatikvah*, Israel's national anthem. They continued to be conducted in Yiddish and remained an important component of the *landsmanshaftn* calendar.

The fight for Yiddish: 'a kind of urgency'

For the pre-war and post-war Yiddish speakers from Eastern Europe, Yiddish was everything. It was their language and their soul. Their families and communities had lived and died with Yiddish on their lips and in their hearts. But not everyone was enamoured of the Yiddish language and its culture. Many Jews were unnerved by the prospect of Jews speaking publicly in any language other than English. As Jacob Rosenberg recalled, 'Yiddish was an anathema to the established Anglo Jewish communities. The question of language became an arena of acute contention'.[15]

Arguments over the appropriateness of the Yiddish language and the promulgation of its culture had been brewing in Melbourne since the early 20th century. At the opening of the Kadimah library in 1912, Rabbi Dr Abrahams of the Melbourne Hebrew congregation inflamed the mostly Yiddish-speaking audience with his controversial

---

15   Rosenberg, *Sunrise West*, pp.160–3.

statement that 'Yiddish was not [our] language' and proudly claimed that the new library would be for 'the advancement of the Hebrew language'. At the same event, Rabbi Danglow acknowledged that while he understood Yiddish, he preferred to address them in English.[16] When Hymie Kolt's family arrived in 1924, they were told by representatives of the Jewish community 'not to speak Yiddish or Russian in public, or if they did, to keep their voices low'.[17] Disputes over the use of Yiddish were not, however, unique to Melbourne; they went back much further.

Moses Mendelssohn (1729–86), the philosophical father of the Haskalah movement, the Jewish version of the European enlightenment in Germany, called Yiddish a 'jargon' and advocated the use of German vernacular. The same debate raged in America a century later between the German Jewish immigrants, who called for the 'Americanisation' of new immigrants and the wholesale adoption of the English language, and their Yiddish-speaking Ostjuden (Eastern) brethren.[18] The speaking of Yiddish in community organisations and at community events was not only a statement of identity but an integral link to the cultural past, a past that had largely been obliterated in Eastern Europe by the Holocaust. As Yiddish advocate and Holocaust survivor Mendl Balberyszki explained, 'The struggle for Yiddish is not simply a technical one but involves the whole question of our existence. Without Yiddish (and Hebrew) there can be no Jewish existence'.[19]

---

16   John S. Levi, *Rabbi Jacob Danglow*, Carlton: Melbourne University Press, 1995, p.63.
17   Julie Meadows, *A Shtetl in Ek Velt*, p.42.
18   Markus and Charak, *Yiddish Melbourne: Towards a History*, p.17.
19   Mendl Balberyszki, *Australian Jewish News*, 1 April 1960.

For many Yiddish speakers, the language signified who they were and what they represented. Michael Gawenda summed it up:

> For most of the Yiddish speakers there was a sense that they were trying to recreate secular Jewishness which was very powerful in Poland – but had been mostly destroyed by the Holocaust. It was different from the Italians and the Greeks because it was a traumatised community . . . there was a kind of urgency about recreating what had been destroyed. They were driven by that. That partly explains the vibrancy at that time.[20]

Yiddish immigrants sensed the urgency with which they needed to act in order to recreate in Melbourne the same Yiddish world that had flourished in the large towns and cities of Poland and Lithuania, such as Warsaw, Lodz, Krakow, Bialystok and Vilna. The loss of language and culture would signal the end of a civilisation. Little wonder that the leaders at the vanguard of Yiddish culture in Melbourne largely came from the urban centres that best represented the Yiddish world. Leading Yiddish identities Aron Sokolowicz, Leo Fink, Mina Fink, Jacob Waks and Yehoshua Rapaport came from Bialystok; Aron Nirens, Jonas Pushett, Nachman Gryfenberg, Symche Burstin, Pinye Ringelblum and Cluwa Krystal came from Warsaw; Samuel Wynn, Pinchas Goldhar, Abraham Cykiert, Jacob Rosenberg and Bono Wiener came from Lodz; Rachel Holzer came from Cracow; Avram Zeleznikow, Mendl Balberyszki and Joseph Giligich came from Vilna, where Genia Wasserman (born in Bielsk-Podlaski) was educated; Jacob Kronhill from Lublin. They had experienced the full expression of Yiddish life. The challenge that they faced was how to pass on their language and its rich culture to a future generation, born into a different world.

---

20 Michael Gawenda, interview 10 March 2011.

A SECOND CHANCE

Yiddishist community leaders did not shy away from heated debate over issues that they perceived to be a direct attack on their Yiddish identity. On 10 May 1948, the Victorian Jewish Board of Deputies passed a motion that permitted delegates to make addresses in Yiddish, which would then be translated into English for those who did not understand Yiddish. There was peace, as the status quo was maintained for 12 years, but on 21 March 1960, the Chairman of the Board, Moss Davis, announced that 'in future no translations of Yiddish speakers would take place where the speaker, in the opinion of the chair, could express himself properly in English'. This was met with outrage and dissent, resulting in a walkout of five Yiddishist delegates – Mendl Balberyszski of Carlton Hebrew congregation, Sender Burstin and Motl Wilenski from the Kadimah, Bono Wiener of the Lodzer Centre and Jacob Kronhill of the Yiddish Schools.[21] As a result of continued lobbying, the motion was amended on 2 May 1960, allowing the delegates to make Yiddish addresses but noting that 'they had to adhere to the standing orders in respect to speaker's time limits'. For Sender Burstin this signalled a victory, 'an example of how determination and sticking to principles can bring positive outcomes'.[22]

Yiddishists also fought to have Yiddish taught at the Mount Scopus Day School, the first Jewish day school in Australia, when it was established in 1948. There were lengthy discussions led by a bloc of Yiddish educators, notably Joseph Giligich and members of the Victorian Jewish Board of Deputies. Consequently, a motion

---

[21] *Australian Jewish News*, 26 March 1960.
[22] Burstin, *Yiddish Melbourne Observed*, p.162.

was passed that offered Yiddish in the extracurricular program. However, as few students chose to take Yiddish as an elective, in 1952 the school decided to drop Yiddish. Pressure from Yiddishists had it reinstated in 1955 in the primary school, where 50 students in years 3 and 4 elected to take Yiddish language instruction in that year, but there were fewer in the upper primary years and no students in the secondary years.[23] Yiddish instruction at Mount Scopus languished as the school's focus was decidedly Zionist and instruction in Hebrew was mandatory. But, as we will see, this did not spell the end of Yiddish education for the Yiddishists who managed to sustain two Yiddish schools throughout the decades following the war.

Even if they spoke other languages, Yiddish remained the language of choice for most post-war Yiddish-speaking immigrants. For writer and author Arnold Zable, the 'heart of the nation was its language'. Yiddish provided 'the glue to keep people together'.[24] For Jack Felman, a general practitioner, Yiddish represented something more: a means of regaining what had been lost forever – a homeland and a community.

> My Greek and Italian patients speak to the Yaya and Nona in Greek and Italian. Greeks and Italians always go back to Italy and Greece and they have dozens and dozens of cousins and relatives. Where would my parents send us back? They knew they could not recapture the life, the culture, the society they had, by going back.[25]

---

23 W.D. Rubinstein, *The Jews in Australia*, Melbourne: William Heinemann Australia, 1991, p.220.
24 Arnold Zable, interview 2 December 2011.
25 Jack Felman, interview 24 March 2011.

A SECOND CHANCE

The survivors had no homeland to which they could return; their lives were now rooted in Australian soil. Their focus was on consolidating and expanding the Yiddish world here in Melbourne, a world that had been recreated and nurtured in the fertile pre-war years. As a consequence of the Yiddish institutions built and fortified prior to 1939, Yiddish culture flourished throughout the 1950s, a period that represented a new era for Yiddish Melbourne.

Chapter 13

ISRAEL: THE GAME-CHANGER

Di Yiddishe gasse, the Jewish street, or Jewish quarter, meant far more than roads, thoroughfares and buildings. It came to define the community's life, its essence. While monumental events would soon challenge political allegiances and redefine Jewish identity, Yiddish cultural life was in full bloom in post-war 1940s Melbourne.

A second Yiddish newspaper, the *Yiddishe Post*, a supplement to the weekly *Jewish Herald*, began publication in 1946, and a second Yiddish school was established, the Sholem Aleichem afternoon and Sunday school, located in St Kilda with Yasha Sher as its headmaster. In order to cope with the increased demand for Yiddish education, Joseph Giligich instigated a two-year training course for Yiddish language teachers in 1947. The I.L. Peretz School, established in November 1935, had its own Yiddish choir, which found fame in the 1940s. Eleven gramophone records of Yiddish songs were made in 1945, which were broadcast on radio station 3XY. To meet the demand of a growing number of young children, the school opened a kindergarten in 1950.

There was also a voracious appetite for entertainment. In 1948 alone the David Herman Theatre put on in the Kadimah hall six classic Yiddish plays, by Jacob Gordin, Abraham Goldfaden and

Itzik Manger, Sholem Aleichem and Peretz Hirshbein, and three reviews – *A Be Men Lebt* (As Long As We Are Alive), *Oyfn Tzimbl* (On the Cymbal – Marionettes), and *Nadir un Vayn Nisht* (Here You Are and Don't Cry). They played to packed houses.[1] The Kadimah held a variety of weekly lectures, recitals, debates and symposiums, with topics ranging from the literary to the political. Purim plays and musical concerts were staged. Popular Yiddish films, such as *Yidl mitn Fidl* (Jew with a Violin) starring American comic actress Molly Picon, were regularly screened and always guaranteed an appreciative audience.

Paid membership of the Kadimah cultural centre was climbing steadily from 360 paid members in 1938 to 1,337 in 1951. The *lebedike tsaytung* (living newspapers) were a regular feature at the Kadimah, 'providing a platform for a free Jewish word in Melbourne'.[2] As has been noted, to cope with the increased demand for Yiddish books, the Bialystoker Centre opened its own library, the Peisach Kaplan library, in 1948, supplementing the existing Kadimah library.[3] In 1951 the Kadimah inaugurated a Jewish children's library, free of charge, with books in both Yiddish and Hebrew.

In spite of an expanding, rich cultural life that saw the transposition of an entire Yiddish cultural world, Jewish Melbourne remained a complex community with disparate political views. 'There were always a lot of [political] fights, a lot of discussions and debates in all the organisations between different factions and groups within the community,' recalled Yiddish teacher and community identity Danielle

---

1 Arnold Zable, *Wanderers and Dreamers: Tales of the David Herman Theatre*, Melbourne: Hyland House, 1998, pp.81–2.
2 Kadimah Annual General Meeting report 1951.
3 Bialystoker Annual General Meeting report 1949.

ISRAEL: THE GAME-CHANGER

Charak, a child survivor who arrived with her family in 1949. In the shadow of the Holocaust, Danielle explained that underlying all the arguments and debates was an abiding 'concern and love for the Jewish people'.

> The discussions were always in Yiddish. You could come from different political points of view but basically you were united in *Yiddishkeit*. This was the main characteristic of these people. The ultimate agenda was, 'What will happen to our people?' One must understand that these were not assimilated Jews, these Jews were passionately involved in what they thought was *best* for the Jews.[4]

One momentous event, however, would galvanise the community and bring political disputations to a head. The perennial questions for a majority of the Jewish population, 'What will happen to our people?' and 'What was best for the Jews?', were finally given a resounding, definitive answer – a Jewish homeland. It was an answer that would redirect Jewish loyalties, reshape Jewish identity and influence the way Jewish youth engaged with the world and what fired their passion. Most significantly, it moved them away from the centrality of a world steeped in Yiddish, with its legacy of murderous antisemitism, towards what it was hoped would be a new, empowering future, free from the tyrannies of the past.

The shift towards a new authoritative, muscular Jewish identity occurred during the war years. Zionist youth groups transformed Australia's Zionist movement, projecting new possibilities for a new future, at a time when there appeared little hope for Europe's Jews. Zionism provided the answer to Jewish survival. The Zionist ideology captured the imagination of many young people. Zionist recruiters

---

4   Danielle Charak, interview 9 February 2009.

targeted not only recent immigrants of Yiddish-speaking background, but also Australian-born youth. Through a structured program of activities, rallies and lectures they appealed to a broad cross-section of the community. Habonim (the builders) was founded by Shmuel Rosenkranz, Isaac Roseby and Gedalia Perlstein and held its first meeting on 31 March 1940 in Herzl hall in Carlton.[5] By the end of 1944, Habonim was a highly structured and well-organised movement that had spread across the Jewish communities of Australia. Local branches were established in Adelaide in 1949 and Brisbane in 1947.

In Melbourne other Zionist movements flourished as well. Right-wing Betar was formed in May 1939 under the leadership of Kalman Parasol and Menachem Shifman. Their first public function was to mourn the death of Russian-born Revisionist Zionist leader Ze'ev Jabotinsky in August 1940. Bnei Akiva, an orthodox religious Zionist movement, had its beginnings in 1944 in Carlton and Elwood and by 1949 was a well-structured organisation and spread rapidly. By the late 1940s Zionist youth movements had consolidated their place within the Jewish community.[6] The champions of Yiddish now had a powerful rival for the hearts and minds of young people, particularly those of Eastern European Yiddish-speaking backgrounds. 'In spite of distancing myself from Yiddish,' explained Ezra Kowadlo, 'Habonim became my link to Judaism and Zionism'.[7]

In the years leading up to Israel's 1948 Declaration of Independence, British-mandated Palestine was embroiled in what became

---

5   Bernard Hyams, *The History of the Australian Zionist Movement*, Melbourne: Zionist Federation of Australia, 1998, p.78.
6   Hyams, *The History of the Australian Zionist Movement*, p.81.
7   Meadows, ed., *Fun Himlen Blayene Tsu Bloye Teg (From Leaden Skies to Blue Days*, p.76.

ISRAEL: THE GAME-CHANGER

a three-way conflict between the British governing forces, Jewish underground resistance groups, and the Arab population. The Jewish resistance movement comprised various groups, including the Haganah, the Irgun and the Lehi (also known as the Stern gang), all fighting for independence but with differing political agendas. The more mainstream Haganah tried to cooperate with the British forces, particularly during the war years. The right-wing Irgun and radical militant Lehi believed that only through armed struggle would they free themselves from British rule and gain independence. At the end of the war these groups formed an uneasy alliance, an anti-British national movement, but the bitter divisions, disputes and rancour between the factions remained unresolved.

Founded in 1929 the Jewish Agency, chaired by David Ben Gurion from 1935 to 1948, was the official representative of the Yishuv (the Jewish community in Palestine prior to independence) during the British mandate and was responsible for security, education and *aliya* (immigration to Israel). It also had a government department that oversaw foreign affairs on behalf of the Jewish community of Palestine. The Jewish Agency was responsible for the illegal entry of more than 150,000 Jewish immigrants into Palestine between 1934 and 1948.[8]

In protest against restrictive immigration laws that limited Jewish settlement in the Yishuv, at a time when European Jews were desperate for sanctuary, Jewish paramilitary groups carried out attacks targeting the British authorities. Their actions soon escalated into a bloody, bitterly fought, widespread insurgency. Indicative of the desperation of Jewish underground paramilitary forces, on 22 July 1946

---

8 Mordecai Naor, *Zionism: The First 120 Years, 1882–2002*, Jerusalem: Zionist Library, 2002, p.34.

the militant right-wing Irgun bombed British administrative headquarters in the south wing of the King David Hotel in Jerusalem. The attack left 91 people dead and 46 injured and brought widespread condemnation. *The Argus* proclaimed the perpetrators as 'Jewish terrorists', while The Adelaide *Advertiser* called it a 'mass slaughter' of 'innocent bystanders who were victims of Jewish fanaticism'.[9]

The Victorian Jewish community also condemned the act. Statements issued in the mainstream press by the Victorian State Zionist Council 'welcomed the denunciation by the Jewish Agency of the recent outrage' and the Victorian Jewish Advisory Board 'strongly denounced and condemned the terrible atrocity in Jerusalem, and earnestly hopes that the perpetrators, whoever they are, are brought to justice'.[10] Jewish community spokesmen not only deplored the acts of brutality but also had concerns about the danger they posed for the establishment of an independent Jewish state.

The insurgency continued unabated, spilling out beyond Palestine, into Britain itself and to Europe. There were bombing attacks on civilian and military targets. Some were thwarted, such as a plan to drop bombs on the British House of Commons from a plane chartered by members of the extreme militant group Lehi; others were not. Successful sabotage attacks were carried out on British Army transportation routes in Germany in late 1946 and early 1947. The British response was swift and they arrested thousands, instigating prison floggings and executions. Following the execution of three Irgun fighters in July 1947, the Irgun exacted its own revenge, kidnapping and murdering two British sergeants the next day and leaving

---

9   *The Argus*, 24 July 1946; *The Advertiser*, 31 July 1946.
10 *The Argus*, 24 July 1946.

their booby-trapped bodies hanging from trees in an orange grove in Netanya. Such actions caused an escalation of antisemitic attacks in Britain; rioting erupted over several days in Liverpool and Jewish property was damaged in several major British cities, including London and Manchester.[11]

Eventually the British recognised that its role in Palestine was futile and costly. On 14 February 1947 British Foreign Secretary Ernest Bevan informed the House of Commons that 'the Palestine question would be referred to the United Nations'. On 31 August the United Nations Special Committee on Palestine (UNSCOP) recommended that Palestine be partitioned into separate Jewish and Arab states and the UN General Assembly voted in favour of partition on 29 November 1947. As the British began to withdraw, civil war erupted between Jews and Arabs, beginning nearly six months of bloodshed and carnage.[12]

Local opposition to Jewish independence

The period of Jewish insurgency and civil war in Palestine generated heated debate in Melbourne, splitting the community between Zionists and anti-Zionists. While Yiddishists were prominent on both sides of the debate, most were supporters of Zionism. In 1946 community leader and Yiddishist Samuel Wynn led the appeal committee of the Victorian branch of the Keren Hayesod, founded in 1920 as the Zionist movement's fundraising arm. His 'call to Australian Jewry' was unequivocal: 'We see ahead of us the one light

---

11   J. Bowyer Bell, *Terror Out of Zion*, London: St Martin's Press, 1976.
12   Arieh J. Kochavi, *Post Holocaust Politics: Britain, the United States and Jewish Refugees 1945–48*, Chapel Hill, NC: University of North Carolina Press, 2001.

around which our spirits can rally: Eretz Israel'.[13] The David Herman Theatre produced popular Hebrew plays translated into Yiddish. Yiddish actor Yankev Waislitz directed a production of *Unzer Erd* (Our Land), a stirring play about young Zionist pioneers by popular Hebrew playwright and poet Aharon Ashman, at the Union Theatre, Melbourne University, on 13 June 1946.[14] It was a resounding success.

Other leaders, also staunch Zionists and committed Yiddishists, directed their considerable energies towards survivors desperate to leave Europe who remained stranded in Europe's displaced persons' camps. Leo Fink, President of the United Overseas Jewish Relief Fund from 1943 to 1947, Jonas Pushett, member of Jewish Welfare board in the 1940s, and David Abzac, Secretary of Jewish Welfare from 1946 to 1950 and Chairman of its migration assistance committee from mid-1948, were among those at the forefront of welfare and relief fund-raising, deeply committed to the rescue and resettlement of Holocaust survivors in Melbourne. In this they shared common ground with the Bund. The Bund, an activist minority within the Yiddish-speaking community, remained opposed to the establishment of an independent Jewish state and unswervingly committed to serving 'the local community'. They did so by 'occupying responsible and important positions in the Hilfs Fond (Welfare Society), the Kadimah, the Yiddish school, Yiddish theatre and the *landsmanshaftn*'.[15]

A small group of influential individuals, members of the conservative Melbourne Jewish establishment, were incensed by what they perceived as the undermining of British rule in mandated Palestine by Jewish extremists. They ran a concerted public campaign opposed

---

13 *Australian Jewish News*, 14 June 1946.
14 *Australian Jewish News*, 4 May 1946.
15 Burstin, *Yiddish Melbourne Observed*, p.148.

to the creation of a Jewish state. Sir Isaac Isaacs, former Governor-General of Australia, Rabbi Danglow of the St Kilda synagogue, and Archie Michaelis, St Kilda's representative in the Victorian parliament, led the attack. They feared that support for political Zionism demonstrated disloyalty and was a betrayal of the British Empire, which they felt had served the Jewish people well. As such, they considered support for Zionism as a betrayal of Australian Jewry, which had integrated successfully into Australian life and had much to lose as a consequence of divided loyalties.

There were claims and counter claims. The Victorian Jewish Advisory Board in 1946 affirmed its 'unswerving support of the Zionist ideal', while Isaacs and Michaelis insisted that all acts of Jewish 'terrorism' led by militant Jewish underground resistance organisations against British forces in mandated Palestine be equally condemned by the community's umbrella body and asserted that large numbers of Jews 'who loyally served the empire in war' were opposed to 'political Zionism'. Adding more fuel to the flames, Danglow, in a fiery address from his pulpit, advised 'migrant Jews' to 'shake the dust off their feet and leave, if they don't like it here'.[16]

The anti-Zionists continued to condemn political Zionism as the natural enemy of Australian Jews who enjoyed the rights and privileges of an egalitarian society and were neither homeless nor stateless. To make matters worse, Isaacs and Michaelis aired their opinions to the wider public in the mainstream press, incurring the wrath of Jewish community leaders who saw this as an internal issue and not for public debate. Michaelis, however, claimed that as a parliamentarian he could speak out on Jewish affairs and would 'not

---

16   *Jewish Herald*, 11 October 1946, cited in Peter Medding, *From Assimilation to Group Survival*, Melbourne: F.W. Cheshire, 1968, p.133.

be dragooned into silence'.[17] When Zionist leader and founder of Sydney's Temple Emanuel, Reform rabbi Max Schenk, made disparaging remarks about British policy in Palestine, Michaelis fired off a stinging rebuke in *The Argus* of 1 April 1948: 'I am confident that the vast majority of Australian Jewry are fully aware of the great debt they owe to Great Britain, and will view with disgust the anti-British sentiments expressed by Rabbi Schenk'. Rabbi Danglow echoed the same sentiments two months later in a letter to the Editor of *The Age*.

> I am confident that the large majority of Australian Jews fully and gladly recognise their privileges and obligations as loyal citizens of the Commonwealth and deplore and keenly resent the violent and irresponsible outbursts against Britain by individual Zionist extremists in this country and elsewhere . . . Australian Jews as a whole dissociate themselves entirely from such ill-considered attitudes and utterances, being gratefully cognisant of all that Britain has done towards successful Jewish settlement in Palestine, and ever remembering the magnificent services unboastfully rendered by it to modern civilisation particularly during the critical years of the recent great war.[18]

Tensions, recriminations and accusations between the Zionist-affiliated Jewish umbrella bodies – the Victorian Jewish Board of Deputies and its federal counterpart, the Executive Council of Australian Jewry – and those opposing the establishment of a Jewish state continued with fiery passion and conviction on both sides. The heat finally came out of the debate with the establishment of the state of Israel in May 1948, which brought to an end attacks on British forces in Palestine and was recognised as a newly created nation by

---

17 *Australian Jewish News*, 23 April 1948, cited in Medding, *From Assimilation to Group Survival*, p.134.
18 *The Age*, 9 June 1948.

Britain and Australia. For all intents and purposes it was the end of the conservative, pro-British, anti-Zionist movement.

The state of Israel is born

At 4 p.m. on 14 May 1948, Zionist statesman and political leader David Ben Gurion stood before some 250 invited guests in what is today known as Independence Hall in Tel Aviv and issued the Proclamation of Independence, declaring the establishment of the state of Israel. The 16-minute address was broadcast live on what was to become the Israeli national radio station, Kol Israel (Voice of Israel). For the first time in 2,000 years Jews had their own homeland.

Following the devastation of the Holocaust, for those immigrant Jews who had direct experience of life without security, without refuge, the impact of the establishment of the state of Israel was profound. The overwhelming majority of Yiddishists embraced the idea of a Jewish state, a Jewish homeland, a country that would defend and protect them. As Sam Lipski reflected, 'The Holocaust and Israel were at the very centre of Jewish life in Carlton . . . for that generation and for the survivors to live to see the establishment of the state of Israel was a defining period'.[19] For many Jews around the world the declaration of Israel's independence was electrifying, prompting celebrations and outpourings of unbridled joy. 'The early-morning news of the declaration spread like wildfire and many spontaneous gatherings were held in various parts of the city', reported the *Australian Jewish News*.[20] In Melbourne, singing and dancing filled the community halls and synagogues. No longer a point of division,

---

19 Sam Lipski, interview 15 August 2011.
20 *Australian Jewish News*, 21 May 1948.

the birth of a Jewish homeland brought together Jews from different walks of life. 'I'll never forget it. There was dancing, the young with the old, the *frum* (orthodox) with the not *frum*. Wild scenes like we would never see again', Rachel Levita recalled of that emotional night in the Kadimah hall.[21]

Festivities and celebrations continued. On 17 May the Samuel Myers Hall in St Kilda was overflowing with well-wishers, with about 1,000 persons filling the hall, its buffet room, annexes and vestibule. Samuel Wynn chaired the meeting, read messages and

> the text of the cable sent to Mr Ben Gurion, first premier of the Jewish state. Carlton synagogue's Rabbi Gurewicz gave a stirring address in Yiddish in the course of which he appealed for support for the Jewish state. He said the Jews will build a state that will be an example of good for the world. The Jewish Men's Choir finely sang 'Hallelujah'.[22]

Benzion Patkin read in Hebrew, with English translations, and Maurice Ashkanasy made a forthright address in which he 'alluded to those Jews who will not stand with us at this historic moment as forfeiting their name as Jews'. He went further, declaring that Israel was now in a fight for its life. The very day after Ben Gurion had declared Israel's independence, five Arab nations who refused to accept the United Nations partition resolution of 29 November 1947 declared war on Israel, instigating the War of Independence. Ashkanasy pronounced that all Jews must be prepared to make the ultimate sacrifice in defence of Jewish nationhood: 'We must all die eventually, but there is no greater manner of dying than in the establishing of *Am*

---

21 Peter Kohn, 'Levita – a Star Remembers: the Peter Kohn interview, *Australian Jewish News*, 17 February 1989, p.11.
22 *Australian Jewish News*, 21 May 1948.

Israel Chai (the nation of Israel is a living state)'. The evening concluded 'in an atmosphere electric with feeling, the entire audience impressively sang Israel's national anthem, the *Hatikvah*'.[23]

On 31 May, a crowd of more than 4,000 people celebrated at the Melbourne Exhibition Building, at a time when the Jewish population of Melbourne numbered approximately 15,000. As the *Jewish News* reported, 'Guests from other states; members of Jewish bodies and organisations; men, women and children from all areas filled the main hall. Held high on the stage was the flag of Israel while the words of Herzl, "We will build a Model State", stood out boldly for all to see'.[24] Rabbi Berkovitz from Sydney reminded the crowd of Israel's greater significance and its role in the world, stating that 'the battle for Palestine was being waged not for a Jewish state alone but for the survival of mankind. The state of Israel is the front line for humanity'. Israel's fate, he concluded, was inextricably tied to the fate of all Jews; 'the Jewish people will meet the crisis for they are the living Jews with faith in the eternal destiny of Israel – in the eternity of the Jewish race'.[25]

The creation of the state of Israel was a source of personal pride and accomplishment, the fulfilment of a people's desire for a Jewish homeland that struck a deep chord with many individuals. 'I was twenty-three in 1948', Warsaw-born Carlton resident Leon Freedman, who arrived with his family in 1927, and recalled that the momentous occasion 'aroused enormous enthusiasm . . . Zionism was boosted. On a personal level we felt so proud to be a Jew'.[26]

---

23 *Australian Jewish News*, 21 May 1948.
24 *Australian Jewish News*, 4 June 1948.
25 *Australian Jewish News*, 4 June 1948.
26 Leon Freedman, interview 24 March 2009.

A SECOND CHANCE

The community quickly rallied behind the fledgling state. Eager to hear news of Israel's battles against the invading Arab armies who vowed to destroy the small state before it could draw its first breath, public events were held to inform the community of the course of the war. In the same way that news was often disseminated during the Second World War, word of mouth played an important part in the information chain. Sam Lipski recalled the weekly information evenings held at the Kadimah throughout Israel's War of Independence, which continued until formal armistice agreements were signed in February 1949, to relay the latest news concerning Israel – presented in Yiddish. The information evenings were

> run by the late Joe Solvey, an important figure in the Zionist history of Melbourne, he was active in the state Zionist council and later president for a number of years, one of the founders of Bialik College, but he was also a great Yiddishist. Solvey conducted the *lebedike tsaytung* (living newspaper) . . . I don't know where he got his information from but he would lecture for two hours every week and all in Yiddish . . . The Kadimah was always full, week after week.[27]

The birth of the state of Israel was a pivotal moment for Australian Jewry. Coming just three years after the Holocaust, the urgent need to secure a Jewish homeland was brought into sharp focus. The Hitler years exposed the total vulnerability and absolute defencelessness of the Jews. While Jews in Australia enjoyed comfort and security, circumstances could always change. Recent history had taught them a devastating lesson. Many now viewed Zionism no longer as an aspiration but as a dire necessity. In a time of great Jewish tragedy, the Zionist message was clear and compelling – a

---

27   Sam Lipski, interview 15 August 2011.

Jewish homeland was imperative to Jewish survival. As historian Bill Rubinstein saw it, 'A world had died but nothing had as yet taken its place'.[28]

Annual Independence Day celebrations – a time to rejoice

Nothing could match the appeal of Israel Independence Day celebrations. While the Jewish calendar was heavily weighted with commemorations and memorial days, a day of pure celebration marking the birth of a Jewish homeland not only gave promise of a better future but was recognition that a new Jewish world order had been created.

When Israeli emissary, Moshe Sharett (Israel's second Prime Minister, from 1954 to 1955), toured Australia in 1957, he drew record crowds. That year Israel Independence Day celebrations at the West Melbourne Stadium attracted 8,000 participants, at a time when Melbourne's Jewish population was about 25,000.[29] By 1957, Israel Independence Day celebrations had become the largest event in the calendar of Melbourne's Jewish community, eclipsing even Holocaust commemorations. Yiddish continued to have a strong presence in celebrations held in these early years. Leon Freedman remembered the excitement he felt when he attended these annual events: 'They had wonderful Yom Ha'atzmaut celebrations. Huge Yiddish-speaking crowds were attracted and you wouldn't hear a single English word'.[30]

---

28 W.D. Rubinstein, *The Jews In Australia: A Thematic History*, Volume 2, Melbourne: William Heinemann, 1991, p.501.
29 Hyams, *The History of the Australian Zionist Movement*, p.108.
30 Leon Freedman, interview 24 March 2009.

The annual celebrations were organised by the State Zionist Council, involved the Zionist youth movements and included Hebrew singing, Israeli dancing and speeches by local and visiting dignitaries. They were a showcase for Israel's achievements. In 1960 the *Australian Jewish News* front-page story recorded that over 5,000 people had attended the Israel Day Rally at Melbourne's Festival Hall.[31] Throughout the 1960s these annual rallies attracted between 4,000 and 7,000 people, and it was claimed that they were the largest indoor Jewish gatherings in the world outside New York.[32]

When Menachem Begin, then leader of the main opposition party in the Israeli Knesset, a faction leader in the War of Independence and the son of Polish Yiddish speakers born in Brest-Litovsk in 1913, visited Melbourne in 1963, he inspired crowds with his public addresses, many of which he gave in Yiddish. As Leon Freedman put it, 'He wasn't Prime Minister yet ... just Menachem Begin of the Irgun. He was a wonderful orator. He tugged at our hearts in Yiddish. We were enthralled. You went away feeling so proud'.[33]

The Bund – a new era

The creation of the state of Israel signalled the triumph of Zionism. As Sam Lipski bluntly put it, 'Zionism and Israel won the argument. Conclusively. The Bund and *doykeit* lost. Overwhelmingly'.[34] In Melbourne the Bund continued its focus on *doykeit*, the here

---

31 *Australian Jewish News*, 6 May 1960.
32 Peter Medding, 'The Melbourne Jewish Community Since 1945: A Political and Sociological Study', MA thesis, Melbourne University, 1962.
33 Leon Freedman, interview 24 March 2009.
34 *Australian Jewish News*, 8 June 2008, cited in David Slucki, 'The Jewish Labour Bund After the Holocaust: A Comparative History', PhD, Monash University, 2010, p.286.

and now of a Yiddish-centric life of the diaspora. For the present it retained its opposition to political Zionism and the establishment of an independent Jewish homeland which prioritised the Jewish state over the diaspora.

Ironically, by the mid-1950s more Bundists were living in Israel than in Melbourne.[35] Yiddish organisations in Israel did exist in spite of the government's strong antipathy towards Yiddish and what it represented for them – a 'failed diaspora', characterised by the downtrodden, powerless ghetto Jew. This negative attitude won Israel no friends among Bundists around the world for whom Yiddish was at the very core of their being. A Jewish homeland without Yiddish close to its heart? Israel was founded on the revival of Hebrew as a modern language, embodying the 'new' Jew, an empowered figure who emerged from the *shtetl* to forge a new life. Despite the Israeli establishment's attitude and an environment generally hostile towards Yiddish activists, Bundists established Yiddish libraries and Yiddish schools in Israel. The Bund journal, *Lebns Fragn* (Life's questions), first appeared in 1951 and a Bund headquarters was opened in Tel Aviv in 1957.[36] Israel was home to a sizable, thriving Bund organisation. So the Bundists faced a conundrum: If the Bund supported all Jews 'here', 'there' and 'now', what of those living in Israel? In response the Bund softened its stance on Israel.

In an announcement in April 1955 that marked a major turning point, at its world conference in Montreal the Bund publicly announced its support for the Jewish state: 'Israel is a significant factor in Jewish life. As a self-contained, self-governing Jewish community, Israel can

---

35 Slucki, 'The Jewish Labour Bund After the Holocaust', p.323.
36 Slucki, 'The Jewish Labour Bund After the Holocaust', p.333.

play an affirmative role in Jewish life'.[37] It advocated for the safety of Jews who happened to be living in Israel: 'When Israel and its Jewish population are threatened with total annihilation, it is the obligation of Jews together with peace-loving people everywhere to give complete support to the state of Israel, and to ensure the physical existence of the Jews in Israel'.[38]

In 1966 Melbourne Bund leader Sender Burstin reiterated the repositioning of the Bund's attitude towards Israel as home to over two million Jews, without relinquishing its concerns about Israel's negation of the diaspora and its denigration of Yiddish.

> Notwithstanding our legitimate criticism of the state of Israel, we must recognise its national significance. Two and a quarter million Jews have their political, economic and cultural lives concentrated in a very small territory. This places a huge responsibility on us to give the Yishuv all moral and material assistance to ensure its healthy development.[39]

Supporting Jews living in Israel was one thing, but it didn't spell the end of the Bund's opposition to political Zionism. Also in 1966, Sender Burstin asked some rhetorical questions in the Melbourne Bund journal *Unzer Gedank* (Our thoughts): 'Is the struggle finished? Has Zionism been victorious on all fronts? Has it fulfilled all the hopes upon which it was based? Far from it!'[40] In this, Sender Burstin put the case for continued support of Jewish life in Australia.

The Bund had to grapple with issues of political relevance in a new world in which Israel now loomed large and in which revolutionary

---

37 Quoted in Slucki, 'The Jewish Labour Bund After the Holocaust', p.348.
38 Moshe Ajzenbud, *60 Years of Bund In Melbourne, 1928–1988*, Melbourne: Jewish Labour Bund, 1996, p.51.
39 Burstin, *Yiddish Melbourne Observed*, p.176.
40 Slucki, 'The Jewish Labour Bund After the Holocaust', p.242.

socialism was not part and parcel of the political realities confronting a democratic and egalitarian country such as Australia. The Bund strengthened its own relevance through strategic alliances, recognising that strength came with unity, and established the World Coordinating Committee of Bund Organizations in Brussels in 1947 to link the dispersed Bund communities around the globe. On a local level the Bund replicated what it had done in Poland by aligning itself with the nation's workers' party, in Melbourne the Victorian branch of the Australian Labor Party.

While the Bund never eclipsed the Zionist juggernaut, it remained a vocal and combative community force. The Bund's influence went beyond its actual numbers. While it failed in its first attempts to join the Victorian Jewish Board of Deputies as an affiliate in its own right (it was labelled a political party thereby making it 'ineligible' under the board's rules), it managed to exert its influence through Bundist delegates to the board who represented other institutions. It was an adaptive approach that worked. Delegates who were Bundists, such as Bono Wiener representing the Lodzer Centre, Mendl Balberyszski from the Carlton Hebrew congregation, Sender Burstin from the Kadimah, and Jacob Kronhill representing the Yiddish schools, ensured that the Bundist Yiddishist vision remained within the board's orbit. Similarly, its members worked within and eventually took over the Kadimah, dominated Jewish Welfare, and ran the Yiddish schools.

Arguably the Bund's greatest achievement in this period was cultural – the preservation and advancement of Yiddish. At a grassroots level they achieved much. They fought for the right to speak Yiddish at meetings of the Board of Deputies, organised cultural and artistic programs and lectures, hosted visiting speakers, chaired political discussions and debates, and organised memorial evenings.

What do you think of Israel?

For postwar Jewish immigrants in Melbourne, the world of Yiddish, the bedrock of cultural life, became irrevocably subsumed within a greater imperative, which offered surety and permanence, security and continuity – Israel. For his landmark demographic study of the Melbourne Jewish community in 1961,[41] sociologist Peter Medding conducted 125 interviews on a range of topics and included the question, 'What do you think of Israel?' The responses were illuminating. They captured the zeitgeist of the times, in which the wounds of the Holocaust were still fresh and raw and the turbulent period before Israel came into existence remained in living memory.

The establishment of a Jewish homeland offered more than physical security, a place to flee in times of persecution, a haven where Jews could live without threat of extermination. Many Jews living in the diaspora felt that their status had changed after 1948; their self-perception was also altered. They felt that they were now viewed differently by others and in turn viewed themselves differently. In particular, Israel gave many immigrant Jews, who had only known a fragile, precarious, itinerant existence, a sense of ownership. 'Makes us feel that we have something that belongs to us', said one; 'Something we own', replied another. They now had a greater sense of pride and self-worth, 'Now we have an address', one explained, 'without it no respect'. 'Israel is the only thing for us. Prestige for the Jews who are not there, prestige we never had', another observed. The future of Israel became inextricably linked with their own future. 'I am a Zionist. Israel is the answer to all Jewish problems in the world',

---

41   Medding, *From Assimilation to Group Survival*.

and 'survival of Judaism is tied up with Israel. The future of all Jews depends on the fate of Israel'.[42]

By the time Medding undertook his study, Zionism was no longer a political entity in search of an address, as it had been before 1948. Israel was an established fact, a place all Jews could call home. While Yiddish provided their link with *yenner velt*, that 'other world', Israel gave them hope of a better future, a new world. Although a small, but steady stream of Jews migrated to the Jewish homeland, most immigrant Jews in Melbourne did not go to live in Israel. While they would rally to Israel's defence, volunteer to fight in its wars, and visit on a number of occasions, they never felt the existential threat that would compel them to flee this land in search of sanctuary and better opportunities. Australia gave them comfort and security, a place where they could express their Jewishness in any manner they wished. They would still continue to support and advocate passionately for Israel; many would visit their Biblical homeland, while others marvelled at the small nation's considerable achievements, from a distance. For Israel had given them the greatest gift of all. These Jews now felt that they had a place in the world, they were no longer cast adrift and rudderless. Israel was their anchor – 'our life line,' another interviewee added, 'without which we sink'.

---

42   Medding, *From Assimilation to Group Survival*, p.145.

Part Three

Generations

Chapter 14

'THE PURSUIT OF HAPPINESS'

There is an old saying: 'Home is where the heart is'. The Jewish heart lies within the sanctity of home and family, which are central to traditional Jewish values and beliefs and form the cornerstone of Jewish life. The Holocaust proved how transitory that sanctity could be and how easily it was crushed into the dust and ashes of the crematoria. Ensuring security for one's home and family was fundamental to Jewish survival. Holocaust survivor Hania explained:

> I have had many lives, and for each of these I have had a different home. My first life was Poland. My second life was during the war. I had no home then. And for my third life, Australia has become my home. It is home because my children were brought up here. It wasn't home in the beginning, but we belong here now.[1]

Hania's sense of belonging was contingent on being able to raise her family in a secure, protective environment. After their world had been torn apart, the desire for a peaceful existence within secure borders was paramount. And while Australia did not always offer the vibrancy of life in European cities, it did offer post-war Jewish immigrants something far more important – a safe place to settle permanently. For Serge Liberman's father it was permanency and

---

1 Rosh White, *From Darkness to Light*, p.201.

stability that mattered most of all: 'It's not Poland,' he said, 'it's not Paris, but it's soil under our feet. It's home'.[2]

What did home and family mean in the context of post-war Melbourne? What sort of culture did these traumatised Holocaust survivors encounter and develop? To understand Melbourne in the 1950s we need to go back to 1942 and the speech that defined the aspiration of the Liberal movement led by Robert Menzies. It was a vision that would govern Australia for over two decades following the Liberal party electoral victory in 1949.

Menzies' vision for a new Australia had an aspirational, independent, self-reliant middle class as the 'backbone of the country'. On the one hand he rejected inherited wealth and privilege, and on the other hand he rejected the privileges of unskilled lower classes 'whose wages and conditions are safeguarded by popular law'. He exalted the middle classes with whom he identified; they were the 'strivers, the planners, the ambitious ones'. These people were Menzies' 'forgotten people'.[3] They were the 'salary earners, shopkeepers, skilled artisans, professional men and women, farmers for the most part unorganised and unself-conscious'. Menzies presented a case in which private aspiration met public benefit. Australian democracy would thrive from an aspirational middle class, but one that was decidedly British in its values and character. It was a muscular and robust vision, one in which 'leaners grow flabby; lifters grow muscles'. Menzies prized initiative, for 'men without ambition readily become slaves'. His vision of Australia was dependent on an all-embracing, growing bourgeoisie.[4]

---

2   Liberman, *On Firmer Shores*.

3   Judith Brett, *Robert Menzies' Forgotten People*, Carlton: Melbourne University Press, 2007; Nick Cater, 'Robert Menzies' Forgotten People', *The Australian*, 22 May 2012.

4   Robert Menzies, 'The Forgotten People, 22 May 1942', http://www.liberals.net/theforgottenpeople.htm, accessed 10 April 2018.

'THE PURSUIT OF HAPPINESS'

Pivotal to Menzies' vision was the importance of home and family. Menzies spoke of 'homes material, homes human, homes spiritual', linking 'home' to a set of moral values.[5] He saw the home as the basis of social stability, 'the foundation of sanity and sobriety; it is the indispensable condition of continuity; its health determines the health of society as a whole'. It was a trope that signified a particular way of life – family, belonging, conformity – a particular set of inclusions and exclusions. For Robert Menzies, Prime Minister throughout the 1950s, 'home' represented family, the bedrock of society: 'My home is where my wife and children are; the instinct to be with them is the great instinct of civilised man'.[6]

Notions of an idealised home and family captured the Australian imagination of the 1950s. Such notions were defined by having a home in a growing suburbia, raising a family, and enjoying steady employment. The rise of consumerism in the 1950s and the abundance of new gadgets and consumables – homewares, electrical appliances, new cars and beauty products for the stay-at-home wife and mother – were all designed to enhance the home and family. Consumerism was the essence of the good life: make money, spend it and enjoy! It was a conservative view that was highly gendered, premised on class, racial hierarchies and enshrined within the values of a white middle class.[7] Popular magazines of the period, *House and Garden* and the *Australian Women's Weekly*, affirmed a white, middle-class Anglo-Celtic British Australia, one that seemed at odds with the immigrant and burgeoning immigrant communities which nurtured distinctively European

---

5   John Murphy, *Imagining the Fifties: Private Sentiment and Political Culture in Menzies' Australia*, Sydney: UNSW Press, 2000, p.136.
6   Robert Menzies, 'The Forgotten People'.
7   Fiona Allon, 'At Home in the Suburbs', *History Australia*, Vol. 11, No. 1 (2014): p.15.

cultures. But there were aspects of this idealised life that were accommodating and transferable.

Middle-class aspirations, self-reliance and independence were traits entrenched in Jewish cultural life. Jews had long been accustomed to living independently, to establishing their own communities and creating their own opportunities. Necessity had taught Jews to be creative and adaptive to changing circumstances and challenging environments. Survival depended on it. While the 'Australian way of life', as Menzies saw it, was comfortably couched within a white Anglo-Celtic middle-class ethos, it posed no threat to the Jewish way of life and Jewish continuity; indeed, it presented a benign environment in which Jews could co-exist and thrive. Just as home and family were valued and prized, so too were private enterprise and personal endeavour. All of this sat comfortably with Jewish sensibilities. It resonated with a Jewish way of life that had long existed in Eastern Europe. Australia in the 1950s was characterised by what one historian called 'the pursuit of happiness'.[8] For Jews coming from a battered, tortured past and in search of a new life in a new continent, it was a pursuit they were keen to join.

While some aspects of Menzies' liberalism – individualism and initiative – dovetailed with Jewish aspirations, there were differences between the general post-war assumption that immigrants would quietly assimilate, and the Yiddishists' imperative to nurture distinctiveness, sustain a sense of community, and promote cultural maintenance and generational transmission. These differences remained unresolved and seemed at odds with an Anglo-centric Australia, because the goal of assimilation operated at the level of public rhetoric

---

8   Murphy, *Imagining the Fifties*, pp. 13–30.

with no means of rigid enforcement. The Australian government was more interested in economic growth and prosperity than it was in the way people lived their lives. So while there was talk of retaining Australia's British character there was no real political will to enforce it.[9]

Jewish immigrants saw Australia as a land of opportunity, a land of freedom: 'We had opportunities here which we did not have in Poland. Hitler did not give me choice. Australia gave me choices,' Rozka recalled.[10] For former Carlton resident Sam Lipski, Holocaust survivors encountered a way of life that was liberating, free of danger and sustainable:

> There was an early recognition that Australia was different to Europe, that you could make a new life here . . . It's tough but work hard and you'll get on. You'll make it. It's better than where you are now, in Germany or anywhere in Europe. The idea that you could be openly, fiercely, proudly Jewish in Melbourne Australia was amazing to them. They enjoyed a complete sense of freedom and what you might call antisemitism in Australia was a joke compared to what they had been through. Along with other European immigrants they struggled in the first years to earn enough money. There was fresh, abundant, affordable food here. You could afford it even on a worker's salary. This was terribly important for people who had starved their way through the camps.[11]

Australia in the 1950s had full employment and business opportunities the likes of which these immigrants had never before experienced. This shaped the way they viewed Australian society. Rather than see a class system that was exclusive, Jewish immigrants

---

9   Andrew Markus and Margaret Taft, 'Postwar Immigration and Assimilation: A Reconceptualization', *Australian Historical Studies*, Vol. 46, Issue 2 (2015): pp.234–251.
10 Rosh White, *From Darkness to Light*, p.179.
11 Sam Lipski, interview 15 August 2011.

encountered a society they believed was devoid of inherited class, a society in which rank was determined by what you could make of yourself. Genek expressed it this way: 'The differences here are between the nouveau riche who made their money in the last fifteen years and the nouveau riche who made it forty or fifty years ago'.[12] While they craved a sense of normalcy, what constituted such a life was also predictable and static and lacked vibrancy: 'Life is so normal. You get up in the morning and you know exactly what you are going to do. You will have breakfast, lunch and supper. And the next day is exactly the same. Things don't happen. We thought it pretty dull. Normal'.[13]

Post-war Jewish immigrants did not feel the oppression of overt antisemitism in Melbourne. Although prejudice existed, it did not pose an existential threat as it had in Europe. Some immigrants saw antisemitism more as xenophobia, as public fear and resentment of foreigners rather than hatred towards them. As one put it, 'I think there is antisemitism here in the same way as there is anti-Irish feeling, for example. The Chinese . . . Irish and Greeks can be attacked as easily as the Jews'.[14]

Although foreigners often faced animosity – Italians and Greeks were sometimes disparagingly referred to as 'dagos' and 'wogs' – many survivors felt that Australians, on a personal level, were generally accepting of foreigners and often helpful. Friendships were formed either in the workplace or through neighbours. When Marysia started work in a factory she recalled the friendship extended to her by other women: 'The women were very helpful and friendly. They

---

12   Rosh White, *From Darkness to Light*, p.179–80.
13   Rosh White, *From Darkness to Light*, p.180.
14   Rosh White, *From Darkness to Light*, p.184.

showed me everything, taught me everything'.[15] Another woman recalled the enduring friendships made in the retail environment of a large department store: 'I met lovely people whilst I worked at Myer, and made some friends for life'.[16] Neighbours could also be supportive: 'I had helpful neighbours, one of whom was a handyman and would repair faulty plumbing for us'.[17] Kuba recalled shifting into his new home in Moorabbin: 'On the day I arrived the neighbour, a man, came in with a plate of food. It was a pie and some stewed fruit. He said, "Here you are. Your first meal in your new home." I liked that'.[18]

For many, Australia was a land of opportunity. Here was a blank canvas, waiting to have a new picture of life drawn upon it. Some immigrants relished the freedom and the opportunity to start again from scratch, seeing the glass half full rather than half empty. For Jacob Rosenberg there was a sense of cultural freedom, one that allowed immigrants to 'assume a pivotal role in the emerging multicultural mosaic'. For Rosenberg, these new immigrants 'breathed fresh meaning into the existing Jewish communities, a new sense of purpose'. A sincere appreciation was felt towards a new, safe and tranquil world that Australia offered; 'Despite all the settling in difficulties we experienced in common with most migrants, we loved Melbourne from day one. I said to Esther, "How can we handle so much freedom, and such peace?"'[19]

For others, Australia offered political and social freedom never experienced before. While Australia was caught up in the global

---

15   Rosh White, *From Darkness to Light*, p.185.
16   Margaret Taft, 'From Displaced Person to New Australian: A Journey Towards Self Determination', MA thesis, Monash University, 2004, interview 5.
17   Taft, 'From Displaced Person to New Australian', interview 3.
18   Taft, 'From Displaced Person to New Australian', p.185.
19   Rosenberg, *Sunrise West*, p.126.

politics of the Cold War, with its talk of an imminent threat posed by subversive fifth columns, 'reds under the beds', and the Petrov spy affair of 1954, its implications for Jewish life in the suburbs of Melbourne were mostly negligible. There were, however, serious repercussions for left-leaning Jews and those identified as communists, such as writer Judah Waten, and for organisations such as the Jewish Council to Combat Fascism and Antisemitism, established at the height of the war in 1942 to fight antisemitism and which by 1952 was largely seen as a pro-Soviet front. But for most, Cold War machinations were benign. Avram Zeleznikow recalled:

> Wherever I was in Europe, I had to have an identity card. When I came to Australia, the first time I was asked for an identity card was in 1959, after eight years, when I went into the library on Swanston Street to borrow some books. This was very symbolic.[20]

Symche Burstin also recalled revelling in a new sense of freedom: 'It was so nice – so different from Poland. We felt so free. We could walk in the streets, meet, speak Yiddish in the streets, sing Yiddish songs even with our poor voices.'[21]

New homes, new communities

Carlton's Jewish population peaked at 3,000 residents in 1947. By 1954 the number had dropped to 2,613, a downward trend that continued into the 1960s. By the mid-1950s, post-war Jewish settlement had spread beyond the centrality of Carlton. But this did not mean there was any diminution of Yiddish culture; rather, it signalled

---

20   Avram Zeleznikow, interview 26 August 2008.
21   Symche Burstin, interview 9 July 2008.

an expansion in the places Jewish immigrants called home. While Carlton remained the beating heart of Yiddish Melbourne, its veins and arteries extended throughout other more diverse suburbs. While some moved east to Kew and Balwyn or south to Caulfield, St. Kilda and Elwood, it was the northern suburbs that saw the flourishing of new Jewish communities. Moonee Ponds, Brunswick, Coburg, Heidelberg, Northcote, Preston and Thornbury all saw Jewish communities grow and expand as places of first settlement. By 1954, the number of Jewish residents in these suburbs was either double or triple those counted in the census of 1933.[22] These working-class suburbs became immigrant enclaves. They were open to new business opportunities, close to the factories and markets, and offered affordable, available housing at a time of acute housing shortage. The post-war years were a time of full employment, in contrast to high levels of unemployment in the early decades of the 20th century and the Great Depression. This was a time for optimism.

Throughout the 1950s and early 1960s, the northern suburbs supported a thriving Jewish community comprised largely of Holocaust survivors, most of whom were Yiddish speakers. Many of them were local shopkeepers and ran small businesses. High Street and the surrounding streets of Northcote and Thornbury were home to Jewish delicatessens, milkbars, fruit shops, clothing stores, fabric stores, bakeries, barbers and shoemakers. Adjacent streets housed businesses such as knitting mills and clothing factories, which were able to thrive because of tariff barriers that protected Australian industry. By one account there were at least a dozen knitting mills in the area.[23]

---

22 Price, 'Jewish Settlers in Australia', Appendix IXa.
23 Max Lasky, 'Remembering the Thornbury *Shul*', *Australian Jewish Historical Society Journal*, Vol. XIV (1997): pp.126–129.

A SECOND CHANCE

In many fundamental ways, Northcote and Thornbury replicated the Carlton of old, with the familiar hum of Yiddish permeating the streets, shops and factories.

Rapidly growing post-war Jewish communities had a pressing need for accessible places of worship that were within walking distance of the homes of the religiously observant. Places of worship were quickly established in suburbs such as Coburg by the late 1940s, Ascot Vale in 1951, and Thornbury in 1954.[24] Often they commenced as *shtibls* (rooms) in private homes that could sustain a *minyan* (in traditional orthodox terms, a minimum of ten men required for a service to be held), then in rented premises when private rooms became too small, and, finally, in dedicated facilities that became synagogues.

The Northcote/Thornbury *kehile* was an example of a community founded almost entirely by post-war Holocaust survivors that began in this way. The first known post-war orthodox religious congregation in Northcote met informally in the Friedlander home about 1949 or 1950, then moved to the Shuster home at 46 Woolton Avenue in Thornbury. By the mid-1950s, when these premises became too small for the high holy days, public halls and reception centres were hired and utilised. Carmella Receptions on the corner of Gooch and High Streets served this purpose as a makeshift synagogue. In 1960 a purpose-built synagogue was established at 41 Rossmoyne Street, Thornbury. The vast majority of the congregation were Polish-born, Yiddish-speaking Holocaust survivors. Changing demographics meant that community numbers dwindled in the 1960s, and the Thornbury synagogue was closed in 1969 and the property sold. Its two Sifrei Torah [handwritten

---

24　Laurie Burchell, 'A Synagogue in Coburg', *Australian Jewish Historical Society Journal*, Vol. XIV (1998): pp.492–4.

scrolls containing the five books of Moses] went to the Yeshivah Centre in Melbourne.[25]

Despite the proliferation of these new communities, Carlton remained the cultural heart of the community throughout the 1950s. Cyla Hartman recalled her early years in Northcote: 'We stayed there (Carlton) for only a few months and then our friends found a house for us to rent in Northcote, where we lived for the next thirteen years, but Carlton remained central to our lives'.[26] The centrality of Carlton as a Yiddishist hub was also recalled by Mary Rodder:

> My time as a Carlton resident was memorable, if relatively short. My parents opened a shop in the newly established Heidelberg Mall and we moved there when I was about six years old . . . Carlton was still a magnet for my family. My mother continued to shop at Kaplan's kosher butcher until a kosher butcher appeared in East Kew and my father was an ever-present coffee-drinker at the University Café in Lygon Street. Until the Carlton *shul* made way for the new high-rise Housing Commission flats, we continued to drive there from Kew for the *yom tovim* [high holy days].[27]

Indicative of this dispersal, when a reception in honour of visiting Israeli delegate Mr Moshe Sharett and in support of the United Israel Appeal was held on 25 May 1957 at the Royal Ballroom in Carlton, it was sponsored by a group calling itself the 'Northern Suburbs, Lodzer Centre and Warsaw Jewish Centre'. Some 150 hosts were named on the invitation, which was written in both Yiddish and English. They were listed under a number of organisations, including the Northcote

---

25 David Havin, *Orthodox Jewry in Carlton and Surrounding Suburbs*, Melbourne: D.J. Havin, 2007, p.51.
26 Meadows, *Fun Himlen Blayene Tsu Bloye Teg,*, p.251.
27 Meadows, *Fun Himlen Blayene Tsu Bloye Teg*, p.234.

Jewish Centre, the Brunswick Group and the Moonee Ponds Jewish Centre.

'A home of our own'

The 'pursuit of happiness' meant different things to different people. For Jewish immigrants, 'happiness' began with the preservation of home and family – the wellspring of Jewish life. For many post-war Jewish immigrants, the cultural flourishing of Yiddish Melbourne in the years immediately after the war was evidence that this small community was not only tolerated but sustainable. The Yiddish world of their past, obliterated by the Holocaust, had been transplanted in new soil in an unlikely continent, on a raw and sunburnt land at the farthest corner of the globe.

Australia offered Holocaust survivors who had themselves been 'forgotten people' a second chance at establishing safe, secure homes for their new, in many cases, newly formed second, families. 'For wanderers like ourselves . . . living from hand to mouth wherever the *goyim* [gentiles] were ready to receive us . . . a home of our own is the nearest blessing to Paradise'.[28]

---

28   Liberman, *On Firmer Shores*, p.25.

Chapter 15

PARNOSEH – EARNING A LIVING

When revered ex-partisan and Yiddishist Avram Zeleznikow arrived in Melbourne from Paris in 1951 with his young wife, Masha, and their eight-month-old son, Yankel (John), they brought few possessions and very little money. Their fares to Australia had been paid by the Joint and their entry permits sponsored by Jewish Welfare. Both Avram and Masha had been university students who had to forego any plans to continue their studies here. Finding a place to live and earning a living were far more pressing concerns. 'We had no profession and no knowledge of the English language', recalled Avram; 'When I asked [Jacob] Waks if we can study here, he replied, "Here you don't need to study. Go and work. It will be for the best."' Waks' advice to the young new arrivals echoed Avram's own impressions of Australia at that time. 'In the 1950s there was great prosperity in Australia. There was no unemployment and plenty of work. Plenty!'[1]

The post-war years in Australia were indeed boom times for business. From 1947 to 1972 Australia enjoyed a buoyant economy. Only two brief periods, cyclic downturns in 1952 and 1961, interrupted this prosperity. High immigration and economic prosperity went hand in hand. The times provided huge opportunities, particularly for

---

1   Avram Zeleznikow, interview 26 August 2008.

immigrants willing to work hard, often at more than one job, in stark contrast with the pre-war decades and devastation of the Holocaust.

Although opportunities were abundant, for many, life continued to be a struggle. Avram recalled:

> I began to make shirts. But I couldn't do it. I had two left hands. I would sew and unpick all day. I tried working for the Smorgons in their meat business. Then I worked in Fink's factory. Friends tried to teach me the knitting business. It also didn't work out. So I had to look for a business [of my own].

After seven years in different labouring jobs, when Avram saw an opportunity to be self-employed he seized it.

> In 1958, 99 Acland Street was a chocolate factory. Then you needed a licence to sell chocolate and it had one. We made it into a milkbar and started making meals. We built up Scheherazade. Soon 30 to 40 single men, Holocaust survivors, ate there each day. They liked Masha's cooking. It became their home.

Most arrived as sponsored immigrants, as was a required for them to obtain a visa. Often sponsors, family or friends, helped them get started. To take advantage of opportunities, capital was needed. As was often the story with immigrants, your success or failure depended on the assistance you received from others. Avram received help from another immigrant and fellow Yiddishist, Lublin-born Jacob Kronhill, who had arrived from Shanghai in 1946 and who guaranteed a bank loan for Avram: 'When we bought Scheherazade we owed money. But Jacob Kronhill helped. The bank manager asked how much I needed. I said I didn't know. He gave me £2,000. Kronhill called the bank manager to give his signature'.[2]

---

2   Avram Zeleznikow, interview 26 August 2008.

PARNOSEH – EARNING A LIVING

The Café Scheherazade quickly became a much-loved fixture in the Jewish landscape, offering a meeting place and home away from home for many Jewish émigrés. An iconic establishment for 40 years, it was immortalised in Arnold Zable's book of the same name.[3] Avram Zeleznikow would go on to leave his mark on many Jewish institutions: the Kadimah, Jewish Welfare, the Jewish Board of Deputies, Mount Scopus College, the Jewish Community Council, and as a leading teacher of Yiddish at the Sholem Aleichem Sunday School.

The achievements of individuals such as the Zeleznikows were enabled by being part of a community that existed within an open and free society, a land of opportunity, far removed from the Eastern European world of closed doors, perpetual economic struggle and murderous violence. By the 1960s the Australian Jewish community was increasingly affluent and upwardly mobile. The 1961 Australian census reveals that close to 50 per cent of Jewish males in the workforce were either employers or self-employed, compared to 22 per cent of the total Australian population. Sociologist Peter Medding believed that, high though they were, the census figures for the Jewish male workforce underrepresented employers and the self-employed due to the way the census questions were framed. His own random sample for 1961 showed a much higher number of employers and self-employed Jewish males, constituting some 75 per cent of the Jewish male workforce.[4]

In 1964 the London *Financial Times* declared Australia the healthiest economy in the Western world.[5] The 1950s and 1960s were years

---

3   Arnold Zable, *Café Scheherazade*, Melbourne: Text, 2001.
4   Medding, *From Assimilation to Group Survival*, pp.20–1.
5   Geoffrey Bolton, *The Oxford History of Australia*, Vol. 5, Melbourne: Oxford University Press, 1990, p.177.

of industrial growth, with increased foreign investment to bolster new technologies. From 1940 to 1960 Australian manufacturing was sheltered from the competition of imports, not only because of tariffs charged but also because of severe controls on the quantity of imports. While quantitative controls were removed in 1960, tariffs continued to protect manufacturing jobs and ensure profitability.[6] In 1966 the manufacturing sector was the biggest employer, providing 27 per cent of total jobs.[7]

Jews from Eastern Europe brought many of their 'old world' occupations with them. They were tailors, weavers, knitters, shoemakers, leather merchants and manufacturers of leather goods. These immigrants gravitated naturally towards textiles and manufacturing. The Jewish *shmatte* business (rag trade) of Flinders Lane began soon after the war and continued to grow in the postwar era, becoming an important centre for Melbourne's fashionable garment industry. Other manufacturing businesses sprang up in the industrial northern suburbs of Northcote, Preston, Brunswick and Collingwood. Holocaust survivors Jack and Chaim Liberman, who arrived in Melbourne in 1949, and Henry Krongold, who escaped Poland during the war and arrived 18 months later in 1941, were among those who seized opportunities to establish lucrative businesses, with both businesses beginning in hosiery manufacturing.[8]

---

6   Alf Rattigan, *Industry Assistance: The Inside Story*, Melbourne: Melbourne University Press, 1986, pp.4–5.
7   *The Australian Encyclopaedia*, Terrey Hills, NSW: Australian Geographic, 1996, p.1149.
8   'A Driven, Successful Life Shaped by the Gulag', *Sydney Morning Herald*, 4 January 2008; James Mitchell, *Henry Krongold*, Crows Nest, NSW: Allen & Unwin, 2003.

Polish-born Auschwitz survivor Nathan Werdiger arrived in Melbourne in 1949, aged 23, after spending four years recovering in a Swiss sanatorium. He was sponsored by his great uncle's family, who had arrived before the war. Together with his cousin Arnold Lederman, he saw an opportunity in the manufacturing of light, bright fabrics favoured by the younger generation. While other bigger mills were still weaving heavy materials for workwear and uniforms, Werdiger ventured into this new line of manufacturing. His company, Classweave Textiles, soon became a market leader and one of Australia's biggest textile businesses, going on to supply prominent fashion designers such as Norma Tullo and Prue Acton. By the 1980s Werdiger had moved into another business enterprise that began its rapid rise in the 1960s – property development.[9]

A number of Jewish immigrants followed a long immigrant tradition that sought financial security and economic advancement through the construction industry and property development. This was linked to another relatively new phenomenon in housing, a move from the suburban to the urban, as 'modern' dwellings – flats and units – rapidly increased in Melbourne, signifying a break with the more traditional single house and garden on large suburban blocks and the influence of European, 'continental' dwelling culture, transforming the streetscapes and sensibilities of inner suburbia. For many Jewish immigrants, property development became their primary source of income; for others, it was a secondary source alongside their manufacturing interests. This became particularly important once the clothing, textile and footwear industries went into decline following the

---

9   Carolyn Ford, *Who Brought the Luck to the Lucky Country?* Melbourne: Red Dog Books, 2011, pp.1–12.

25 per cent tariff cut by the Whitlam government in 1973. Growth in manufacturing, property development and investment throughout the 1960s and into the 1970s was reflected in the economic and social successes of many Jewish immigrants in a particularly accessible, fluid business environment.[10]

One manufacturer who experienced the downturn and made a calculated decision to leave manufacturing in the 1970s was Israel Kipen. Bialystok-born Kipen arrived from Shanghai in May 1946, sponsored by his mother's cousin, Rivke Dorevitch. When war broke out in 1939, Kipen was a university student in Warsaw. Failing to persuade his family to leave, he fled east to Lithuania. With the assistance of Lithuania's Japanese consul Chiune Sugihara, who, against his government's orders, saved thousands of Jewish lives, Kipen was fortunate to secure a visa ostensibly to Dutch Curacao. He made his way to Japan. From there he was deported in September 1941 to the Jewish refugee colony of Shanghai.[11]

Upon his arrival in Melbourne, Kipen began working as a 'middle man', selling goods manufactured in the burgeoning local textile trade, from businessmen such as knitwear manufacturer Aron Nirens and socks manufacturer Sender Burstin, to large retailers such as Myer, Foy and Gibson, Woolworths and Georges.[12] Kipen displayed entrepreneurial nous and, sensing a great need for knitted garments in a consumer-hungry society, soon set himself up as a knitwear manufacturer. He recalled the 1960s as a time of great prosperity: 'During the 60s my productive potential was pushed to capacity to

---

10   Seamus O'Hanlon, 'A Little Bit of Europe in Australia: Jews, Immigrants, Flats and Urban and Cultural Change in Melbourne, c1935–75', *History Australia*, Vol. 11, No. 3 (2014): pp.116–133.

11   *Australian Jewish News*, 10 July 2017.

12   Israel Kipen, *A Life to Live*, Melbourne: Chandros Publishing, 1989, pp.153–6.

meet demand and throughout that decade I did not know a single slack period'.[13]

By the 1970s, however, after the cut in tariffs, cheap imports from Asia exposed the vulnerabilities of the textile and footwear industries. Labour costs in Australia could not compete. As Kipen recalled, 'One scarcely needed to be an economist to understand that labour costing $2 per hour could not compete with labour costing a mere 20 cents'.[14] In 1977 he finally wound up his business with the auction of his machinery.[15] What followed for Israel Kipen was a successful return to university and the education that had been disrupted by war, and a continued passion and advocacy for modern Zionism, the Hebrew language and the Jewish day school movement. It also saw his role as a substantial philanthropist grow and develop. Economic prosperity did more than provide security for home and family; it was a great social enabler, providing opportunities and pathways to explore a more expansive range of cultural pursuits and philanthropic interests.

By the mid-1960s, Jewish life was one of increasing affluence. In Peter Medding's 1967 sociological survey of Melbourne's Jewish community, 74 per cent of those interviewed identified as upper- or middle-class.[16] Prosperity, however, existed alongside economic struggle. Although many were self-employed, working for oneself often involved a gruelling work schedule with little respite. Milkbar owners and those with stalls at Victoria market, for example, often worked exhausting hours for a meagre income, and a substantial

---

13 Kipen, *A Life to Live*, p.294.
14 Kipen, *A Life to Live*, p.295.
15 Kipen, *A Life to Live*, p.297.
16 Peter Medding, Melbourne Jewish Sociological Survey 1967.

25 per cent of Jewish males were employed as labourers, on wages that were sustaining but not wealth-creating. Nevertheless, this was a community that not only perceived itself as part of a solid middle class but was actively pursuing a broader range of initiatives that it could and did support. For Yiddish Melbourne, the 1960s and 1970s was a complex period of cultural continuity and expansion, tempered by significant change.

Chapter 16

ZENITH

When Avram arrived in Melbourne in 1951, he found cultural and educational organisations very similar to those he had known in pre-war Poland, albeit on a much smaller scale.

> I went to work in a Yiddish Sunday school soon after I arrived. So although I had changed countries, my social environment had not changed. I even found that I was working again with some of the people I had known in Poland. This sheltered me. It was like a cocoon.[1]

The protective cocoon that Avram immediately experienced was the result of a rapidly growing community whose founders had laid deep cultural roots in the pre-war years and whose labours were bearing fruit after the war. So, while Avram may have been surprised at the similarities he encountered between Melbourne Yiddish life and his pre-war existence, it really was a logical progression.

As a result of immigration patterns, by the 1950s the majority of Jewish adults in Melbourne came from a Yiddish-speaking (and Holocaust) background. By 1961 only 38 per cent of Jews were Australia-born. Yet the transformation of the community was greater than this statistic suggests. The vast majority of those under the age of 21, comprising some one-third of the Jewish population, were born

---

1   Rosh White, *From Darkness to Light*, p.177.

in Australia, whereas very few of the adults were. Peter Medding's 1961 survey of the Melbourne Jewish community indicated that only 12 per cent of Jews over the age of 21 were born in Australia.[2] In 1967, a community survey found that 60 per cent of the Jewish community's adults spoke Yiddish. Consequently community power dynamics shifted, up to a point. Yiddishists had become board members on all major community organisations, although they only really controlled Jewish Welfare, the Kadimah, the Bund and their own *landsmanschaftn*. The Victorian Jewish Board of Deputies' key office-bearers remained members of the Jewish establishment throughout the 1950s and 1960s, with the exception of Leo Fink who was Vice-President in 1954 and 1955. There were, however, Yiddishist delegates to the VJBD who advocated fiercely for Yiddish causes, such as the use of Yiddish at public events and the importance of maintaining Yiddish cultural activities.

The rapid growth in the number of Yiddish speakers gave greater impetus, a sense of purpose, and meaning to the cultural activities of Yiddish Melbourne. Yiddish-speaking post-war immigrants demonstrated the same steadfast commitment to the preservation of Yiddish culture and a passion for community organisation that the pre-war immigrants had shown. But instead of having to carve out a new cultural space for themselves, they could build upon the institutions and cultural initiatives that had sprung up in the pre-war period and replicated the world that immigrants like Avram had lost.

The Yiddish press

Jews have long been called 'people of the book'. The written word has always been close to the heart of Jewish life. Jews are a literate

---

[2] Medding, *From Assimilation to Group Survival*, p.19.

community. The growth in a Yiddish readership meant that the demand for Yiddish newspapers, journals and books also grew. By 1950 the Melbourne community supported two Yiddish weekly newspapers, *Di Yiddishe Nayes*, which commenced in 1935 and was published until 1995, and *Di Yiddishe Post*, published from 1946 until 1961. This was a far cry from the 1920s and 1930s when it had been extremely challenging to establish a Yiddish newspaper and number of attempts had failed. The significance of having two Yiddish papers was not lost on writer and journalist Sam Lipski, who reflected on their differences.

> There were two Yiddish newspapers circulated within the community. There was *Di Yiddishe Nayes* and *Di Yiddishe Post*, which was a companion to the *Jewish Herald*. There were differences between them. Both had reputations for being very important in the period immediately after World War Two. People read Yiddish. The news was heavily geared to news in Australia, what the Australian government was doing. They concentrated on national politics and also represented the community because the community had an injection of writers and poets. The difference between the *Nayes* and the *Post* was the *Post* was the more literary of the two because Shia Rapaport was a significant international writer, polemicist, literary critic and his material was republished everywhere there was a Yiddish press. There was also a political divide between the *Nayes* and the *Post* and that was because Rapaport was very anti-Communist and the paper reflected a strong anti-Soviet line from the start. *Nayes* was not pro-Soviet, but more left-leaning.[3]

Yiddish writers were held in the highest esteem, as the written word was revered. Publications were encouraged and supported. While a number of seminal Yiddish publications had appeared before 1945,

---

3   Sam Lipski, interview Jewish Museum of Australia, 10 August 1992.

including the collections of essays published in the *Almanacs* of 1937 and 1942 and the published works of Pinchas Goldhar, Yossel Birstein, Herz Bergner, the number of Yiddish publications flourished in the post-war period. Among them were the works of a diverse group of writers whose interests ranged from political polemic to autobiographical works, reflective pieces and works of fiction. Prominent writers included Yehoshua Rapaport, Gedalia Shaiak, Yitzhak Kahn, Lew Frydman, Moshe Ajzenbud, Abraham Cykiert, Jacob Rosenberg and I.M. Lewin, who enriched the Melbourne Yiddish literary scene with their powerful poetry and prose. It has been estimated that more than 40 Yiddish books were published in Melbourne after 1950.[4] Yiddish journals also appeared. *Oifboy*, (Reconstruction), a 32-page literary journal, was published monthly between 1945 and 1948. *Unzer Gedank* (Our Thoughts), a Bund journal, first appeared in 1947 and continued until 1981. The Bund youth group SKIF began publication of *Chavershaft* (Friendship) in 1953.

Throughout the 1960s and 1970s the Yiddish press still had a substantial readership. In 1968 *Di Yiddishe Nayes* had a circulation of some 4,000, with a readership well in excess of that number. Yiddish journals continued to be published. A literary periodical *Der Landsman* provided a voice for the *landsmanshaftn* in 20 issues published between December 1964 and September 1970. The *Melburner Bleter*, the Yiddish section of the *Melbourne Chronicle*, was launched in 1975, sponsored by the Kadimah. It was edited, from its inception, by Moshe Ajzenbud, a short-story writer and novelist. The third and last *Yiddishe Almanac*, a collection of Yiddish essays, was published

---

4   W.D. Rubinstein, *The Jews in Australia*, p.334.

in 1967. Although the sale of Yiddish books was in decline, there were still three Jewish bookstores in Melbourne, each catering to a Yiddish readership.[5]

Further growth of the Kadimah

In 1956 the leader of the Bund, Jacob Pat, visiting Melbourne from New York, noted the crowds who came to hear him speak:

> The Kadimah hall in Lygon Street is overfilled already for the eighth time. People stand on the steps and in the hallway. No vacant seats left. So one [was] permitted to sit on the stage. Why have the people come? What do they want to hear? They listen as if spellbound. They hear about five million Jews in the great distant America, about the general and the Jewish worker movement, about Jewish problems and achievements, about Jewish literature, Eretz Israel, the Diaspora. The hall is no longer a mere meeting place. It creates the impression of a packed hall of Hasidism. It seethes; in the silence a pot boils. It is a quiet murmur of hearts, here in the furthermost corner of the world.[6]

The importance of the Kadimah as a vibrant, diverse Yiddish oasis was enhanced by the arrival of large numbers of Yiddish speakers, causing its outreach and output to grow. As discussed in previous chapters, the dynamic cultural centre of the Kadimah commenced in 1911 and hosted a Yiddish library, a theatre and an annual calendar of lectures and community forums. After the Second World

---

5   Manfred Klarberg, 'Yiddish in Melbourne', in Peter Medding, ed., *Jews in Australian Society*, Melbourne: Macmillan, 1973, pp.103–112.

6   Jacob Pat, 'Impressions of a Visit, 1956', translated from the Yiddish by Serge Liberman, *Australian Jewish Historical Society Journal*, Vol. XVI, Part 1 (2001): pp.48–61.

War, it further expanded its offerings to meet increased patronage and demand. In 1950 alone 213 public functions were held at the Kadimah and the number of people attending it in that year, including those using the newspaper/reading room and club room, was 41,900. While the Kadimah's membership in the 1950s peaked in 1952 with 1,341 members, the numbers of members remained high (well over 1,000) throughout the 1950s and well into the 1960s.

During the 1950s and 1960s the Kadimah annual reports recorded sponsored visits of over 30 overseas academics, artists, actors, singers and writers, who entertained and gave lectures to local audiences craving a meaningful connection with the wider Yiddish world. In 1955 the Kadimah hosted H. Triwaks, who lectured on Jewish life in Argentina. In the same year academic Dov Ber Malkin from Israel delivered a series of ten lectures on a range of subjects related to Yiddish literature and theatre. In 1958 Leib Rochman, also sponsored by the Kadimah, delivered three lectures on Israel.[7] The Kadimah continued its robust and engaging program of broader community activities. Social and educational programs – lectures, discussion groups, memorial evenings, welcome and farewell events, United Israel Appeal evenings and Purim concerts – were particularly well patronised. In 1964 alone, 72 functions were held at its premises with a total of 17,500 attendees.[8]

Yiddish theatre

> At the Kadimah hall, lights blaze from the arched windows and upstairs rooms. The foyer is choked with perfumed women

---

[7] Kadimah Annual General Meeting Reports, 1955–8.
[8] Kadimah Annual General Report, February 1965, p.14.

and men in winter overcoats. Kalman the baker bends over and pinches Josh on the cheek. Zlaterinski pats him on the shoulder. 'Tonight you get an education', he says. 'Little do the *goyim* [gentiles] know what wonders we possess. Little do they understand that our Yiddish theatre is world class!'[9]

Yiddish theatre reached its zenith in post-war Melbourne. Arnold Zable has attributed this to the fact that Yiddish theatre was 'alive', the 'living expression of [Yiddish] culture' often bringing into stark reality the social issues connected with everyday life. Yiddish theatre was transformative. It was both a celebration of life and a commemoration of that which had been lost. It touched all members of the community.[10]

For the Yiddish actors it also became a haven, a home away from home. As Shulamis Sher, wife of Yasha Sher, recalled:

> The David Herman Theatre was like a family. Everyone knew one another. We rehearsed three or four times a week and when we could get the stage if the children weren't using it, we'd have Sunday rehearsal as well. After every play we'd have a party, each time in another house. We were very close. Everyone helped another with money, food.[11]

Throughout the early post-war period, the plays performed were largely traditional and often well known to the audiences. Plays such as *Tzvay Hundert Toyzent* (Two Hundred Thousand), staged in 1951 and again in 1956, is a story of bourgeois excess and working-class morality conveyed in the tale of a poor tailor who wins 200,000 rubles in a lottery only to be swindled out of his fortune. Favoured playwrights were Sholem Aleichem, Sholem Asch, I.L Peretz, S. Ansky,

---

9 Arnold Zable, *Scraps of Heaven*, Melbourne: Text, 2004, p.193.
10 Arnold Zable, interview 2 December 2011.
11 Shulamis Sher, interview 21 July 2008.

J. Gordin, A. Goldfaden and I.S Singer. Occasionally contemporary plays were translated into Yiddish, such as Arthur Miller's *Death of a Salesman* (*Der Toyt fun a Salesman*), performed in 1960 under the direction of Yankev Waislitz.[12] Throughout the 1960s and 70s the David Herman Theatre group provided two to three seasons each year, each of about 10 to 12 performances, which were supported by some 3,000 patrons.

Another theatrical initiative that emerged during this period involved a core group of the younger generation. Coinciding with the revival of local Australian theatre in the late 1960s, actress and director Fay Mokotow, a prominent member of SKIF-Tsukunft, staged a hugely successful production of the great Yiddish poet Itzik Manger's *Megillah Lider*, with music by Dov Seltzer. She staged it in an avant-garde, minimalist fashion with the youth of SKIF-Tsukunft. It proved a big hit in the Melbourne and Sydney Yiddish communities and motivated Fay Mokotow, Alex Dafner and others to form the Melbourne Yiddish Youth Theatre (MYYT) at the Kadimah in 1969, a group that remained very active throughout the 1970s.[13]

Era of the visiting impresarios

There was also a significant rise in the number of visiting impresarios in the 1950s and 1960s. In 1955, theatre director Zygmunt Turkow and his wife, actress Rosa Turkov, undertook the first of many tours, organised under the auspices of the David Herman Theatre.

---

12   Arnold Zable, *Wanderers and Dreamers*, p.82.
13   'Yiddish Theatre in Australia', *Yiddish Melbourne*, http://future.arts.monash.edu/yiddish-melbourne/culture-yiddish-theatre-in-australia/, accessed 11 April 2018.

They enthralled audiences with their productions of *Uncle Moses*, *Zing Mayn Folk* (Sing My People), *Goldfaden's Cholem* (Goldfaden's Dream), *Oyf di Moyrn fun Yerushalayim* (At the Walls of Jerusalem), and *Scenes from Sholem Aleichem*. In 1957 Chayele Grober, an actress from Sweden, gave five performances of her own play, *Oyf Fridlecher Erd* (On Peaceful Soil) and gave two lectures.

When acclaimed Yiddish actress Ida Kaminska arrived in Melbourne for a six-week tour on Sunday, 7 August 1960, she was treated like royalty. Her flight arrival details were published in advance on the front page of the *Australian Jewish News*, so that she could be greeted by enthusiastic fans as well as by community dignitaries. Shortly after her arrival, hundreds of invited guests attended a reception at the Kadimah to honour her visit and to hear an address by the 'Grande Dame' herself. Melbourne felt privileged to play host to this star of the Yiddish stage, whose career had begun in the early 1900s and was to continue to the end of the 1960s. As director of the State Jewish Theatre in Warsaw from 1949 to 1968, she had overseen the rebirth of Yiddish theatre in Poland in the aftermath of the Holocaust. Kaminska's arrival was hailed in the Jewish press as 'one of the greatest events in Jewish communal life in Melbourne', her name being 'synonymous with the best the theatre has to offer'.[14]

Kaminska brought with her to Melbourne an entourage that included her husband, Yiddish actor Meir Melman, and Ruth Kaminska-Turkow, her daughter from her earlier marriage to Zygmunt Turkow. Kaminska and her troupe performed two productions to

---

14 *Australian Jewish News*, 29 July 1960.

sell-out crowds at St Kilda's Palais Theatre, with a capacity of just under 3000: *Baymer Starbn Stayendik* (Trees Die Standing), a contemporary Spanish play, written by Alejandro Casona and translated into Yiddish, which focused on family, blackmail and deceit, and the well-known classic by Jacob Gordin, *Mirele Efros,* often referred to as the 'Jewish Queen Lear' in which the title character, a powerful matriarch, becomes bitterly estranged from her family. The title role was one of Kaminska's signature pieces. The troupe played both productions twice.

By the time Kaminska arrived in Melbourne, she was one of the most influential Yiddish actresses in the world. She had already won many acting awards, including the Gold Medal of the International Festival of Drama in Paris. Daughter of renowned actress Ester Rachel Kaminska, often called 'the Mother of the Jewish Stage', and director and stage producer Abraham Izaak Kaminski, Ida Kaminska took over the mantle of theatre leadership from her mother and carved out an illustrious career of her own. By the mid-1960s she secured a starring role in the 1965 Czech film *The Shop on the Main Street,* for which she received an Academy Award nomination for best actress in a lead role in a foreign film. In 1967 she directed and played the lead role in a Broadway production of Bertolt Brecht's *Mother Courage and Her Children.*[15] That someone of Ida Kaminska's professional stature would come to this far-flung corner of the globe and perform to capacity crowds was testament to the strength and vibrancy of Yiddish cultural life in Melbourne in 1960. Her path to Melbourne was soon followed by other notable Yiddish celebrities.

---

15   Ida Kaminska, *My Life, My Theatre,* New York: MacMillan, 1973.

Yiddish cultural activity reached new heights in the 1960s. The number of international visitors performing to Melbourne audiences significantly expanded the cultural offerings the city could experience and enjoy. While there were only six visitors in the 1950s, the number more than quadrupled to more than 26 actors, theatre directors, singers, poets, artists and academics on extended tours from Canada, the United States, Israel and Argentina in the 1960s. Through the 1970s the number of visiting Yiddish performers and academics continued to grow to more than 35 as demand for cultural activities continued unabated.[16] The international visitors came because there was a voracious appetite for cultural pursuits of the highest calibre and an appreciative, sizable audience of increasingly affluent pre-war and post-war Eastern European Yiddish-speaking immigrants who could sustain and support their visits. Audiences were drawn to overseas visitors who brought the surviving remnants of the Yiddish world – no longer in the cities of Warsaw, Lodz and Vilna, but in Montreal and New York – just that little bit closer. The visiting impresarios, entertainers, academics and dignitaries linked the wider Yiddish world with a new world now deeply rooted in Australian soil. Their visits were a part of a much larger social movement and cultural development sweeping across Australia.

A Yiddish education – 'the natural thing to do'

The community also provided for the needs of the younger generation. It was recognised that the transmission of *Yiddishkeit* to the next generation was fundamental to rebuilding and sustaining the

---

16   'International Visitors', *Yiddish Melbourne*, http://future.arts.monash.edu/yiddish-melbourne/international-visitors/, accessed 11 April 2018.

world destroyed by the Holocaust. The community that could sustain two Yiddish newspapers in the immediate postwar period had two Yiddish schools.

The I.L. Peretz School, which commenced in 1935 in Carlton, opened a kindergarten in 1950. Throughout the late 1940s and 1950s, its Sunday and afternoon school in Carlton flourished, with enrolments increasing steadily. In 1946 the school had 140 students in eight classes, necessitating a split between the younger students who remained at the Kadimah and the senior students in a Drummond Street building. As the school continued to expand, the initial staff of three grew to include new immigrants, but the staff was still insufficient to meet increased demand. It was decided that headmaster Giligich would run a two-year course to train teachers, basing the training on the traditions of the CYSHO Schools in Eastern Europe. Cluwa Krystal, who had trained in the pre-war Yiddish schools of Poland and had survived the war in Shanghai, was appointed kindergarten director in 1950. The school continued to gather momentum. Expansion exacerbated the space problem, which was solved by the Australian Jewish Welfare Society's gift of a building in Drummond Street, Carlton, formerly used as a hostel but no longer needed. A new school was built on the land and opened on Sunday, 1 July 1956. Over 225 students attended the new campus. Enrolments at the I.L. Peretz School peaked in 1961 when there were 262 students.[17]

Arnold Zable captured the vibrant atmosphere of the school in the 1950s:

---

17 David Burstin, 'I.L. Peretz Yiddish School 1935–84', *Australian Jewish Historical Society Journal*, Vol. X, Part 1 (1986): pp.15–27.

> On Wednesday evenings and Sunday mornings, the two-storey building at 885 Drummond Street was buzzing with activity – parents delivering their kids and staying on to help with voluntary work; children playing on any piece of concrete clearing that we could find until the bell dragged us into classes. There we learned to form the letters of the *alef-beis* and to converse, write and study in Yiddish, that warm mother tongue of Eastern European Jewry. It was our home away from home, our school away from the state school system, an added dimension to our lives.[18]

For other students, such as Rachel Caplan, it not only taught the rudiments of the Yiddish language but also provided a moral compass: 'For at least a third of my life, the I.L. Peretz *shul* played a major role in my development, not only in the Yiddish sphere, but also as a human being, a *mentsh*.'[19] Others, however, had less positive memories. Some students resented having to attend additional classes when they could be out playing with friends. One recalled trying desperately hard to feign illness or to find ingenious hiding places to avoid capture.

As the Jewish population south of the Yarra steadily grew, it became necessary to establish another Yiddish school closer to the community's new homes. In 1946 the Sholem Aleichem School opened as a supplementary and Sunday school, operating initially from rented premises in Blanche Street, St Kilda. The first principal of the school was Yasha Sher, Giligich's son-in law, an active member of the Kadimah and one of the luminaries of Yiddish culture in the post-war period. The school flourished and grew quickly. On its opening day, Sunday,

---

18 Markus and Charak, *Yiddish Melbourne: Towards a History*, p.96.
19 Julie Meadows, ed., *Fun Himlen Blayene Tsu Bloye Teg*, p.239.

5 May 1946, it had 23 students. In 1953 it opened a kindergarten with some 30 children in a newly acquired property in Elsternwick. The director was Genia Wasserman, a trained and experienced teacher from Eastern Europe who had survived the war in Kazakhstan. By 1960 the school had over 200 students in 11 classes.

Newcomers from Eastern Europe had no hesitation in sending their children after school hours to a Yiddish school. Leon Goldman, who arrived in Australia in 1948 as a 10-year-old with his widowed mother, recalled his immediate enrolment in the Sholem Aleichem School:

> We arrived on Sunday and by Wednesday, three days after arriving, I was in the Sholem Aleichem School in a little cottage in Blanche Street, St Kilda, in Yiddish afternoon school until I finished grade 10 in the mid-1950s and then I went on to the Peretz school ... It was the natural thing to do.[20]

Both the I.L. Peretz School and the Sholem Aleichem School taught a uniform curriculum with flexible teaching methods. Students mostly spoke Yiddish in their homes, so the emphasis was initially on teaching them to read and write Yiddish. Older students were introduced to Yiddish literature, poetry and prose, Bible stories, ethics and religion. Jewish festivals were celebrated with Yiddish songs and appropriate activities, the *driter seyder* (the third seder, an additional Passover meal) was held annually, there were Purim parades, Warsaw ghetto commemorations, as well as concerts and plays based on the work of Yiddish writers. The school choir was active both within and outside the Yiddish communities, cutting gramophone records, singing on radio, and appearing at communal functions.

---

20   Leon Goldman, interview 5 May 2009.

Their repertoire included Yiddish folk songs, songs from the ghettos of Europe, the Partisan's hymn and school songs. The curriculum at the schools was rich and deep. It did not merely teach students how to speak, read and write the Yiddish language; it provided the basis of their Jewish education and nurtured their Jewish identity, all within the tenets of all-embracing *Yiddishkeit*.

A Yiddish youth group

Yiddishists also saw the need to establish their own youth group, separate from the Zionist groups, Habonim and Betar, which had been established a decade earlier and focused on inculcating a love of Israel and the Hebrew language. In response the Sotsyalistisher Kinder Farband (Socialist Children's Union, SKIF) was established in 1950 by Tsukunft, the youth organisation of the Bund. Symche Burstin and Pinye Ringelblum were the first *helfer* (leaders), modelling Melbourne's SKIF on the organisation they had known in pre-war Poland and post-war France, and in accordance with Bund ideals of socialist development and knowledge. Central to its mandate was the promotion of Yiddish language and culture. The key to their success was close and personal contact among members of the movement. Five young pioneers began meeting every Sunday and, by the time of the first SKIF camp in December 1950 held in Anglesea, there were 17 children who attended the first summer camp.

From 1953 SKIF had enough members for *kraizn* (discussion groups) to meet in Carlton at the Kadimah and in St Kilda at Jewish Welfare House in Herbert Street. The rapid growth in membership drove the establishment of a two-year, 8-hour course for *helfer*. In 1954 SKIF gave its first major concert in Melbourne. Held in the

Kadimah Hall, it included songs, choral recitals, gymnastic displays and a variety of presentations. In 1956, to mark the 30th anniversary of the establishment of SKIF in Poland, a huge concert was held. Presentations at these concerts included: *Bontshe Shvaig* (Bontshe the Silent One), *Der Shpakchler* (The Granary) and *Mister Tvister*. The future for Yiddish youth looked secure.

Chapter 17

SIGNS OF CHANGE

The 1960s in Australia was a time of accelerating social change, from which a more outward-looking society emerged from its insular Anglo-Australian myopia. The change was underpinned by a buoyant economy, a prosperous middle class, and the coming of age of a generation of more radical 'baby boomers', seen as champions of political protest and sexual freedom. Often mythologised excessively as the revolutionary 'swinging 60s', it was, nevertheless, a transitional decade that challenged the conservatism and blandness of the 1950s and brought a new sense of internationalism, diminished attachment from the British Commonwealth, and greater alignment with American and European popular culture and politics.[1]

Indicative of the beginnings of this realignment, Melbourne's International Film Festival had, by 1964, attracted a loyal audience of over 4,000 patrons who clamoured for the limited number of tickets and enjoyed more than 150 different feature films and documentaries by continental and avant-garde filmmakers, such as Fellini, Bergman, Bunuel, Wajda and Antonioni. While the festival arguably only catered to a cultural elite always at the vanguard of

---

1   Shirleene Robinson and Julie Ustinoff, eds, *The 1960s in Australia: People, Power and Politics*, Newcastle upon Tyne: Cambridge Scholars Publishing, 2012, pp.xi-xvii.

social change, it signalled a new sense of internationalism and cosmopolitanism that was spreading across Melbourne society.[2]

In another sign of the times, in 1967 the word 'British' was removed from Australian passports. Australia was modernising itself, more accepting of change and the effects of increased affordable travel, new technologies and non-British migration. This 'cosmopolitan influence', a term coined by Australian writer George Johnston in his 1966 bestseller *The Australians*, was largely a result of post-war migration which helped propel Australia into a new, more ethnically diverse era, in which (among a number of advancements) the arts gained greater significance, Australians travelled more and in turn welcomed more visitors to its shores. The divide between Australia and the wider world was narrowing.[3] Yiddish Melbourne's engagement with Europe and the Americas paralleled the reshaping of Australia's social and cultural landscape through its own growing international interests and connections.

Throughout this period, demand for spoken Yiddish remained high. A new development in 1975 was the inauguration of a Yiddish radio program. Its early audiences were the enthusiastic Yiddish speakers of the post-Holocaust migration and some of their children, who had grown up in Australia and attended the I.L. Peretz and Sholem Aleichem schools. Yiddish Radio began with Ethnic Community Radio 3ZZ, soon after transferring to 3EA, which became SBS Radio in the late 1980s. The main Melbourne presenters over the years have included SKIF founder and Yiddish teacher Pinye Ringelblum, actor Yasha Sher, poet and writer Abraham Cykiert,

---

2   Erwin Rado, 'Eyestrain for Art's Sake', *The Bulletin*, 13 June 1964.
3   Tanja Luckins, 'Cosmopolitanism and the Cosmopolitans: Australia in the World, the World in Australia,' in Robinson and Ustinoff, *The 1960s in Australia*, p.56.

SIGNS OF CHANGE

Yiddish teachers and community figures Danielle Charak, Alex Dafner, Mira Zylberman, Chana Mrocki, Reene Zufi, Michael Zylberman, and Bobbi Zylberman.[4]

At the same time, the Hazomir Choir, which began in 1947 as the Men's Jewish Choir, quickly grew into a popular mixed choir with a repertoire of Yiddish, Hebrew, classical and folk songs. Among its high-calibre conductors were Henry Portnoy, Felix Werder, Dolf Brenner, Pinchas Sharp, Jacques Berlinski, Baruch Kalushyner, Ben Segaloff, and Adrian Bartak. From its earliest days, pianist Miriam Rochlin accompanied the choir at rehearsals and performances. In 1979, 73 members of Hazomir participated in the International Choral Festival, Zimriah, in Israel, performing in Yiddish, Hebrew and English. A special rendition of 'Waltzing Matilda' was warmly appreciated by former Melbournites living in Israel.[5]

Although Yiddish Melbourne appeared to be thriving during the 60s and 70s, there were early signs of decline. While the Yiddish community was still sustaining itself, there was no substantial growth to replenish it. Israel and the Zionist movement continued to engage the passions of the youth. In the 1960s the Australian Jewish Welfare Society, now in the capable hands of the indefatigable Walter Lippmann, the pre-war German Jewish refugee discussed in an earlier chapter, shifted focus from immigration and resettlement to the growing social needs of an ageing community. In 1964, 28 flats for the aged were completed in Herbert Street, St Kilda; the complex became known as Rose Court. In 1965 a decision was made to purchase additional property for aged-care residences. A property with

---

4. 'Yiddish Radio', *Yiddish Melbourne*, http://future.arts.monash.edu/yiddish-melbourne/media-and-creative-writing-yiddish-radio/, accessed 11 April 2018.
5. *Melbourne Chronicle*, September-October 1981.

33 flats for singles and seven flats for couples was purchased at 3/5 Herbert Street, St Kilda, to be named Pras Court. The 1966 annual report noted that demand for aged-care accommodation was high, with applicants far exceeding the accommodation available. There was a push for aged-care facilities to be centralised. The 1969 annual report noted the change in Jewish demography, with a 'greater proportion moving from the middle-aged group into pensionable ages' and a concomitant need for a 'widening of the range of services available for elderly citizens'. Both Rose Court and Pras Court were quickly filled to capacity with a long waiting list, so further necessary planning for more aged-care accommodation was undertaken.[6]

When Walter Lippmann reported that Jewish Welfare was in 'the process of adjusting our thinking and administration to the changing needs of the times', he was, in part, talking about Yiddish Melbourne.[7] Economic prosperity alone did not ensure cultural continuity. Membership of the Kadimah remained over 1,000 in the 1960s, peaking at 1,379 in 1967, but over time very few new members joined its ranks. The library remained open twice a week, with over 100 active Yiddish book readers, but the number of people borrowing books was falling. The Kadimah annual report for 1960 noted that 'those who are mostly interested in the Kadimah's activities are Jews from Eastern Europe who form a large section of our community and belong mostly to the *landsmanshaftn*'. It recognised a problem with youth disengagement.

> [With] The meagre activities of our youth ... in the field of national and cultural work, the outgoing committee looks with great anxiety to the future of our Jewish community. A few

---

6   Australian Jewish Welfare Annual Reports 1960s.
7   Australian Jewish Welfare Annual Report 1963–64, p.14.

attempts of the committee to attract Jewish youth to the premises of the Kadimah by proposing that they conduct cultural activities at the Kadimah on broad inter-organisational basis did not yield satisfactory results.[8]

Talk of relocating the Kadimah to a site south of the Yarra, in keeping with the shifting Jewish demographic, gained traction in the late 1950s and was put to a vote at a general meeting in 1958, but lacked majority support. The Kadimah voted again in 1961 but still again fell short of getting an outright majority in favour of relocation. At the 1963 annual general meeting the motion was finally passed.

By this time the Jewish population in the City of Melbourne, which included Carlton, was in steep decline. In numerical terms the Jewish population of Carlton and the northern suburbs peaked in 1954, growing from 3,564 to 5,190. By 1961 the number of Jewish residents had fallen to 1,677 and in 1971 the number decreased further to 1,403. In the context of the rapid population growth of the late 1930s and after 1947, the decline is even more significant. In 1933, 40 per cent of Melbourne's Jewish population lived in Carlton and the northern suburbs; in 1954 the population fell to 22 per cent. In contrast, there was a growing concentration in the south eastern suburbs, including Caulfield and St Kilda, where the established Jewish population and immigrants from Germany, Austria and Central Europe lived. The population of these suburbs increase from 12,986 Jewish residents in 1954 to 17,732 in 1961. The 1967 Jewish community survey revealed the greatest concentration of the Jewish population resided in the south eastern suburbs – some 68 per cent. Only 14 per cent lived in the eastern suburbs of Kew, Balwyn and

---

8   Kadimah Annual General Report, February 1961, p.3.

Doncaster. The smallest concentration of Jews, less than 5 per cent lived in Carlton and the northern suburbs.[9]

In 1967 the Kadimah opened at a temporary site in Gordon Street, Elsternwick. In 1972 it officially opened its new premises on its current site in Selwyn Street, Elsternwick. The Kadimah of Carlton was no more, but in a pragmatic and adaptive move, the Kadimah had repositioned itself in the shifting heartland of Jewish Melbourne, which was increasingly ensconced in the middle-class leafy suburbia of the southern and eastern suburbs of Melbourne. As it repositioned itself, the Kadimah sought to retain its relevance.

The face of Jewish education was also changing as the Yiddish-speaking community continued to reposition its priorities, shifting loyalties away from the old *shtetl* world of Yiddish towards Israel and Zionism. Modern Hebrew now provided the pathway to a new world and a new future. The early attempts and ultimate failure to have Yiddish taught at Mount Scopus College revealed that there was little demand for Yiddish instruction in a mainstream orthodox Zionist school. Hebrew instruction was, however, mandatory. With the growth of the Jewish day-school system, by the 1960s there were seven day-schools, six of which were Zionist, with 2,700 enrolled students – Mount Scopus, Yeshivah/Beth Rivkah, Yavneh, Moriah, Bialik and Adass Israel. With the exception of Bialik College which was non-denominational and staunchly Zionist, all were orthodox. By 1964, 36 per cent of all Jewish children aged between six and 17 were enrolled in Jewish day-schools.[10]

---

9 Price, 'Jewish Settlers in Australia', Appendix IXa; Walter Lippmann, 'The Demography of Australian Jewry', *Australian Jewish Historical Society Journal*, Vol. VI, Part 5 (1968): pp. 253–66, Table 5; Commonwealth Bureau of Census and Statistics, *Census of Population and Housing, 30 June 1971: Bulletin 7, Characteristics of the Population and Dwellings. Local Government and Areas, Part 2, Victoria*, Canberra, 1973.

10 Medding, *From Assimilation to Group Survival*, p.103.

SIGNS OF CHANGE

A substantial proportion of parents had the economic means to support and sustain full-time Jewish private school education for their children. This network of day-schools continued to be supplemented by part-time schools – 14 Hebrew schools (six under the auspices of the United Jewish Education Board), five run by orthodox congregations, three by Liberal congregations, but just two part-time Yiddish schools, I.L. Peretz School and Sholem Aleichem School, which struggled with declining numbers. The I.L. Peretz School reached its peak enrolment in 1961 with 262 pupils, dropping to 110 in 1968. Sholem Aleichem reached 200 students in 1960 and maintained that number throughout the decade. Overall, the number of children receiving Yiddish instruction dropped between 1960 and 1968 from 450 to 300.[11]

What did this all mean? This was the era when the 'baby boomers', the second generation, was reaching maturity. Those born in 1948–50 were aged 15 to 17 in 1965. The falling numbers in the I.L. Peretz School reveal a generational shift in Yiddish acquisition. In 1970, the year that Joseph Giligich retired, the I.L. Peretz School had only 70 students. In 1972 a junior school was opened in Balwyn to cater for families who had moved to the eastern suburbs. The senior school moved to Balwyn the following year and in 1977 a new school building was opened. Despite this move, enrolments fell from year to year until, in 1984, the I.L. Peretz School and kindergarten were absorbed into the Sholem Aleichem School.[12]

In the context of the growing strength of the Jewish day-school movement, with its focus on Zionism and traditional mainstream

---

11   Manfred Klarberg, "Yiddish in Melbourne', in Peter Medding, ed., *Jews in Australian Society*, Melbourne: Macmillan, 1973, p.105.

12   'Yiddish Schools in Melbourne', *Yiddish Melbourne*, http://future.arts.monash.edu/yiddish-melbourne/education-yiddish-schools-in-melbourne/, accessed 11 April 2018.

orthodoxy, it is not surprising that the part-time schools became less attractive to parents seeking a Jewish education for their children. Coupled with the fact that fewer students acquired *mame loshen* in their homes, for those attending Yiddish classes the depth of Yiddish acquisition inevitably declined. But the leaders of the Yiddish-speaking community were not about to give in. In an attempt to maintain the viability of Yiddish, their response was to join the day-school movement and establish a Yiddish day-school.

In 1974 Holocaust survivor and Yiddish activist Nachman Gryfenberg, together with a group of committed co-workers, set about establishing a day-school that would promote Yiddish language and Yiddish culture and ensure that Yiddish education would be permanently accessible in Melbourne. It was to be a Yiddish school for all, not one aligned to Bundist ideology. To accommodate a wider range of interests and to attract a broader clientele, the school, located in Elsternwick, would provide a secular liberal and general education including Yiddish, Hebrew, Jewish history, literature and ethics. There were 10 students when Sholem Aleichem College opened as a day-school in February 1975.[13]

If the immediate post-war period had been one of revival and regeneration for the Bund, the bastion of Yiddish language and culture, there were signs of problems to come for the organisation. Yiddish was spoken less and less, evident in the growing reliance on English in its youth movement SKIF. The annual general report of the Bund noted in 1967 that 'Yiddish is a problem in our children's and youth work'.[14] The SKIF movement's journal, *Chavershaft*, moved from a

---

13   'Yiddish Schools in Melbourne'.
14   Cited in David Slucki, 'The Jewish Labour Bund After the Holocaust: A Comparative History', PhD, Monash University, 2010, p.273.

predominantly Yiddish publication to one in which English was the preferred language. Furthermore, the Bund's working-class socialist ideology was losing its relevance in an upwardly mobile, increasingly affluent Australian Jewish community. 'The Bund became a mass movement without a mass', commented Michael Gawenda; 'It was a working-class movement without a working class . . . But they [Bundists] were remarkable people and they did produce something unique'.[15] What they produced, however, was not consistent with the way the Bund had been conceived. Danielle Charak remarked that most of the leaders of the Bund in Melbourne, such as her father Nachman Gryfenberg, Sender Burstin and Bono Wiener, had become small business owners, not members of the proletariat.[16] Political ideals did not always match reality or practice. David Slucki observed that the decline of the Bund could be traced in the diminishing size of the Bund's annual reports, published in its *Bulletin* each year. By the 1980s the calendar of events had far fewer 'lectures, fundraisers, celebrations, commemorations and political engagement'.[17]

The SKIF youth movement also repositioned itself, moving away from the hard-line socialist manifesto advocated by the early Bundists to one that was less politically charged, where Yiddish was more symbolic than spoken. Melbourne SKIF has remained the only active Bund youth movement in the world, partly because of its willingness to adapt, keeping in step with a shifting demographic. SKIF had to compete not only with other popular youth groups but with lifestyle choices that were not underpinned by the political agency that propelled the movement it in its earliest days. The

---

15 Michael Gawenda, interview 17 May 2011.
16 Danielle Charak, interview 4 February 2009.
17 Slucki, 'The Jewish Labour Bund After the Holocaust', p.280.

younger generation were, according to Arnold Zable, 'products of a liberal democratic, affluent, postwar world and post messianic environment'.[18] For David Slucki, 'SKIF had to become more of a social group than a political and cultural movement'.[19] In order to survive it had to remain relevant to a new generation with shifting priorities and had to compromise some of its political base, while retaining its ties to *Chavershaft, Doykeit* and *Yiddishkeit*. The fiery rhetoric of a workers' party with its 'combative style of activism' had to make way for 'equality and empathy, democratic socialism and social awareness'.[20]

Jewish consciousness and Israel

While Yiddish struggled to retain its relevance, Israel continued to strengthen its hold on Melbourne's Jewish consciousness. From the time the state of Israel was established the community's extensive fundraising focus and annual appeals targeted Israel's myriad needs, from absorption of new immigrants to reclaiming the desert. Different groups within the community, in particular the *landsmanshaftn*, were substantial supporters of the United Israel Appeal. Israeli dignitaries and emissaries were frequent visitors, charged with reinforcing the strong connection between the Zionist reality and the Melbourne Jewish community.

As previously argued, for some 20,000 Holocaust survivors who made Australia their home, the Holocaust and Israel sat front and

---

18   Cited in Slucki, 'The Jewish Labour Bund After the Holocaust', p.279.
19   Slucki, 'The Jewish Labour Bund After the Holocaust', p.282.
20   Slucki, 'The Jewish Labour Bund After the Holocaust', p.232; 'What is SKIF?', http://www.skif.org.au/what-is-skif, accessed 11 April 2018.

centre. When former SS officer Adolf Eichmann, the 'desk murderer' of the Third Reich who had orchestrated the deportation of European Jewry to the killing centres of Poland, was captured by Israel's spy agency Mossad in 1960 and put on trial in Jerusalem in 1961, Israel effectively stamped its sovereignty and jurisdiction over world Jewry, giving it the legal authority to represent the Jewish people. Eichmann was indicted on 15 criminal charges, including crimes against humanity, war crimes, crimes against the Jewish people, and membership of a criminal organisation.[21] When Israel's prosecutor Gideon Hausner declared in his opening address that he speaks for the 'six million', he irrevocably linked the Holocaust with the state of Israel. The Eichmann trial brought the testimonies of 112 witnesses to a world audience with electrifying results. Not only did it validate their experiences as never before, but it proved a timely reminder that a strong and authoritative Israel was now guardian of the Jewish people.

In Melbourne the *Australian Jewish News* ran consistently on its front page stories about Eichmann, from the time of his capture to the horrific witness testimonies throughout his trial, the announcement of the tribunal's verdict on 12 December 1961, his death sentence by hanging on 15 December and his execution in the early hours of 1 June 1962. There was no escaping the pervasive nature of the trial, Israel's role in the proceedings and its penetrating impact on Melbourne's Holocaust-conscious Jewish community. By the mid-1960s, when Melbourne Jewry was asked in a survey what Israel means to them personally, over 77 per cent replied that they saw Israel as

---

21 Hanna Yablonka, *The State of Israel vs Adolf Eichmann*, New York: Schocken Books, 2004.

their national home, a place of refuge, as representative of the Jewish people, a source of pride and sentimental attachment. Over 61 per cent said they would like to live there,[22] but very few left Melbourne to live there.

In June 1967 Jewish revival was threatened with another Holocaust. In the weeks and days leading up to the Arab–Israeli Six-Day War, Arab leaders threatened Israel with its destruction, vowing to unleash a 'war of annihilation', 'to blot out its [Israel's] entire presence' and to 'wipe Israel off the map'.[23] Israel's 2.7 million residents, many of whom were Holocaust survivors and refugees from Arab lands, were surrounded by Arab armies on all fronts. Israel's back was to the sea. All its cities were within range of Arab artillery. Internationally, Israel was isolated. China, India, the Soviet Union and the Soviet bloc countries were all hostile. The United States was 'friendly', but not militarily aligned. Israel's main arms supplier, France, decided to switch sides just days before hostilities erupted. In preparation for an apocalyptic battle, Israel distributed gas masks to its civilians and dug some 10,000 graves.[24] For the third time in its short existence, Israel was bracing itself for the fight of its life.

The Arab rhetoric of annihilation conjured up images of the Holocaust and struck at the heart of the local Jewish community. 'Nasser [President of Egypt] is trying to finish Hitler's job,' Israeli emissary Brigadier General Rabbi Shlomo Goren told a hushed audience at a United Israel Appeal evening in Melbourne on 23 May; 'and he aims not only to destroy the sovereign state of Israel'.[25] It

---

22 Peter Medding, Melbourne Jewish Sociological Survey 1967.
23 Cairo Radio, 22 and 27 May 1967.
24 Michael Oren, 'Six Days that Helped Put Palestinians on the Map', *The Australian*, 12 June 2017.
25 *Australian Jewish News*, 26 May 1967.

wasn't just the Jewish homeland that was under siege. Jews everywhere again felt isolated and targeted for extermination. Nothing less than Jewish survival was at stake. Goren emphasised that this was not Israel's fight alone. It was imperative for diaspora Jews to stand ready to assist their Israeli brothers and sisters: 'We in Israel are prepared to make every conceivable sacrifice. We are ready to give our blood and our property in order to preserve Israel for the entire Jewish nation. Are you with us in this task?'[26]

The community gave an unequivocal positive response to Goren's rhetorical question. At a time of growing dissent and disillusionment over Australia's involvement in the Vietnam War, with an increasing number of anti-Vietnam rallies protesting against a war many Australians considered unjust and unnecessary, the Six-Day War was seen as a moral war, a David and Goliath battle. The mainstream press saw Israel as the underdog, the Israeli soldiers as the 'unsung heroes'.[27] This wasn't about fighting a dubious, contentious foreign war in a foreign land. Australian Jewry was heavily invested in Israel's fate. This was about averting another Holocaust. 'Every man and woman who was fighting in the Israeli forces in the war last week knew that they were fighting not merely for the national sovereignty of the state but for Jewish survival', United Israel Appeal (UIA) emissary A. Abrahamson told an emergency appeal meeting.[28]

The war united the generations in their resolve to fight for Israel with money and blood. Huge rallies in support of Israel were staged in capital cities, with record attendances: 7,000 in Melbourne, 6,000 in Sydney, and 650 and 600 respectively in smaller Jewish communities

---

26 *Australian Jewish News*, 26 May 1967.
27 *Canberra Times*, 24 May 1967.
28 *Australian Jewish News*, 16 June 1967.

of Brisbane and Adelaide. Recruitment drives to attract young volunteers were endorsed by the Australian Zionist Youth Council, the Jewish Students Societies of the University of Melbourne and Monash University, B'nai B'rith Young Adults, UIA Young Adults and the Association of Victorian Jewish Youth. Their duty was spelt out in the *Australian Jewish News*:

> Call to All Jewish Youth: The call for your active participation in the current emergency has been made by the People of Israel. It is your duty as an individual to attend a meeting of all Jewish Youth this Monday 5 June 1967, where the magnitude of the crisis will be presented in its full context and your obligation will be clarified.[29]

The Executive Council of Australian Jewry and the Zionist Federation of Australia and New Zealand also asked the youth to assist Israel in its hour of need.

> Young Jews and Jewesses prepared to answer the request of the World Zionist Organization for working hands to take the place of Israel's working youth who have been mobilised for defence, to register with the offices of the Jewish Board of Deputies or State Zionist councils in their respective states.[30]

By the end of June, some 4,000 volunteers from 26 countries had arrived in Israel and been placed in over 177 *kibbutzim* (collective farms).[31] In Australia, some 1,500 volunteers registered at state and federal Zionist council offices by late June, with approximately 250, mainly young people, selected to go to Israel's aid.[32] While most

---

29 *Australian Jewish News*, 2 June 1967.
30 *Australian Jewish News*, 2 June 1967.
31 *Australian Jewish News*, 7 June 1967.
32 Hyams, *The History of the Australian Zionist Movement*, p.135; *Australian Jewish News*, 29 June 1967.

volunteers were deployed in civilian duties, one group of Habonim leaders was sent to repair damage done to buildings, orchards and classrooms on Kibbutz Yisrael. Those who had experienced Israeli life or had served in the Israeli armed forces were able to join combat units. The *Australian Jewish News* told the story of 23-year-old Max Redlich, a Melbournian who had previously lived in Israel for five and a half years and served as a paratrooper during that time. Redlich managed to get on one of the last planes into Israel, arriving on 1 June 1967. When hostilities broke out on 5 June, he was reinstated with the rank of sergeant, 'moving from group to group ... his unit [was] moved to Jerusalem. Max was wounded although not badly, but the traces of war will stay in his leg for the rest of his life'. Max stayed in Israel for the following two months before returning to Melbourne.[33]

Recruitment of volunteers continued well after the war was over, with 'new registrations, particularly of young people prepared to work wherever required still being accepted at the Zionist offices in all states'.[34] Of those who had offered to put their lives on the line, a number were unlikely candidates, including the chairman of the Bund, Holocaust survivor Bono Wiener.

Fundraising went into overdrive. An emergency appeal called for 'funds on an unprecedented scale ... every Jew in our community must not fail to answer Israel's desperate call for maximum support'. The appeal announced in the *Jewish News* pledged to raise $2,000,000 and was endorsed by 55 signatories, which included synagogues, sporting organisations, Jewish Welfare, the Kadimah, WIZO, B'nai

---

33   *Australian Jewish News*, 18 August 1967.
34   *Australian Jewish News*, 30 June 1967.

B'rith and the *Landsmanshaftn*.[35] Fundraising dinners were held, schoolchildren donated pocket money, non-Jewish supporters contributed as they 'sympathised with our cause'.[36] By the end of the emergency period, the amount raised trebled the amount pledged. In a show of great solidarity, the Bund, although still opposed to political Zionism, donated $1,000 to the United Israel Emergency Appeal, citing 'the special circumstances in Israel'. The President of the Emergency Appeal, Henry Krongold, responded:

> It is brotherly and good for every Jew in our city to know and to feel that such an important movement as yours, identifies and stands shoulder to shoulder with us, at this troublesome but historically vital hour in the life of the state of Israel. With sincere appreciation for your honourable and generous act of solidarity for Jewry in the state of Israel.[37]

Annie Gawenda recalled how Bundists in Melbourne were deeply affected by the war and the threat it posed to all Jews, and how their attitudes toward Israel changed as a result.

> It impacted on those who had a pretty hard attitude towards Israel before ... but that changed towards an understanding of how important Israel was to Jews ... I think 1967 was a turning point ... there was a huge groundswell of nationalist feeling that if you lost the country [Israel] then what?[38]

For this war touched all their lives and demonstrated that what united all Jews was far greater than that which divided them. The devastating impact of the Holocaust and the emergence of a Jewish

---

35 *Australian Jewish News*, 2 June 1967.
36 *Australian Jewish News*, 21 July 1967.
37 Moshe Ajzenbud, *60 Years of the 'Bund' in Melbourne 1928–1988*, Melbourne: Jewish Labour Bund, 1996, pp.52-3.
38 Annie Gawenda, interview 17 May 2011.

homeland was an especially powerful and defining time in the history of world Jewry. Here in Melbourne the threat to Jewish survival served to bring together a small, often fractious community in ways that were previously unimaginable.

Chapter 18

'YIDDISH HAS NOT YET SAID ITS LAST WORD'

The United Nations Educational, Scientific and Cultural Organisation (UNESCO) currently lists Yiddish among the world's 'definitely endangered' languages, defined as such when children no longer learn the language as their mother tongue in their homes.[1] Threatened with extinction, Yiddish is a language deemed to be in its death throes – dying but not yet dead. UNESCO's dire prediction simplistically assumes that the Yiddish language cannot and will not survive, in any shape or form, but the continuing saga of Yiddish in a place like Melbourne is far more complex than UNESCO has understood or predicted.

Jewish community surveys have been conducted in Melbourne in 1967, 1991, 2008 and 2017 to gauge attitudes, practices and the transmission of values across the generations. They show that in the decades following the 1960s there was a sharp decline in Yiddish language competency, so that between 1967 and 1991 the proportion of the Melbourne Jewish community that usually spoke Yiddish in the home had halved, going from 28 per cent down to 14 per cent. The 2008 community survey revealed a further decline to 11 per cent, and in the

---

1 'UNESCO Atlas of the World's Languages in Danger', http://www.unesco.org/languages-atlas/index.php, accessed 11 April 2018.

survey of 2017 the proportion dwindled to 7 per cent. Of those who could *understand* Yiddish, the 1967 survey indicated a high 60 per cent. In the 2017 survey, that had fallen to 21 per cent, largely people over the age of 60, although an interesting finding was that close to 10 per cent remain in the younger age groups. Albeit at a diminished level, the transmission of language is continuing.

The overall decline of Yiddish should not surprise. The intergenerational switch to English occurred because Jews in Australia enjoyed a very different way of life to that experienced in the closed *shtetl* world of Eastern Europe. There, they were forced to live independent of their neighbours, with a heightened sense of being different. The language Jewish immigrants brought with them survived, complete with its own consciousness and a culture that quickly became a cherished and much loved way of life. But here, in the land of opportunity and equality there was no need for such separateness. In an open, free society, the migrants adopted the language of their new homeland. It was a similar story in America, as Ruth Wisse, Professor of Yiddish at Harvard University has explained:

> Jews changed their language to English in America much as people adapt their wardrobe to a new climate. America was so much warmer and so much more welcoming than Europe, Jews did not feel they needed insulation from their neighbours. Yiddish had learned to resist persecution, to defend its constituency with cunning, and courage. But America proved relatively hospitable; why shouldn't Jews function in the common language of the land.[2]

While the outlook for the future of Yiddish competency in Melbourne, as in America, may appear bleak, a closer examination

---

2   Edward S. Shapiro, ed., *Yiddish in America*, Scranton and London: University of Scranton Press, 2008, p.17.

reveals a complex, diverse picture. What exists in Melbourne is rare but not unique. Though smaller in scale, it is similar to the handful of other remaining Yiddish centres around the globe, notably New York, Montreal and London. Yiddish language competency may be under threat in the mainstream, but certainly not in one sector of the community.

Yiddish in the ultra-orthodox community

Within Melbourne's ultra-orthodox *haredi* community, Yiddish continues to grow and thrive. Joel Friedman, a member of this community observes that 'Yiddish lives . . . young couples speak Yiddish to their children'. For Raizl Fogel, whose family are members of this community, 'Yiddish is a tradition passed down through the generations. It binds us together. If you don't know Yiddish you are lost in our community. Yiddish unites us with the past and is our connection to the old world'.[3] The term *haredi* means 'fearful', with reference to fear of God – 'Hear the word of the Lord, you will *tremble* [haredim] at his word' (Isaiah 66:5). A biblical term, its contemporary use began in the second half of the 20th century to describe a particular group of ultra-orthodox Jews whose lifestyle, worldview, ethos and beliefs went beyond what many understood as 'orthodox'.[4]

Haredim first emerged as a post-enlightenment phenomenon, as an anti-assimilationist response to the secularisation of Jewish identity. The emancipation of Jews meant that some, particularly in Western Europe, could live full secular lives free from the constraints and confines of the ghettos and the restrictions of religious

---

3 Interviews with Joel Friedman, 17 May 2009, and Raizl Fogel, 27 May 2011.
4 Simeon D. Baumel, 'Black Hats and Holy Tongues: Language and Culture Among British *Haredim*', *European Judaism*, Vol. 36, No. 2 (2003).

observance. Jews could now express their Jewish identity in different ways. The new secular world that Jews now inhabited brought ultra-orthodoxy into sharper focus.

The *haredi* community in Melbourne comprises more than 12 different sects that come under the inclusiveness of the Adass Yisroel (the congregation of Israel) umbrella. While each sect adheres to the leadership of its own rabbi, they are united by their particular brand of ultra-orthodoxy. Adass Yisroel in Melbourne began with the arrival of ultra-orthodox Hungarian holocaust survivors in 1950. In 1956 the *kehile* claimed to have 800 members.[5] Today the *haredi* community number some 500 families with a conservative estimate of 2,500–3,000 individuals. Over 80 per cent of this community live within a small geographic area, in the suburbs of St Kilda East, Ripponlea, Elsternwick and Caulfield North.

The *haredim* are differentiated from mainstream orthodox Judaism by a number of distinctive characteristics. Their dress code is highly prescriptive and makes them easily identifiable. Different sects choose their own particular 'style', with men mostly dressed in black with white shirts; they wear black hats, have beards and long ear locks. They choose to wear the garb that their ancestors wore in Russia and Poland, believing that it keeps them closer to the heart of their faith. Women adhere to the laws of modest dress and wear long skirts and sleeves, high necklines, and, if married, some form of hair covering. Ideologically, some, such as the Satmar in Melbourne, do not recognise Israel as a modern, secular Jewish state. In keeping with a literal interpretation of biblical text, the establishment of the state in their understanding should only come with the arrival of the Messiah. They

---

5   Suzanne D. Rutland, 'The Emergence of Ultra-Orthodox Judaism in Post-War Australia', *Australian Jewish Historical Society Journal*, Vol. XIII, Part 4 (1997).

do not embrace broad secular knowledge and their level of secular education is minimal. Their use of technology is highly selective and only to support their ends – they typically oppose the viewing of television and films and make very little use of the internet, often only for business purposes. Torah study is their top priority.

The specific role of women within public life and the religious congregation is highly regulated and prescriptive. They are completely conversant in the rituals of religious life but they do not study Torah as the men do. They live segregated lives. The role and nature of work in daily life is seen as a means to an end rather than a way of improving one's social standing. The *haredi* are not socially aspirational and do not seek upward mobility. They are not an affluent community, although its members are highly supportive of each other. The few who are in a position to assist others struggling economically do so. In Melbourne, of those who responded to the 2017 Jewish Community survey questionnaire, only a third of men and women are fully employed, a third work part time, and a third are unemployed. Some 42 per cent claimed to experience financial hardship.[6]

Within the *haredi* community, Yiddish is spoken in the home, the schools and the synagogue. In the 2017 Jewish community survey, of the 390 Victorian *haredim* who completed the questionnaire some 57 per cent indicated that they could speak and understand Yiddish 'very well' or 'quite well'. For a majority it is their mother tongue, contrary to UNESCO's limited understanding of the use of Yiddish. The Yiddish of the ultra-orthodox *haredi* is, however, a functional language with none of the secular literary, artistic resonances reflected in the theatre, publications or culture of pre-war and

---

6   Jewish Community Survey, 2017.

post-war Yiddish Melbourne and in the flourishing Yiddish world of interwar Poland.

Yiddish in these *haredi* communities provides an all-embracing inclusiveness. For Joel Friedman, Yiddish is all or nothing: 'there is Yiddish and there is *goyish* (gentile)'. Yiddish serves to maintain boundaries, preserving their existing social structures within a strictly isolationist, exclusive society of their own making. This is in stark contrast to the imposition of Jewish isolation upon Eastern European Jewish communities by external forces before their emancipation. Here, separation comes from within.

Yiddish remains the spoken language of choice across the generations and is the means for cultural and religious transmission; *chumash* (the Torah) and *gemara* (the Talmud) are translated into Yiddish for study and discussion. Sermons, speeches and announcements in the community's synagogue are in Yiddish, as are speeches at life cycle events. Boys undertaking their *bar mitzvah* will deliver their *pshetel* (the exegesis of the weekly Torah portion) in Yiddish. This builds on the model established in the Adass Yisroel boys' school, first registered as a day-school in 1953, where, from preparatory class onwards, all text learning is done in Yiddish. 'In Adass they acquire an excellent command of Yiddish for life', Raizl Fogel commented. Thus the holy texts, written in Hebrew, are discussed and studied using Yiddish language. This is not the case in the girls' Adass Yisroel school, where the girls are taught in English and only study Yiddish as a 'language other than English'.

In 2010 a group of ultra-orthodox families concerned that the standard of Yiddish education offered at the Adass schools was inadequate, opened a kindergarten named Divrei Eminah (Matters of Faith) with the aim of specifically teaching Yiddish in an immersion program to both boys and girls. The impetus for the school came out of a strong desire to ensure that girls obtain a thorough knowledge of Yiddish, equal to the boys, including rules of grammar, so that when they reach marriageable age they are able to sustain Yiddish-speaking homes and language transmission to their children. The school is registered as a bi-literate school, meaning that they use Australian curriculum outcomes equally for both Yiddish and English. The school leaders liaise with similar communities in Belgium, the United States and Israel to share resources and experience. The kindergarten and day-care centre expanded in 2011 to include a pre-preparatory class and in that year had 40 enrolments.[7] Since then the school has grown, adding additional primary year levels, and is currently registered to grade 5 and seeking registration for grade 6. Its current prep to grade 5 enrolment is 92 students; the day-care centre in Brighton is registered to take 69 children per day and states that it is full with a waiting list.

Just as the Yiddish language is a cohesive factor within the *haredi* community in Melbourne, it also provides a conduit that connects *haredim* around the world. 'With Yiddish you are not a stranger wherever you go', Raizl Fogel explained about the networking role Yiddish played amongst *haredi* families around the world. Families who are unable to find suitable partners for children in the local community, seek and find marriage partners for their children within the network of the global *haredi* community. Families may employ a *shadchen* (matchmaker), much in the same way their ancestors did, who act as the go-between for families with marriageable children.

---

[7] 'Yiddish in the Ultra-Orthodox Community', *Yiddish Melbourne*, http://future.arts.monash.edu/yiddish-melbourne/yiddish-in-the-ultra-orthodox-community/, accessed 11 April 2018.

For Joel Friedman the comparatively small size of the Melbourne ultra-orthodox community means marriage partners have to be found amongst overseas likeminded communities, 'finding *shidduchim* (marriage partners) is a big problem in Melbourne'. Some of his own children and grandchildren have found partners in Montreal, where he has family. The Yiddish vernacular is also a direct connection with specific aspects of a Jewish life of the past. For these Jews it signifies a rejection of modernity, acculturation, secularisation and religious reform in all its forms.

The demographic picture

Yiddish in the rest of the community has followed a very different trajectory. The Jewish community survey of 2017 reveals the significant polarisation of those for whom Yiddish is fundamental to their way of life. Spoken Yiddish retains its relevance for minorities from a wide spectrum of Jewish life – from those who adhere to a strict religious orthodoxy to those who do not define themselves by religious denomination, but are secular or non-practising Jews. More than three in ten over the age of 60 and identifying as modern Orthodox, traditional, or secular indicated that they could understand Yiddish 'very well' and 'quite well'. But it is within the secular segment of the community that Yiddish cultural life continues to be actively promoted.[8]

One secular family that has bucked the trend of diminishing language acquisition are the Ringelblums, who have undertaken to raise their children entirely in Yiddish. Doodie Ringelblum, who was raised in a strict Bundist home and grew up in the world of secular Yiddish,

---

8   Jewish Community Survey, 2017.

is the son of Pinye Ringelblum, a dedicated Yiddish teacher, Principal of I.L. Peretz School 1971–78 and President of Sholem Aleichem College 1985–89, founder of SKIF in Australia in 1950 and Yiddish radio broadcasting in Melbourne. For Doodie and his wife Ruth, the means to experience a full Jewish life lies in language: 'I believe that you cannot live a meaningful life in that culture without the language of that culture'. Doodie explained this further, 'an authentic Jewish life is not just a religious life . . . Yiddish is a means, a tool to a full Jewish life for me and my family'.

The Ringelblum family faces great challenges in this regard as there are no other like-minded families living locally; 'the Adass families wouldn't play with our kids' and 'there is a dearth of suitable contemporary Yiddish publications for children and young adults', but their commitment to a life lived in Yiddish remains unswerving. In their early years the family travelled to America every two years to partake in Yiddish Vokh (Yiddish Week), where they subsequently formed an internet group *'mames un tates'* (mothers and fathers), made up of about 60 families worldwide who had also decided to immerse their children in Yiddish. The group comprised a broad spectrum of interests and beliefs from strictly modern orthodox Jews to communists.[9]

Learning Yiddish today

With the rapid growth of the Jewish day-school movement and the decline of the part-time afternoon and Sunday school system, Yiddishists were rightly concerned that Yiddish language instruction would falter. In response, they established Sholem Aleichem

---

9   Doodie Ringelblum, interview 23 April 2009.

College in 1975 in Sinclair Street Elsternwick. The Yiddish language continues to be taught at this flourishing day-school, which has about 250 students, from kindergarten up to grade 6. It is only one of a handful of secular Yiddish day-schools in the world. Helen Greenberg, Principal of the school and daughter of Yiddish stalwarts and Holocaust Centre volunteers, Cesia and Abe Goldberg, 'grew up with Yiddish all around me . . . I have a deep love and appreciation for Yiddish and I am doing everything I can to promote it'. Helen's passion for a Yiddish school came from 'my early years growing up in this community, attending Sholem kindergarten, SKIF, my family and seeing the importance of Yiddish and its culture'.[10]

Yiddish is taught daily at Sholem Aleichem College at all levels, including in the preschool. Preps study Yiddish/Jewish Studies for five lessons per week, Years 1 and 2 study Yiddish/Jewish Studies six lessons per week, and Years 3 to 6 study Yiddish/Jewish Studies seven lessons per week. The school employs a thematic approach to the teaching of Yiddish, integrating themes from the general studies curriculum. Internationally prescribed textbooks as well as readers, computers, supplementary worksheets and activities provide the language framework for Yiddish competency. Yiddish learning programs and word-processing programs are also used in the computer laboratory. Yiddish is taught as a living language and therefore incorporates an important oral component. In the upper primary years the children undertake creative writing both as an individual activity and in group activities. Whenever possible, the children are provided with opportunities to interact with adult Yiddish speakers from within the school community, teachers, parents and grandparents, as well as from the

---

10   Helen Greenberg, interview 4 May 2009.

broader community. The aim is that, by the time they graduate from primary school, students should be conversant in Yiddish, with a firm understanding of its significance as part of a multifaceted, contemporary Jewish identity.[11] Helen Greenberg pointed out that the school subscribes to the Yiddish ideal of *'menschlikhkeit* – teaching children how to be good, decent people'.

Yet, of the nearly 3,000 primary school students currently attending Jewish day-schools in Melbourne, Sholem Aleichem students are only a very small number, less than one in ten. Beyond primary school, Yiddish education struggles to survive. Yiddish is currently taught as a Victorian Certificate of Education (VCE) subject, but numbers are small with only eight to 10 students completing their VCE examination in 2017, all of whom were mature-age students. Yiddish is also taught at the tertiary level. With community funding, a Yiddish program was established at Monash University in 2004, but it too only attracts a handful of students. The program offers undergraduate language training, scholarships for overseas intensive study, postgraduate supervision, and an annual Kronhill Visiting Scholar in Yiddish Culture. It also provides the language skills for any future Yiddish teachers.

Yiddish across the generations

Third-generation Yiddish speaker David Slucki summed up the current state of Yiddish in the secular world as 'different'. 'I wouldn't say that Yiddish is dead. Yiddish is different and plays a different role in Jewish life . . . Yiddish becomes a cultural indicator rather

---

11 'Sholem Aleichem College Primary School Curriculum', http://www.sholem.vic.edu.au/wp-content/uploads/2014/06/D911173246.pdf, accessed 11 April 2018.

than a fact of daily life'.[12] In Slucki's view, while Yiddish as a spoken language is under threat, its cultural importance and significance as an identity marker live on. Contemporary Yiddish has adapted. Rutgers University's Professor of Jewish History, Jeffery Shandler, echoes Slucki's assessment: 'Yiddish hasn't simply dwindled, and it certainly hasn't died, although it is often characterized in such terms. Yiddish has become something significantly different from what it once was'.[13]

Shandler sees the post-Holocaust era as a period when the Yiddish language diminished as the primary means for transmitting ideas, opinions and information, while the importance of Yiddish as a cultural symbol continues to expand.[14] Yiddish language and Yiddish culture may appear to have taken divergent pathways, but in reality they exist in a form of symbiosis. Yiddish culture emerged within the language. For Anna Epstein, curator of the 2012 Melbourne Jewish Museum exhibition *Mameloshn: How Yiddish made a home in Melbourne*, 'language is something that has a culture attached to it, literature, poetry, theatre and public speaking'. For some, there is a substantive attachment to Yiddish culture that comes directly through its literature, either through the study of translations or by actively learning Yiddish, or partaking in study groups that seek to rediscover the mysteries of the writers and intellectuals of the lost Yiddish world. For others, there is an emotional attachment to a cultural heritage that is no longer language-based. This form of attachment is largely symbolic, through artefacts or the use of easily understood idioms,

---

12 David Slucki, interview 27 May 2011.
13 Jeffery Shandler, *Adventures in Yiddishland: Postvernacular Language and Culture*, Los Angeles: University of California Press, 2006, pp.4–5.
14 Shandler, *Adventures in Yiddishland*, p.4.

such as *shlep* or *schmooze*, or expressions that have crept into the English vernacular, like 'I need it like I need a hole in the head, or proverbs such as 'the apple never falls far from the tree'. Yiddish may no longer be an accessible, spoken language for many, but its value system, its cultural aspects, its meanings live on.

'Yiddish will survive as a secular expression of culture,' Anna Epstein elaborated, 'more and more people are saying "I want to capture my culture. I want to reconnect."'[15] Secular Yiddish culture provides a younger generation with a visceral link to the past, in most cases not through the language itself, but through what that language represents. For many it is an act of remembrance that engages the sights, sounds and rhythms of a way of life once lived by their parents and grandparents and from which they are now removed.

The 'post-vernacular' age

In the secular world, Yiddish has evolved and adapted, mostly as a 'post-vernacular' phenomenon, having moved on from being a language spoken amongst immigrants and in the home to their children. While the survey of Melbourne's Jewish community provides a clear demographic picture of who still understands and/or speaks Yiddish and who does not, it does not tell us the extent and depth of Yiddish cultural life in Melbourne.

The spread of a popular culture based in Yiddish with an increasing dependence on performance, translation and, to a lesser extent, scholarship has become an important component of mainstream Jewish popular culture supported by specific interest groups, without being the dominant spoken language of what is now a well settled and

---

15   'Growing a Yiddish Heritage', *The Australian*, 1 August 2011.

integrated community. In Melbourne, and similarly in Montreal and New York, this is most visible in the performing arts, most notably in Yiddish theatre in the form of lively cabaret or musical theatre and Klezmer music, old and new.

Popular Yiddish culture

Klezmania, a group of singers and musicians who describe themselves as 'a riot of a band, breaking down genres and styles in its path, filling the room with energy and passion whenever they play', was formed in 1993. Lead singer is Yiddish teacher Freydi Mrocki, a passionate advocate for Yiddish: 'I now commit myself to do whatever I can in my lifetime to keep Yiddish alive'.[16] The group's repertoire is extensive; they claim to sing and play 'klezmer, blues, ska [precursor of reggae], Gypsy swing and waltzes, jazz, Australian folk music, romantic ballads, whirling frenetic traditional dance tunes and more'. The group has attracted a substantial following among young and old, extending its reach beyond the Yiddish community to those for whom modern interpretations of classic Yiddish folk songs and a range of other music styles appeal. The group appear regularly at community functions and within the broader Jewish and non-Jewish community.[17] The band's success is partly attributable to Freydi's own attitude towards Yiddish: 'I never saw Yiddish as an old fogey language, never saw it as *booba* (grandmother) language. I saw it as a vibrant, creative means of expressing yourself as a young, modern Jewish person'.

The Mir Kumen On Yiddish choir began meeting in June 2008, under the auspices of the J. Waks Cultural Trust. It is led by Yiddish

---

16   Freydi Mrocki, interview 4 August 2009.
17   'Klezmania', http://www.klezmania.com.au/, accessed 11 April 2018.

teacher and musician Tomi Kalinski, who was raised in a Zionist home with Yiddish-speaking parents. For her, 'music and Yiddish are always connected... the world of Yiddish music touches your soul'. The choir specialises in old and new Yiddish songs and performs at a variety of functions in Melbourne. Singers in the choir do not need to be fully literate in Yiddish as transliterated versions of the songs are available.[18] The choir is for 'all people who love Yiddish, young university students to older people', Tomi explained.[19]

The Kadimah Yiddish Radio Show, produced and presented by community identity Alex Dafner, goes to air on Thursdays at 4 p.m. on Jewish Australia Internet Radio (J-Air). Dafner was born in Lodz in 1949 and educated there at the Peretz Yiddish School before arriving in Melbourne as a 10 year-old in 1959. For the first year of their resettlement, the Dafner family lived at the Bialystoker Centre in Robe Street, St Kilda, while Alex's parents found work in the *shmatte* (clothing) business. Alex has built a life in Yiddish as a SKIF member and youth leader, teacher of Yiddish, a long-serving former President of the Kadimah, Vice-President of the Holocaust Centre and curriculum adviser on VCE Yiddish.[20] He has performed on stage and has been an executive producer of Yiddish radio programs at SBS since 1980. He is currently is at the helm of Yiddish broadcasting on J-Air, which features reports from Australia, Israel and other Jewish communities from around the world, as well as songs, stories, comedy, interviews, celebrations and commemorations.[21]

---

18   'Mir Kumen On Yiddish Choir', https://mirkumenon.weebly.com/, accessed 11 April 2018.
19   Tomi Kalinski, interview 30 July 2009.
20   'Alex Dafner (1949–)', *Yiddish Melbourne* http://future.arts.monash.edu/yiddish-melbourne/biographies-alex-dafner/, accessed 11 April 2018.
21   'Kadimah Radio', http://www.kadimah.org.au/radio, accessed 11 April 2018,

'YIDDISH HAS NOT YET SAID ITS LAST WORD'

In 2004 the first Sof Vokh Oystralye, a Yiddish immersion weekend retreat based on the successful Yugntruf Yidish Vokh held annually in the Catskills in New York State, was held in the Dandenongs. Since then, annual weekends away for Yiddish enthusiasts consistently attract some 60 to 80 attendees. Activities include sports, games, discussions, walks, communal singing and literary readings, and a day program for high-school students in years 9 to 11. All are conducted in Yiddish.[22]

The great champion of Yiddish language and culture in Melbourne, the Bund, in 2017 celebrated 120 years since its beginnings as a socialist political party in Vilna. In Melbourne it remains engaged with a small, yet active part of the community, promoting *frayhayt, glaykhhayt* and *gerekhtikayt* (freedom, equality and justice), with a focus on secular Jewishness and Yiddish language and culture. The Bund's activities include its annual 19 April Holocaust commemoration, lectures, concerts and publications (including *Undzer Gedank*).[23] SKIF, the Bund's youth organisation, continues to run programs for eight to 18 year-olds with weekly meetings on Sundays between 3 and 5 p.m. at Waks House, named for Bund leader Jacob Waks and home to the Bund and SKIF, in Caulfield and runs three camps every year.

Inevitable casualties

While aspects of popular Yiddish culture continue to attract the patronage of a small yet committed segment of Melbourne's Jewish community, a number of Yiddish organisations have not survived into the 21st century. Melbourne no longer boasts a weekly Yiddish

---

22 'What is Sof-Vokh?', https://yiddishaustralia.weebly.com/what-is-sof-vokh.html, accessed 11 April 2018.
23 'Jewish Labour Bund Melbourne', https://www.bundist.org/about, accessed 11 April 2018.

newspaper. *Di Yiddishe Nayes* ceased publication in 1995, when it could no longer sustain a viable readership. For devoted Yiddishist Freydi Mrocki, 'it was like a knife had gone through me'. The David Herman Theatre staged its last production, *In Hartz fun Tel Aviv* (In the Heart of Tel Aviv) in 1992, having fallen victim to declining audiences and a diminishing number of aging actors who could no longer tread the boards. For Tomi Kalinski, 'this was tragic. We are one of the last communities which still has native Yiddish speakers and children of native speakers. There should still be a place for Yiddish theatre'. The part-time Yiddish schools, I.L. Peretz and Sholem Aleichem, closed their doors decades ago.

The Kadimah in the new millennium

The Kadimah remains the bedrock of Yiddish culture, as it continues to support a robust, broad-based cultural program, while celebrating revered Yiddish actors, writers and poets who left their mark on the Yiddish world. Iconic figures such as Sholem Aleichem and I.L. Peretz, two of the greatest Yiddish writers of the late 19th and early 20th centuries, are revered and commemorated for their fine examples of Yiddish literature from the period that was the zenith of secular Yiddish culture. Sholem Aleichem was the pen name of Shalom Rabinowitz, born in 1859 in the Ukraine. He wrote popular stories, sketches, critical reviews, plays and poems. He also wrote in Hebrew and Russian, but is best loved for his poignant, often comic Yiddish stories. In 1906 he toured America where he was dubbed the 'Jewish Mark Twain'. His stories around the character of Tevye the milkman formed the basis for the popular stage and film musical *Fiddler on the Roof*.[24]

---

24 'Sholem Aleichem (1859–1916)', *Jewish Virtual Library*, http://www.jewishvirtuallibrary.org/shalom-aleiche m, accessed 11 April 2018.

'YIDDISH HAS NOT YET SAID ITS LAST WORD'

Itzhak Leib Peretz was born in 1852 in Zamosc, Poland. Greatly influenced by the Jewish enlightenment, Peretz wrote stories, poems, essays, folk tales and plays. His sympathies lay with the labour movement and he was often a social critic. He influenced the direction of modern Yiddish theatre in Eastern Europe, taking it in a more serious direction. Set in a Jewish *shtetl*, his 1907 Yiddish play, *Bay Nakht Oyfn Altn Mark* (A Night in the Old Marketplace), brings into play questions concerning life and death in Peretz's own inimitable tragicomic style. Peretz is best remembered for his retelling of traditional stories in a modern context, in which he meshed old-world symbolism and psychological realism, creating a new literary Yiddish style. Themes of forgiveness, self-sacrifice, modesty and purity recur in his stories and continue to resonate with modern audiences.[25]

Testament to their enduring relevance in the Yiddish world of the 21st century, both Aleichem and Peretz have had institutions named after them in Melbourne, where their birthdays are celebrated and their literary works continue to be read and discussed. Indicative of the Kadimah's ongoing activities, it organised an evening in 2015 dedicated to the memory of I.L. Peretz, and throughout 2016, it ran a program celebrating the life and works of Sholem Aleichem, entitled 'Sholem Aleichem: 100 and not yet dead'. The activities included readings, musical performances and a comic re-enactment of Sholem Aleichem's fictional town, Kasrilivke. On 13 August 2017, the Kadimah staged 'A Zeyde Like No Other: Yankev Waislitz on the World Stage' as a tribute to the life and work of the popular Yiddish actor. The actor's great-grandson spoke in Yiddish at the event, as did many others. Live

---

25   Payson R. Stevens, 'I.L.Peretz: The Contributions of I.L. Peretz to Yiddish Literature', *My Jewish Learning*, https://www.myjewishlearning.com/article/i-l-peretz/, accessed 11 April 2018.

entertainment, such as *S'Brent* – Love Burns, *Balaganeydn*, a tribute to avant-garde Polish Yiddish cabaret, and 'Ghetto Cabaret: A Night to Remember', played to appreciative, capacity crowds.

The Kadimah continues to host guest speakers and artists, reading circles, and discussion groups. In 2014 a book of Yisroel Shtern's collected poems was launched, edited by Melbourne Yiddish community stalwart, Dr Andrew Firestone, who initiated and drove the Yisroel Shtern project. Shtern was one of Warsaw's leading Yiddish poets and essayists in the interwar period and was murdered by the Nazis in 1942. In February 2017 a translation of the collected stories of Pinchas Goldhar was published. Goldhar was an acclaimed Yiddish writer, profiled in an earlier chapter, who left his birthplace, Lodz, to settle in Melbourne in 1928.

The Kadimah National Library holds the largest collection of Yiddish books, periodicals, reference, audio and video materials in Australia. It is difficult to estimate the exact number of books it holds, as cataloguing is not yet complete, but is thought to exceed 100,000. The library has become the repository for Yiddish books after their owners have passed away. It has amassed tens of thousands of books otherwise destined for oblivion, in a way similar to the Yiddish Book Center in Amherst, Massachusetts, established in 1980 to rescue and preserve Yiddish books, which has recovered more than a million volumes and receives thousands of books each year from all over the world, including from Melbourne. Since 1997 it has developed a digital library now comprising over 12,000 Yiddish texts, which is heavily used.[26]

---

26   'Our Story', Yiddish Book Center, https://www.yiddishbookcenter.org/about/saving-literature, accessed 11 April 2018.

'YIDDISH HAS NOT YET SAID ITS LAST WORD'

The Kadimah library is currently open twice a week and is staffed by the indefatigable Rachel Kalman and a team of enthusiastic Yiddish-speaking volunteers. While the library has a very small number of visitors from week to week, it has some 140 registered 'borrowers' who are predominantly second-generation Yiddish speakers. Few first-generation readers remain and only two or three are third-generation. The library also houses a sizeable collection of Judaica and Holocaust books and references in English, Hebrew, Russian and Polish. Key individuals in the flourishing years of Yiddish Melbourne are commemorated throughout the library; there is the Yasha Sher Reading Room, the Bono Wiener Collection, the Genia and Chaim Borensztajn Holocaust Memorial-Yizkor Collection, Moishe Rabinowicz Multimedia Research Centre, and the Dafner Family Yiddish Audio-Visual, Radio Collection. The library also supports the Giligich Foundation.[27]

Some may question the viability and rationale of an expanding Yiddish library when the number of potential readers continues to diminish. Can the library continue to exist for such small numbers of readers? But there is significance beyond the needs of the present. For Jews, the 'people of the book', books represent life. The rescue of books signifies the preservation of an entire civilisation. For a small, dedicated group of Yiddishists who continue the Kadimah's mission, preserving what remains of their Yiddish world is an uncompromising commitment. For them, the Kadimah library is the last vestige of a life that once was, the last trace of a community

---

27 'Library and Collections', Kadimah Cultural Centre and National Library, http://www.kadimah.org.au/library, accessed 11 April 2018.

that must be preserved, to provide the means for a much-hoped-for Yiddish revival.

The future

Clearly, Yiddish Melbourne has continuing relevance for segments of the Jewish community. Weathering the winds of social change, popular Yiddish culture remains a feature of the secular Jewish landscape, where it has retained relevance. Cultural elements survive within a secular Jewish world while language competency diminishes. Within the *haredi* community, it is the opposite. It is Yiddish language, the spoken word that serves the needs of a tight-knit and devout religious group.

With virtually no intermarriage outside their own communities, a high birth rate and very few leaving their world, *haredi* numbers are growing rapidly. Contrary to UNESCO's understanding, the fastest-growing segment of Melbourne's Jewish population has Yiddish as its mother tongue. The estimated global population for *haredi* communities is currently 1.3–1.5 million, close to 10 per cent of the world's Jewish population. In Israel *haredim* numbered 750,000 in 2007. In the United States their numbers were estimated in 2006 at 468,000, or 9.4 per cent of the total Jewish population and their percentage is increasing, mostly living in the greater New York metropolitan area. In Montreal a conservative estimate of *haredim* in 2004 was 20,000. A 2007 study in the United Kingdom estimated there to be 45,500 *haredim*, or 17 per cent of the Jewish population, with a second study in 2010 establishing that there were 9,049 *haredi* households with a population of 53,400. In the United Kingdom *haredi* families have an average of 5.9 children, compared to the national average of 2.4. Over 30 years, from 1966 to 1996, the number of Jewish children learning in Yiddish jumped from one in nine to almost one in every three Jewish children in the United Kingdom. For all *haredi* communities, Yiddish is the mother tongue.

When Yiddish scholar and linguist Dovid Katz asked American Yiddish writer Avrom Shulman before his death in 1999 about the future of Yiddish in the United States, Shulman replied,

> Neither Hitler nor Stalin came to America. Here there are no excuses. Yiddish can't survive without a *shtetl*. If you want to save Yiddish, you have to build a *shtetl*, with a town square with its pump and stalls, and with the drunken *goyishe* peasants we would never want to be like, and then you will have your Yiddish.[28]

For the *haredim*, Shulman's assessment rings true. They have constructed a *shtetl*, complete with its own boundaries and prescriptive lifestyle, away from a secular world they 'never want to be like'. Those few who make the decision to leave find it very difficult to do so. Closed communities do not tolerate apostates who challenge their authority and way of life. Those who do leave typically encounter hostility, being shunned and cut off from family and friends; they face a difficult transition to a new life in a secular world that is foreign to them. Organisations such as Footsteps in New York, Forward in Montreal, Mavar and Gesher in London, and Pathways in Melbourne are support groups founded to facilitate entry into mainstream society. But the few who do leave the *haredi* fold do so with a sound level of Yiddish language competency that may be passed on to future generations.

---

28 Dovid Katz, *Words on Fire: The Unfinished Story of Yiddish*, New York: Basic Books, 2004, p.353.

A SECOND CHANCE

Yiddish continues to hold a prized place within a relatively small number of the children of the secular Yiddish pioneers, the second generation who were inculcated with a love of and attachment to a world that belonged to their parents and which they were privileged to share. As a member of that generation, Tomi Kalinski still believes that there is

> a need and desire for some kind of Yiddish in our community, not necessarily academic . . . anytime you do something Yiddish in Melbourne, people come out of the woodwork. There is a hunger for it. There is so much potential . . . The more I learn about Yiddish the more passionate I am about preserving it.

But the question of relevance lies not with this second generation of Yiddish enthusiasts who 'come out of the woodwork' whenever a cultural event is staged, but with the many third- and fourth-generation descendants of Yiddish speakers. Fewer and fewer have the same passion for or proficiency in Yiddish. Freydi Mrocki's children still 'understand but don't speak it [Yiddish] as well as I did at their age'. Yet the spark of Yiddish is not entirely extinguished. For Jess, another third-generation descendant of Yiddish speakers, Yiddish holds a special place in her heart.

> I don't speak or understand Yiddish but I grew up hearing it all the time, as did so many of my school friends. It was the language of my grandparents, both Holocaust survivors, who spoke Yiddish to my mother. I loved them dearly and so formed an emotional attachment to the language they spoke. I haven't discounted learning it one day, bringing me closer to the world they inhabited. Who knows? Maybe.[29]

---

29 Jessica Taft, interview 1 December 2017.

'YIDDISH HAS NOT YET SAID ITS LAST WORD'

Very few of the fourth generation, however, hear Yiddish spoken by grandparents. For them the emotional attachment and historical relevance of Yiddish is still further removed.

In his acceptance speech for the Nobel Prize in Literature in 1978, celebrated Yiddish writer Isaac Bashevis Singer alluded to future possibilities:

> There are some who call Yiddish a dead language, but so was Hebrew called for two thousand years. It has been revived in a most remarkable, almost miraculous way. Aramaic was certainly a dead language for centuries but then it brought to light the Zohar, a work of sublime value... Yiddish has not yet said its last word. It contains treasures that have not been revealed to the eyes of the world. It was the tongue of martyrs and saints, of dreamers and Kabbalists – rich in humour and in memories that mankind may never forget. In a figurative way, Yiddish is the wise and humble language of us all, the idiom of frightened and hopeful humanity.[30]

Here in Melbourne, in *ek velt* (a corner of the world), there are many who share Bashevis Singer's passionate belief that 'Yiddish has not yet said its last word'.

---

30 'Isaac Bashevis Singer – Nobel lecture, 8 December 1978', https://www.nobelprize.org/nobel_prizes/literature/laureates/1978/singer-lecture.html, accessed 11 April 2018.

BIBLIOGRAPHY

Primary sources
Newspapers
Australian Jewish Herald
Australian Jewish News
Canberra Times
Daily Telegraph
Melbourne Herald
Sydney Morning Herald
Sydney Jewish News
Sydney *Sun*
Sydney *Truth*
Sunday *Truth*
The Advertiser (Adelaide)
The Advocate
The Age
The Argus
The Australian
The Bulletin
The Sydney Morning Herald
The West Australian
Undzer Vort

Community surveys
Medding, Peter Y. Melbourne Jewish Sociological Survey, 1967.
Gen 08 Jewish Community Survey, 2008–9.
Gen 17 Jewish Community Survey, 2017.

Interviews
Sam Lipski, 10 August 1992, Jewish Museum of Australia.
Yasha Sher, 30 July 1992, Jewish Museum of Australia.
Shmuel Rosenkranz, 4 August 1992, Jewish Museum of Australia.
Erwin Rado, 25 January 1987, conducted by Andrew Markus.

Yankel Pushett, 20 March 2009, conducted by Miriam Munz.
Symche Burstin, 9 July 2008, conducted by Rachel Kalman.
Nuritt Borsky, 20 November 2014, conducted by Miriam Munz.
Jack Felman, 27 May 2011, conducted by Andrew Markus and Miriam Munz.
Annie and Michael Gawenda, 10 March 2011, conducted by Andrew Markus and Miriam Munz.
Annie Gawenda, 3 June 2009, conducted by Miriam Munz.
Arnold Zable, 2 December 2011, conducted by Andrew Markus and Miriam Munz.
Avram Zeleznikow, 26 August 2008, conducted by Danielle Charak and Miriam Munz.
Shulamis Sher, 21 July 2008, conducted by Rachel Kalman.
Leon Goldman, 5 May 2009, conducted by Miriam Munz.
Danielle Charak, 9 February 2009, conducted by Andrew Markus.
Leon Freedman, 24 March 2009, conducted by Miriam Munz.
Joel Friedman, 17 May 2009, conducted by Miriam Munz.
Raizl Fogel, 27 May 2011, conducted by Miriam Munz.
Doodie Ringelblum, 23 April 2009, conducted by Miriam Munz.
Helen Greenberg, 4 May 2009, conducted by Miriam Munz.
Freydi Mrocki, 4 August 2009, conducted by Miriam Munz.
Tomi Kalinski, 30 July 2009, conducted by Miriam Munz.
David Slucki, 27 May 2011, conducted by Miriam Munz.
Freda Freiberg, 22 July 2015, conducted by Margaret Taft.
Jessica Taft, 1 December 2017, conducted by Margaret Taft.

Archives and manuscripts

National Archives of Australia (NAA). Series A434, 1947/3/21, Reports from Shanghai on Alien Immigration.
National Archives of Australia (NAA). Series A434, 1949/3/3196, Admission of Jews to Australia.
National Archives of Australia (NAA). Series A433, 1943/2/43, Aliens arriving in Australia holding passports not visaed by a British Consul.
National Archives of Australia (NAA). Series A445, 235/5/4, Admission of Jews Policy, Part 3.
National Archives of Australia (NAA). Series A445, 235/5/9, Alleged discrimination against admission of Jews – Question of Jewish or not on departmental forms.

BIBLIOGRAPHY

Commonwealth Parliamentary Debates, House of Representatives, 2 Aug 1945, Hansard, Vol. 31.
United States Holocaust Memorial Museum. USC Shoah Foundation Institute Testimony of Chaim Sztajer, Interview code 5184.
University of Melbourne Archives: Fink, Mina and Leo, 1990.0091.
YIVO Institute for Jewish Research (New York), Archives and Library Collections, RG 108, Frishman, Dovid, *Briv fun Poyln* [A letter from Poland], early 1920s.

Annual reports

Bialystoker Annual General Report, 1949.
Kadimah Annual Reports 1934–1965.
Australian Jewish Welfare Annual Report, 1963–4.

Secondary sources

Ajzenbud, Moshe. *60 Years of 'Bund' in Melbourne 1928–1988*. Melbourne: Jewish Labour Bund, 1996.
Ajzner, Hania. *Hania's War*. Melbourne: Makor Jewish Community Library, 2003.
Allon, Fiona. 'At Home in the Suburbs', *History Australia*, Vol. 11, No.1 (2014).
Alroey, Gur. 'Out of the *Shtetl*: In the Footsteps of Eastern European Jewish Emigrants to America, 1900–1914', *Leidschrift*, Vol. 22, No. 1 (2007).
Altman, Kitia. *Memories of Ordinary People: For Those Who Have No One to Remember Them*. Melbourne: Makor Jewish Community Library, 2003.
The Australian Encyclopaedia. Sydney: Australian Geographic Pty Ltd, 1996.
Bartrop, Paul. '"Good Jews and Bad Jews": Australian Perceptions of Jewish Migrants and Refugees, 1919–1939', in *Jews in the Sixth Continent*, edited by W.D. Rubinstein, Sydney: Allen & Unwin, 1987.
Baumel, Simeon D. 'Black Hats and Holy Tongues: Language and Culture Among British *Haredim*', *European Judaism*, Vol. 36, No, 2 (2003).
Benjamin, Rodney. *'A Serious Influx of Jews': A History of Jewish Welfare in Victoria*. St Leonards, NSW: Allen & Unwin, 1998.
Bennett, Shmuel. *Chronicles of a Life*. Melbourne: S. Bennett, 1999.
Berk, Leon. *Destined to Live*. Melbourne: Paragon Press, 1992.
Berman, Judith. *Holocaust Remembrance in Australian Jewish Communities 1945–2000*. Perth: University of Western Australia Press, 2001.

Bialik, H.N. *Complete Poetic Works of Hayyim Nahman Bialik*, edited by Israel Efros. New York: Histadruth Ivrith of America, 1948.

Blainey, Geoffrey. *A History of Victoria*. Melbourne: Cambridge University Press, 2013.

Bolton, Geoffrey. *The Oxford History of Australia*. Vol. 5. Melbourne: Oxford University Press, 1990.

Bowyer Bell, J. *Terror Out of Zion*. London: St Martin's Press, 1976.

Brett, Judith. *Robert Menzies' Forgotten People*. Carlton: Melbourne University Press, 2007.

Burchell, Laurie. 'A Synagogue in Coburg', *Australian Jewish Historical Society Journal*, Vol. XIV (1998).

Burstin, David. 'I.L. Peretz Yiddish School 1935–84', *Australian Jewish Historical Society Journal*, Vol. X, Part 1 (1986): 15–27.

Burstin, Sender, *Yiddish Melbourne Observed*, translated by Ben and David Burstin, Melbourne: Australian Centre for Jewish Civilisation, Monash University, 2013.

Caplan, Debra. 'The Sun Never Sets on the Vilna Troupe', *PaknTreger: Magazine of the Yiddish Book Centre*, Summer 2014. http://www.yiddishbookcenter.org/language-literature-culture/pakn-treger/sun-never-sets-vilna-troupe.

Cater, Nick. 'Robert Menzies' Forgotten People', *The Australian*, 22 May 2012.

Cohn-Sherbok. Dan. *Anti-Semitism*. Stroud, Gloucestershire: History Press, 2009.

Commonwealth Bureau of Census and Statistics. *Census of Population and Housing, 30 June 1971: Bulletin 7, Characteristics of the Population and Dwellings. Local Government and Areas, Part 2, Victoria*. Canberra, 1973.

Cooke, Steven and Donna-Lee Frieze. *The Interior of Our Memories: A History of Melbourne's Jewish Holocaust Centre*. Melbourne: Hybrid Publishers, 2015.

Cowen, Zelman. *Isaac Isaacs*. St Lucia: University of Queensland Press, 1993.

Cowen, Zelman. 'Isaacs, Sir Isaac Alfred (1855–1948)', *Australian Dictionary of Biography*, National Centre of Biography, Australian National University. http://adb.anu.edu.au/biography/isaacs-sir-isaac-alfred-6805/text11773.

Dapin, Mark. *Jewish Anzacs: Jews in the Australian Military*. Sydney: NewSouth Publishing, 2017.

BIBLIOGRAPHY

Defining Moments in Australia History. National Museum Australia. http://www.nma.gov.au/online_features/defining_moments.

Dinnerstein, Leonard. 'Anti-Semitism Exposed and Attacked', *American Jewish History*, Vol. 71, No. 1 (1981).

Dunstan, David. 'Wynn, Samuel (1891–1982)', *Australian Dictionary of Biography*, National Centre of Biography, Australian National University. http://adb.anu.edu.au/biography/wynn-samuel-9207.

Eisfelder, Horst. *Chinese Exile: My Years in Shanghai and Nanking.* Melbourne: Makor Jewish Community Library, 2003.

Encyclopaedia Judaica, edited by Michael Berenbaum and Fred Skolnik (2nd ed.) Vol. 16. Detroit: Macmillan Reference, 2007.

Feniger, Saba. *Short Stories: Long Memories.* Melbourne: Vista, 1999.

Fishman, David E. *The Rise of Modern Yiddish Culture.* Pittsburgh: University of Pittsburgh Press, 2005.

Ford, Carolyn. *Who Brought the Luck to the Lucky Country?* Melbourne: Red Dog Books, 2011.

Forsyth, Donelson R. *Group Dynamics.* Belmont CA: Wadsworth Cengage Learning, 2014.

Foster, John. *Community of Fate: Memoirs of German Jews in Melbourne.* Sydney: Allen & Unwin, 1986.

Getzler, Israel. *Neither Toleration nor Favour: The Australian Chapter of Jewish Emancipation.* Melbourne: Melbourne University Press, 1970.

Goldhar, Pinchas. *The Collected Stories of Pinchas Goldhar.* Melbourne: Hybrid Publishers, 2016.

Goldhar, Pinchas. 'The Press of the Jewish Community in Australia', *Yiddishe Almanac 1937,* translated by Danielle Charak.

Goldlust, John. *The Melbourne Jewish Community: A Needs Assessment Study.* Canberra: Australian Government Publishing, 1993.

Golvan, Colin. *The Distant Exodus.* Crows Nest, NSW: ABC Enterprises, 1990.

Gutman, Yisrael. 'Polish Antisemitism Between the Wars: An Overview', in *The Jews of Poland Between Two World Wars,* edited by Yisrael Gutman, Ezra Mendelsohn, Jehuda Reinharz and Chone Shmeruk. Hanover, NH: University Press of New England, 1989.

Haberfeld, Lusia. *Lauferin: The Runner of Birkenau.* Melbourne: Makor Jewish Community Library, 2002.

Havin, David. *Orthodox Jewry In Carlton and Surrounding Suburbs.* Melbourne: D.J. Havin, 2007.

Hertz, J.S. *Doyres Bundistn 3.* New York: Unzer Tsayt, 1968.

Hirshbein, Peretz. 'Travel Stories: Pictures', in *Australian Yiddishe Almanac, 1937.*

Holocaust Encyclopedia. United States Holocaust Memorial Museum. https://www.ushmm.org/learn/holocaust-encyclopedia.

Hyams, Bernard. *The History of the Australian Zionist Movement.* Melbourne: Zionist Federation of Australia, 1998.

Ivany, Susan. *Melbourne Chronicle*, June-July 1981.

Jedwab, Lou. 'The Kadimah Youth Organisation in Melbourne: Reminiscences 1942–53', *Australian Jewish Historical Society Journal*, Vol. XII, Part 1 (1993): 179–187.

Jewish Virtual Library: A Project of AICE. http://www.jewishvirtuallibrary.org/.

Jockusch, Laura and Tamar Lewinsky. 'Paradise Lost? Postwar Memory of Polish Jewish Survival in the Soviet Union', *Holocaust and Genocide Studies*, Vol. 24, No. 3 (2010).

Jona, Walter. 'The VAJEX Story: Achievements in War and Peace', *Australian Jewish Historical Society Journal*, Vol. XII, Part 1 (1993).

Jupp, James. *From White Australia to Woomera: The Story of Australian Immigration.* Melbourne: Cambridge University Press, 2002.

Kaminska, Ida. *My Life, My Theatre.* New York: MacMillan, 1973.

Kassow, Samuel. 'The Interwar *Shtetl*,' in *The Jews of Poland Between Two World Wars* edited by Yisrael Gutman, Ezra Mendelsohn, Jehuda Reinharz and Chone Shmeruk, Hanover, NH: University Press of New England, 1989.

Katz, Dovid. *Words on Fire: The Unfinished Story of Yiddish.* New York: Basic Books, 2004.

Katz, Jacob. 'Freemasons and Jews', *Jewish Journal of Sociology*, Vol. 9, No. 2 (1967).

Katz, Jacob. *Jews and Freemasons in Europe 1723–1939.* Cambridge: Harvard University Press, 1970.

Kellermann, Natan P.F. 'The Long-Term Psychological Effects and Treatment of Holocaust Trauma', *Journal of Loss and Trauma*, Vol. 6, No. 3 (2001).

Kipen, Israel. *A Life to Live.* Melbourne: Chandos Publishing, 1989.

Klarberg, Manfred. 'Yiddish in Melbourne', in Peter Y. Medding, ed. *Jews in Australian Society.* Melbourne: Macmillan, 1973.

BIBLIOGRAPHY

Kochavi, Arieh J. *Post Holocaust Politics: Britain, the United States and Jewish Refugees 1945–48*. Chapel Hill, NC: University of North Carolina Press, 2001.

Kohn, Peter. 'Levita – a Star Remembers: the Peter Kohn interview, *Australian Jewish News*, 17 February 1989, p.11.

Landau, David. *Caged: A Story of Jewish Resistance*. Sydney: Pan Macmillan, 2000.

Laqueur, Walter. *History of Zionism*. New York: Schocken Books, 1989.

Laqueur, Walter. *The Terrible Secret: An Investigation into the Suppression of Information About Hitler's 'Final Solution'*. London: Weidenfeld and Nicolson Ltd, 1980.

Lasky, Max. 'Remembering the Thornbury *Shul*', *Australian Jewish Historical Society Journal*, Vol. XIV (1997).

Levi, John S. *These Are The Names: Jewish Lives in Australia 1788–1850*. Melbourne: The Miegunyah Press, 2006.

Levi, John S. *Strike Me Lucky! Judaism in Australia*, Adelaide: Charles Strong Memorial Trust, 1998.

Levi, John S. *Rabbi Jacob Danglow*. Melbourne: Melbourne University Press, 1995.

Levi, John S. and G.F.J. Berman. *Australian Genesis: Jewish Convicts and Settlers 1788–1860*. Melbourne: Melbourne University Press, 2002.

Liberman, Serge. 'Seventy Years of Yiddish Theatre in Melbourne (1909–1979)', Part 2, *Melbourne Chronicle*, January 1981.

Liberman, Serge. *On Firmer Shores*. Melbourne: Globe Press, 1981.

Lippmann, Walter. 'The Demography of Australian Jewry', *Australian Jewish Historical Society*, Vol VI, Part 5 (1968).

Lipstadt, Deborah E. *Beyond Belief*. New York: The Free Press, 1986.

Loewald, Klaus. 'The Eighth Australian Employment Company', *Australian Journal of Politics and History*, Vol. 31, Issue 1 (1985): 78–89.

Luckins, Tanja. 'Cosmopolitanism and the Cosmopolitans: Australia in the World, the World in Australia', in Shirleene Robinson and Julie Ustinoff, eds, *The 1960s in Australia: People, Power and Politics*. Newcastle upon Tyne: Cambridge Scholars Publishing, 2012.

Maclean, Pam. 'Pinchas Goldhar: His Yiddishist Vision – a Flawed Nationalism?', *Australian Journal of Jewish Studies*, Vol. 5, No. 1 (1991).

Marks, Eva. *A Patchwork Life*. Melbourne: Makor Jewish Community Library, 2002.

Markus, Andrew. 'Fink, Miriam (Mina) (1913–1990)', *Australian Dictionary of Biography*, National Centre of Biography, Australian National University. http://adb.anu.edu.au/biography/fink-miriam-mina-12493.

Markus, Andrew. 'Jewish Migration to Australia 1938–1949', *Journal of Australian Studies*, Vol. 7, No. 13 (1983): 18–31.

Markus, Andrew. *Australian Race Relations*. St. Leonards, NSW: Allen & Unwin, 1994.

Markus, Andrew and Danielle Charak, eds. *Yiddish Melbourne: Towards a History*. Melbourne: Monash University, 2008

Markus, Andrew and Margaret Taft, eds. *Walter Lippmann, Ethnic Communities Leader*. Melbourne: Australian Centre for Jewish Civilisation, Monash University, 2016.

Markus, Andrew and Margaret Taft. 'Postwar Immigration and Assimilation: A Reconceptualization', *Australian Historical Studies*, Vol. 46, Issue 2 (2015).

Marrus, Michael. *The Unwanted: European Refugees in the Twentieth Century*. New York: Oxford University Press, 1985.

Masel, Danny and Debbie Masel. 'Alec Masel', *Australian Jewish Historical Society Journal Journal*, Vol. XIX, Part 2 (2008).

Meadows, Julie. ed., *A Shtetl in Ek Velt: 54 Stories of Growing up in Jewish Carlton*. Melbourne: Australian Centre for Jewish Civilisation, Monash University, 2011.

Meadows, Julie. ed., *Fun Himlen Blayene Tsu Bloye Teg (From Leaden Skies to Blue Days) 45 Stories growing up in Jewish Carlton*. Melbourne: Australian Centre for Jewish Civilisation, Monash University, 2014.

Medding, Peter Y. *From Assimilation to Group Survival: A Political and Social Study of an Australian Jewish Community*. Melbourne: F.W. Cheshire Publishing, 1968.

Medding, Peter Y. 'The Melbourne Jewish Community Since 1945: A Political and Sociological Study'. MA thesis, Melbourne University, 1962.

Melbourne Chronicle, September-October 1981

Melzer, Emanuel. *No Way Out: The Politics of Polish Jewry 1935–1939*. Cincinnati: Hebrew Union College Press, 1997.

Mendes, Philip. *Jews and the Left*. Basingstoke: Palgrave Macmillan, 2014.

Menzies, Robert, 'The Forgotten People, 22 May 1942'. http://www.liberals.net/theforgottenpeople.htm.

Mitchell, James. *Henry Krongold*. Crows Nest, NSW: Allen & Unwin, 2003.

BIBLIOGRAPHY

Murphy, John. *Imagining the Fifties: Private Sentiment and Political Culture in Menzies' Australia.* Sydney: UNSW Press, 2000.

Naor, Mordecai. *Zionism: The First 120 Years, 1882–2002.* Jerusalem: The Zionist Library, 2002.

Oeser, O.A. and S.B. Hammond. *Social Structure and Personality in a City.* London: Routledge, 1954.

O'Hanlon, Seamus. 'A Little Bit of Europe in Australia: Jews, Immigrants, Flats and Urban and Cultural Change in Melbourne, c1935–75'. *History Australia*, Vol. 11, No. 3 (2014).

Oren, Michael. 'Six Days that Helped Put Palestinians on the Map', *The Australian*, 12 June 2017.

Orwell, George. 'Anti-Semitism in Britain', *Contemporary Jewish Record*, Vol. 8, No. 2 (1945).

Pat, Jacob. 'Impressions of a Visit, 1956', translated from the Yiddish by Serge Liberman, *Australian Jewish Historical Society Journal*, Vol XVI, Part 1 (2001).

Patkin, Benzion. 'From Advisory Board to Board of Deputies in Victoria'. *Australian Jewish Historical Society Journal*, Vol. IX, Part 1 (1981): 39–50.

Price, Charles A. *Southern Europeans in Australia.* Melbourne: Oxford University Press, 1963.

Price, Charles A. 'Jewish Settlers in Australia', *Australian Jewish Historical Society Journal*, Vol. V, Part 8 (1964): 357–412.

Rado, Erwin, 'Eyestrain for Art's Sake', *The Bulletin*, 13 June 1964.

Rapke, Trevor. 'The Pre-War Jewish Community of Melbourne', *Australian Jewish Historical Society Journal*, Vol. VII, Part 4 (1973): 291–301.

Rattigan, Alf. *Industry Assistance: The Inside Story.* Melbourne: Melbourne University Press, 1986.

Ravitch, Melech. 'Australia and I', *Yiddishe Almanac 1942*, translated by Dvora Zylberman

Reilly, Joanne. *Belsen: The Liberation of a Concentration Camp.* London: Routledge, 1998.

Robinson, Shirleene and Julie Ustinoff, eds. *The 1960s in Australia: People, Power and Politics.* Newcastle upon Tyne: Cambridge Scholars Publishing, 2012.

Rogozinski, Shimon, 'The Lodzer Centre in Melbourne 1953–1974', Melbourne: 1974.

Rosenbaum, Yankel. 'Religiously Carlton, Jewish Religious Life in Carlton 1919–1939', *Australian Jewish Historical Society Journal*, Vol. XII, Part 3 (1994): 519–535.

Rosenberg, Jacob. *Sunrise West*. Sydney: Brandl & Schlesinger, 2007.

Rosenstein, Chaim. 'Yiddish Theatre in Australia', *Yiddishe Almanac 1942*, translated by Dvora Zylberman.

Rosh White, Naomi. *From Darkness to Light: Surviving the Holocaust*. Melbourne: Collins Dove, 1988.

Rosner Blay, Anna. *Not Paradise: Four Women's Journeys Beyond Survival*. Melbourne: Hybrid Publishers, 2004.

Rubinstein, Hilary L. *The Jews In Australia: A Thematic History, Volume 1: 1788–1945*. Port Melbourne: William Heinemann Australia, 1991.

Rubinstein, W.D. *The Jews in Australia*. Melbourne: Australian Ethnic Heritage Series, 1986.

Rubinstein, W.D. 'The Revolution of 1942–44: The Transformation of the Australian Jewish Community', *Australian Jewish Historical Society Journal*, Vol. XI, Part 1 (1990): 142–154.

Rubinstein, W.D. *The Jews in Australia: A Thematic History, Volume 2: 1945 to the Present*. Melbourne: William Heinemann Australia, 1991.

Rutland, Suzanne D. *Edge of the Diaspora* (2nd rev. ed.). Sydney: Brandl & Schlesinger, 1997.

Rutland, Suzanne D. 'Postwar Anti-Jewish Refugee Hysteria: A Case of Racial or Religious Bigotry?', *Journal of Australian Studies*, Vol. 27, Issue 77 (2003).

Rutland, Suzanne D. 'Are You Jewish?', *Australian Journal of Jewish Studies*, Vol. 5, No. 2 (1991).

Rutland, Suzanne D. 'I Am My Brother's Keeper: The Central Role Played by Overseas Jewry in the Reception and Integration of Post-war Jewish Immigration to Australia', *Australian Jewish Historical Society Journal*, Vol. XI, Part 4 (1992).

Rutland, Suzanne D. 'Resettling Survivors of the Holocaust in Australia', *Holocaust Studies: A Journal of Culture and History*, Vol. 16, No. 3 (2010).

Rutland, Suzanne D. '"I Never Knew A Man Who Had So Many Cousins": Differing Attitudes to Postwar Survivor Migration: Melbourne and Sydney', *Australian Jewish Historical Society Journal*, Vol. XII, Part 2 (1994).

Rutland, Suzanne D. 'The Emergence of Ultra-Orthodox Judaism in Post-War Australia', *Australian Jewish Historical Society Journal*, Vol. XIII, Part 4 (1997).

BIBLIOGRAPHY

Rutland, Suzanne D. and Sol Encel. 'Three Rich Uncles in America', *American Jewish History*, Vol. 95, No. 1 (2009).

Sarna, Jonathan D. *American Judaism*. New Haven: Yale University Press, 2004.

Schneer, Jonathan. *The Balfour Declaration: The Origins of the Arab-Israeli Conflict*. New York: Random House, 2010.

Shandler, Jeffrey. *Adventures in Yiddishland: Postvernacular Language and Culture*. Los Angeles: University of California Press, 2006.

Shapiro, Edward S. ed., *Yiddish in America*. Scranton and London: University of Scranton Press, 2008.

Slucki, David. 'The Jewish Labour Bund After the Holocaust: A Comparative History'. PhD thesis. Monash University, 2010.

Taft, Margaret. 'From Displaced Person to New Australian, A Journey Towards Self Determination'. MA thesis, Monash University, 2004.

Taft, Margaret. *From Victim to Survivor: The Emergence and Development of the Holocaust Witness 1941–49*. London: Vallentine Mitchell, 2013.

Tulchinsky, Gerald. *Canada's Jews: A People's Journey*. Toronto: University of Toronto Press, 2008.

'UNESCO Atlas of the World's Languages in Danger'. http://www.unesco.org/languages-atlas/index.php.

Virtual Shtetl. POLIN Museum of the History of Polish Jews. https://sztetl.org.pl/en/.

Wasserstein, Bernard. *On The Eve: The Jews of Europe Before The Second World War*. New York: Simon & Schuster, 2012.

Weinstein, Miriam. *Yiddish: A Nation of Words*. South Royalton, VT: Steerforth Press, 2001.

Wilton, Janis. 'Refugees', in *Australians 1938*, edited by Bill Gammage and Peter Spearritt. Sydney: Fairfax, Syme & Weldon Associates, 1987.

Wischnitzer, Mark. *To Dwell In Safety: The Story of Jewish Migration Since 1800*. Philadelphia: The Jewish Publication Society, 1949.

Wynn, Samuel. 'The Melbourne Kadimah', *Yiddishe Almanac 1937*, translated by M Lipkies.

Yablonka, Hanna. *The State of Israel vs Adolf Eichmann*. New York: Shocken Books, 2004.

Yiddish Melbourne. Faculty of Arts, Monash University. http://future.arts.monash.edu/yiddish-melbourne/.

The YIVO Encyclopedia of Jews in Eastern Europe. http://www.yivoencyclopedia.org/.

Zable, Arnold. *Café Scheherazade*. Melbourne: Text, 2001.

Zable, Arnold. 'Queen of the Yiddish Stage'. *Australian Jewish News*, 4 December 1998.

Zable, Arnold. *Wanderers and Dreamers: Tales of the David Herman Theatre*. Melbourne: Hyland House, 1998.

Zable, Arnold. *Scraps of Heaven*. Melbourne: Text, 2004.

INDEX

A Be Men Lebt (review) 200
A Night in the Old Marketplace (play) 293
A Zeyde Like No Other (Waislitz tribute) 293
Abrahams, Leslie 120
Abrahams, Rabbi Dr 193
Abrahamson, A. 271
Abzac, David 166, 171, 206
actors (Yiddish) 51–2, 57, 60, 62, 63, 248, 249, 253, 292
    Braizblatt, Abraham 52, 63
    Ginter, Nosn 62
    Ginter, Yankev 52, 60–2, 71, 77
    Grober, Chayele 251
    Holzer, Rachel 52, 58–9, 60, 78, 195
    Kaminska, Ida 251–2
    Levita, Rachel 63, 64, 210
    Melman, Meir 251
    Sher, Yasha *see* Sher, Yasha
    Turkow, Rosa 250–1
    Waislitz, Yankev *see* Waislitz, Yankev
    Weissberg, Shmuel 60
Adass Yisroel schools 264, 281
Advocate (Tasmania) 113
aftermath (WWII)
    Claims Conference 164
    displaced persons *see* displaced persons' camps (post WWII)
    Eichmann trial 269
    Harrison Report (1945) 136
    survivors *see* survivors (Holocaust)
Agudas Yisroel (Poland/Israel) 35, 43, 121

aid, welfare and fundraising (Jewish refugees) 50, 100–2, 117, 119–22, 128, 206
    Bialystoker Centre 183
    German Jewish Relief Fund 101–2
    international Jewish organisations 164–5
    Jewish Welfare *see* Australian Jewish Welfare and Relief Society (AJWRS); Australian Jewish Welfare Society
    Kadimah centre 183
    Lodzer Centre 185
    PJRF 100–1
    UJORF 100, 120–1, 162, 167
    Welcome Society *see* Welcome Society
    Yiddishist takeover 120–1, 162, 244
AJWRS *see* Australian Jewish Welfare and Relief Society (AJWRS)
Ajzenbud, Moshe 150, 246
Ajzner, Hania 147, 172–3, 223
Aleichem, Sholem 61, 62, 64, 66, 179, 200, 249, 251 *see also* Sholem Aleichem schools
    Scattered and Dispersed 61, 64
    Tevye the Milkman 61, 292
    tribute to 293
    Tzvay Hundert Toyzent 62, 249
Allied forces (WWII) 113, 117, 118, 131, 132, 135, 199
    Australian Imperial Force 123
    Jewish Brigade (British Army) 137

Royal Australian Air Force 123, 124
Royal Australian Navy 123
Altenburg (Germany) 13
Altman, Kitia 146, 173, 174
Altshul, David 69
America *see* United States
American Jewish Joint Distribution Committee (JDC) 121, 139, 164, 235
   established (1914) 105
Annaberg labour camp (Poland) 146
Ansky, S. 249
   The Dybbuk 54–5, 64
Anstey, Frank 31
antisemitism 201
   America 27–8, 135
   Australia 27, 30–3, 96–7
      post WWII 139–42, 156, 227, 228
   Britain 135, 139–40
   Canada 27–8
   displaced persons' camps 136
   Europe 8, 9, 11–12, 80, 81, 135, 230
   Germany 36, 134–5
   Holocaust *see* Holocaust
   pogroms *see* pogroms (Eastern Europe)
   Poland 12, 36–7, 90, 134
   post WWII 139–42
   Protocols of the Elders of Zion (book) 37
Arab-Israeli conflict *see* Six-Day War (1967); War of Independence (Arab-Israeli)
Argentina 25, 248, 253
As Long As We Are Alive (review) 200
Asch, Sholem 249
Ashkanasy, Maurice 87, 158, 159–60, 210

ECAJ 158, 159
Ashman, Aharon 206
Assembly Hall (Carlton) 189
Association of Victorian Jewish Youth 191, 272
At the Walls of Jerusalem (play) 251
Auschwitz concentration camp (Poland) 114, 133, 137, 146–7, 148, 172–3, 177, 239
Australia (a snapshot) *see also* Melbourne Jewry (a snapshot)
   1920s 9, 39–40
   1930s 32, 42, 91 *see also* immigration policy (pre WWII)
   1940s 167, 224, 231 *see also* immigration policy (post WWII)
   1950s 224–30, 233, 235, 259
   1960s 237–8, 240–1, 259–60
   1970s 240, 241
Australia (Jewish migration)
   1910-1939 50–3, 116
   antisemitism 27, 30–3, 96–7
      post WWII 139–42, 227, 228, 230
   census (1954) 161, 231
   census (1961) 237
   community building 42–5, 46–53, 178, 181 *see also landsmanshaftn*
   early Jewish community *see* first Australian Jews
   Holocaust survivors *see* survivors (Holocaust)
   immigration policy *see* immigration policy (post WWII); immigration policy (pre WWII)
   Jewish community, divided opinion 97–100

INDEX

post WWII *see* post WWII Jewish immigrants
Australian Club 32
Australian Imperial Force 123
   Employment Companies 124–5
   8th Company 124, 125
   Labour Corps 124, 125–6
   Royal Army Medical Corps 133
Australian Jewish Almanac (book) *see The Australian Yiddish Almanac* (book)
Australian Jewish Herald 16, 28–30, 69, 74, 118–19, 120, 199, 245
   established (1879) 68
   Nazi campaign in Europe 110, 111
   Yiddish supplement 30 *see also Di Yiddishe Post* (newspaper)
Australian Jewish News 69, 120, 154–5, 251, 273
   antisemitic incidents 135
   concentration camps 133–4
   displaced persons' camps 136
   Displaced Persons' Program 154–5
   Eichmann trial 269
   Israel, independence of 209, 211
   Israel Day Rally 214
   Six Day War (1967) 272, 273
Australian Jewish Welfare and Relief Society (AJWRS) 166, 168–9, 183, 187, 190, 217, 235, 237, 254
   aged-care homes 261–2
   establishment (1947) 162
   fundraising 164–5, 273
   sponsorship of survivors 162–4, 206
   Welfare House 169, 257
   Yiddishist control 162, 168, 244
Australian Jewish Welfare Society 51, 99, 101, 139
   Larino children's home 102, 122
   PJRF, disputes with 101
   response to Holocaust survivors 152, 154, 159, 161
   UJORF, merge with *see* Australian Jewish Welfare and Relief Society (AJWRS)
   welfare services 102, 122
   Women's Auxiliary 102
Australian Labor Party (ALP) 18, 31, 71, 217
   Chifley, Ben 160
   Chifley government *see* Chifley government
   Curtin (John) 118
   Melbourne Bund, alliance with 79, 80, 121–2
   Scullin government 19, 32
   Whitlam government 240
Australian Life (newspaper) 69
Australian Natives' Association 141
Australian Stock Exchange 32
Australian Women's Weekly (magazine) 225
Australian Zionist Youth Council 272
Austria
   Germany, annexation by 93
   Güssen concentration camp 147
   Kristallnacht pogrom (1938) 93, 94, 104
   Mauthausen concentration camp 147, 148
authors (Yiddish) *see* writers (Yiddish)

Baer, Herbert 32
Bain, Robert 103
Balaganeydn (cabaret) 294
Balberyszki, Mendl 170, 194, 195, 196, 217
Balberyszki, Theo 170–1

Balfour Declaration (1917) 48, 81
Baltic states *see* Estonia; Latvia; Lithuania
Bar-Cohen, Aaron 21
Baranovichi (Byelorussia) 146
Bartak, Adrian 261
Bay Nakht Oyfn Altn Mark (play) 293
Baymer Starbn Stayendik (play) 252
Beendorf concentration camp (Germany) 146
Begin, Menachem 214
Belzec concentration camp (Poland) 112
Ben Gurion, David 203, 209, 210
Bennett family
    Australia, migration to 53, 90, 104–6
    Moshe 90–1, 105
    Rachel 90, 91, 105
    Shmuel 34–5, 36, 46, 49, 51, 53, 90, 104–5, 180
Bergen Belsen concentration camp (Germany) 133, 134, 137, 146, 177
Bergner, Herz 49, 51, 53, 67, 101, 129, 246
    Between Sky and Sea 68
Bergner, Ruth 33
Bergner, Yosl 33, 67, 125, 129
Berk, Leon 146
Berkovitz, Rabbi 211
Berlin (Germany) 13, 149
Berlinski, Jacques 261
Berry, Walter 103–4
Betar (Zionist youth group) 202, 257
Beth Din (Jewish religious court) 86, 118
Beth Israel synagogue 88
Bevan, Ernest 205
Biale Podliaske *landsmanshaftn* 186
Bialik, Chaim Nachman 37
Bialik College 82, 149, 185, 212, 264

Bialkower, M. 184
Bialystok Lending Society 182
Bialystok (Poland) 5, 6, 13, 15, 16, 21, 51, 79, 103, 117, 150, 163, 195
    pogroms 92
Bialystoker Centre (St Kilda) 167, 169, 182–4, 200, 290
    community arbitration 183
    events and activities 183
    Peisach Kaplan Library 182–3, 200
    president 183
Bialystoker *landsmanshaft* 15, 139, 180, 182
    Bialystok Lending Society 182
    hostel 169, 182
Bielsk-Podlaski (Poland) 195
Birobidjan (Soviet Union) 77
Birstein, Yossel 126, 246
Bloustein, Lazer 77
B'nai B'rith 191, 273–4
B'nai B'rith Young Adults 272
Bnei Akiva (Zionist movement) 202
Boas, Isaac H. 56, 98
Boer War 81
Bogatin, Yacov 127
Bolshevik Revolution (1917) 31, 48, 155
Bolshevism 38, 78
Bono Wiener Collection 295
Borsky, Nuritt 174
Braizblatt, Abraham 52, 63
Brecht, Bertolt 252
Brenner, Dolf 261
Brest-Litovsk (Poland) 214
Brilliant, Simche (Samuel) 51, 87
    Kadimah 21
Britain
    antisemitism 135, 139–40, 205
    ICA 164
    immigration policy (1921) 38–9

INDEX

Jewish Brigade 137
Jewish insurgency 204
kehilot 43
British House of Commons 204, 205
British Jewry 4, 38
   Kindertransport 148
British Mandate of Palestine *see*
  Palestine (British Mandate)
British Union of Fascists 32
Brodie, Rabbi Israel 16, 26, 49
Brown, Chaim 115
Brown, Malcha 115, 130
Bruce, Lord (Stanley) 94
Bruce government 19
Brunswick Group 234
Brunswick (Melb)
   Jewish community 62, 127, 231, 234, 238
Buchara (Uzbekistan) 150
Buchenwald concentration camp (Germany) 134, 137
   Buchenwald boys 167
Bund/Bundists 8–9, 12, 13, 43, 51, 74–80, 206
   Australia, in *see* Melbourne Bund
   Communist faction 77–8
   doykeit (here and now) 9, 75–6, 80, 214–15, 268
   Folks Tsaytung 78
   GEZERD, participation in 77–8
   Israel, support for 215–16
   leaders 75, 77, 115, 151, 247
   new era (1950s-60s) 214–17
   origin 74–5, 291
   PJRF *see* Polish Jewish Relief Fund (PJRF)
   Poland, in 9, 18, 35, 75, 76, 79, 217
   reports about WWII 110–11
   schools (Eastern Europe) 76
   SKIF 151

   socialism *see* socialism/socialists
   World Coordinating Committee of Bund Organizations 217
   yiddishism *see* Yiddishism/Yiddishists
   youth groups
      SKIF 257, 258
      Tsukunft 76, 257
Burstin, Ben 15, 128
Burstin, Fayge 9, 12
Burstin, Sara 15
Burstin, Sender 3, 4, 5, 7, 68–9, 78, 88, 100, 117, 162, 230, 240
   Australia, early employment in 9–11
   Bund (Melbourne) 51, 77, 121–2, 216, 217, 267
   Bund (Poland) 9, 12, 76
   Kadimah 76, 196
   Poland, reasons for leaving 11–13, 18, 76
   Tsukunft 76
   union member 18–19
Burstin, Symche 150, 165, 195, 230
   SKIF Melbourne 257
business and employment 19, 91, 96, 231, 235
   Australian economy 121, 153, 235–6, 237, 259
   clothing, textiles and manufacturing 238–41, 290
   construction and property 239–41
   first Australian Jews 9–11, 40, 98, 102
   post WWII Jewish immigrants 225, 226, 227, 228–9, 231, 236–42
   unemployment 19, 91, 96, 225, 231

Café Lipski (Carlton) 3–4, 10, 13, 20
Café Scheherazade (St Kilda) 236–7
Calwell, Arthur 121–2, 141, 152–8, 159, 163
Camberwell House (hostel) 169, 170
Canada 25, 27, 72, 96, 253
    antisemitism 27–8
capitalism/capitalists 8, 18, 31, 75, 140
Caplan, Rachel 255
Carlton (Melb) 168, 169, 209
    Assembly Hall 189
    Café Lipski 3–4, 10, 13, 20
    early migrant groups 5–7, 22, 48, 53, 83
    Herzl Hall 84, 202
    Jewish community 230–1, 233, 263, 264
    Kadimah centre *see* Kadimah centre
    Royal Exhibition Building 192, 211
    school (Yiddish) *see* I.L. Peretz School
    Yiddishe Yidn 5–6, 7
Carlton Synagogue 86, 88, 101, 102, 118, 196, 210, 217, 233
Casona, Alejandro 252
Ceber, Reisel 168, 169
Central Yiddish School Organisation *see* CYSHO schools (Poland)
Charak, Danielle 147, 200–1, 261, 267
    Yiddish radio 261
Chasidic tradition 34, 43, 54
    The Dybbuk (play) 54–5, 64
Chavershaft (journal) 246, 266–7
Chelmer *landsmanshaft* 168, 169
Chifley, Ben 160
Chifley government 152, 159
    Calwell, Arthur 121–2, 141, 152–8, 159, 163

China 270
Chinese Exile (book) 149
choirs (Yiddish) 77
    I.L. Peretz School 199, 256
    Jewish Men's Choir 210, 261
    Mir Kumen On Yiddish choir 289–90
Churchill, Winston 38, 118
Claims Conference 164
Clarke, Marcus 30
Clarke, Sir Frank 97
Cohen, Lt-Col Harold 27
Cohen, Rabbi F.L. 97–8
Cohen, Sir Samuel 99
Cold War 230
commemorations (Holocaust) 213, 217, 248, 291
    Genia and Chaim Borensztajn Collection 295
    landsmanshaftn 193
    Lodz ghetto 186
    ownership of 189–92
    'The Republic of Memory' 187–93
    Warsaw ghetto 187, 188, 189, 190, 191, 256
    Yiddish then English, held in 188
Commonwealth Munitions (factory) 127
Communism/Communists (Aust) 78, 80, 140, 230, 284
    GEZERD 77–8
Communist Party (Aust) 17–18
    Bund faction 77–8
Concentration Camp Inmates 191
concentration camps (WWII) 156, 227 *see also* labour camps (WWII)
    Auschwitz (Poland) 114, 133, 137, 146–7, 148, 172–3, 177, 239
    Beendorf (Germany) 146

INDEX

Belzec (Poland) 112
Bergen Belsen (Germany) 133, 134, 137, 146, 177
Buchenwald (Germany) 134, 137, 167
Dachau (Germany) 147
Güssen (Austria) 147
liberation of 131, 133, 134, 136, 147
Majdanek (Poland) 146
Mauthausen (Austria) 147, 148
personal stories *see* survivors (Holocaust)
Ravensbruck (Germany) 146
Sobibor (Poland) 112
Stutthof (Poland) 146, 170
survivors *see* survivors (Holocaust)
Treblinka (Poland) 112, 133, 143–6, 172–3
Vajhingen (Germany) 147
congregations *see* synagogues
Contemporary Jewish Record (journal) 139
Counihan, Noel 67
Cracow (Poland) 16, 42, 58, 195
Cracower *landsmanshaftn* 180, 186
Croatia 111
Cullen, Major-General Paul Alfred 124
culture and identity (Yiddish) 55–6, 87, 257, 277, 287, 288
actors *see* actors (Yiddish)
choirs *see* choirs (Yiddish)
contentious issue, as 193–8
intertwined entity 5, 55–6, 89, 181, 200
Israel, and 188–9, 201
J. Waks Cultural Trust 289
Kadimah *see* Kadimah centre
Klezmania (folk group) 289

landsmanshaftn *see* *landsmanshaftn*
language *see* language (Yiddish)
plays *see* plays (Yiddish)
playwrights *see* playwrights (Yiddish)
poets *see* poets (Yiddish)
popular culture 288–91
'post-vernacular' age 288–9
SKIF Melbourne *see* SKIF (Melbourne)
theatre *see* theatre (Yiddish)
writers *see* writers (Yiddish)
Yiddishkeit see Yiddishkeit
Curtin (John) 118
Cykiert, Abraham 195, 246, 260
Yiddish radio 260
Cyrenia (ship) 170
CYSHO schools (Poland) 71, 78, 254
Czechoslovakia 95, 138, 148, 158
Czestochower (Poland) 143

Dachau concentration camp (Germany) 147
Dafner, Alex 250
SKIF Melbourne 290
Yiddish radio 261, 290
Dafner Family Yiddish Audio-Visual, Radio Collection 295
Daily Telegraph (UK) 110
Danglow, Rabbi Jacob 26, 29, 30, 85, 88, 91–2, 102, 118, 194, 207, 208
WWI and WWII 124
Darwin 112
David Herman Theatre 64, 199–200, 206, 249–50 *see also* Yiddishe Bine (theatre group)
Baymer Starbn Stayendik 252
final production (1992) 292
Goldfaden's Cholem 251

– 319 –

In Hartz fun Tel Aviv 292
Mirele Efros 252
Oyf di Moyrn fun Yerushalayim 251
Scenes from Sholem Aleichem 251
Tzvay Hundert Toyzent 249
Uncle Moses 251
Zing Mayn Folk 251
Davis, Haskiel 77
Davis, Moss 196
Davison, Frank Dalby 67
Death of a Salesman (play) 250
Declaration of Human Rights (UN) 160
Declaration of Independence 1948 (Israel) 202, 209, 210, 213
  celebrations 209–11
Department of Immigration 158, 160–1
  Heyes, Sir Tasman 160–1
  immigration policy (post WWII) *see* immigration policy (post WWII)
  immigration policy (pre WWII) *see* immigration policy (pre WWII)
  Lamidey, Noel 157
  Ministers
    Calwell, Arthur 121–2, 141, 152–8, 159, 163
    Holt, Harold 159, 160
Department of the Interior 104
der alter heym 34, 44, 46, 51, 53, 100, 128
Der Landsman (journal) 246
Derna (ship) 166
Di Kishefmacherin (play) 63
Di Yiddishe Nayes (newspaper) 69, 78, 79, 82, 100, 245, 246
  final issue (1995) 292
Di Yiddishe Post (newspaper) 199, 245

diaspora 3, 7, 25, 76, 96, 180, 181, 189, 215, 216, 247
  Israel, support for 218–19, 271
displaced persons' camps (post WWII) 135–7, 206
  antisemitism 136
  Lingen (Germany) 137
  Santa Maria di Bagna (Italy) 148
Displaced Persons Program 154–6
Divrei Eminah kindergarten 281–2
  expansion 282
Dorevitch, Rivke 240
doykeit (here and now) 9, 75–6, 80, 214–15, 268
Dyskin, Mr 132
Dyskin, Mrs 132

East Melbourne synagogue 85–6
Eastern European Jews
  Australia, migration to *see* Australia (Jewish migration)
  culture *see* culture and identity (Yiddish)
  der alter heym 34, 44, 46, 51, 53, 100, 128
  diaspora *see* diaspora
  kehile see kehile/kehilot
  language *see* language (Yiddish)
  self-reliance 7–8, 29, 42, 181–2, 226
  shtetl 17, 55, 215, 264, 277, 293, 297
  WWI, exodus during 37
  Yiddishkeit see Yiddishkeit
ECAJ *see* Executive Council of Australian Jewry (ECAJ)
education (Yiddish) 21, 48, 52, 55, 253–7
  schools *see* schools (Yiddish)
  teachers *see* teachers (Yiddish)
Edward VIII (King) 105

INDEX

Eichenbaum, A. 184
Eichmann trial 269
Einhorn, David 77
Einhorn, I. 184
Eisfelder, Horst 149
El Misr (ship) 169
Ellinson Brothers (factory) 127
Elsternwick (Melb)
   Holocaust Museum 192
   Jewish community 279
   Sholem Aleichem schools *see*
   Scholem Aleichem schools
Elwood Talmud Torah (school) 183
employment *see* business and employment
Endecja (Polish political party) 92
England *see* Britain
Epstein, Anna 287–8
Eretz Israel *see* Israel
Estonia 25, 138, 157, 170
Eureka Stockade 18
Evans, Bernard 191
Evian conference (1938) 94
Executive Council of Australian Jewry (ECAJ) 152, 155, 158, 159–60, 208, 272
   presidents 152, 158, 159
Ezra Association 119

Falk, Rabbi 122
Federal election (1929) 19
Federation of Australian Jewish Welfare Societies 163
Federation of Landsmanshaftn 185, 191
Federation of Polish Jewry 192
Felman, Jack 175, 176, 177, 197
Feniger, Saba 146, 192
Festival Hall (Melbourne) 214
Fiddler on the Roof (film/musical) 292
   see also Tevye the Milkman (play)

Financial Times (UK) 237
Fink, Leo 22, 80, 81, 103, 155, 195
   AJWRS 162
   Australia, migration to 13–16
   Jewish Welfare 51
   Kadimah 51, 84
   sponsorship of survivors 162–4
   UJORF 120–1, 206
   VJBD 244
Fink, Mina 80, 103, 106, 195
   Holocaust survivors 163–4
   meeting and resettlement 166–7, 192
   sponsorship of 163–4
Fink family 236
   Australia, migration to 13–16
   Jack 14
   Laibl 15
   Leo *see* Fink, Leo
   Masha 15
   Mina *see* Fink, Mina
   Mordechai 15
   Simche (Sid) 14
   Wolf 14, 120
   Zina 15
Firestone, Dr Andrew 294
first Australian Jews 21–2
   1881-1914 25, 181
   antisemitism 30–3
   blending in 22, 25–30
   convicts 24
   employment 9–11, 40, 98, 102
   free settlers 24
   intermarriage 29
   WWI, enlistment in 26–7, 41, 122
First World War 26–7, 31, 41, 57, 77, 81
   Australian Jewish enlistment 26–7, 41, 122
   Eastern European Jews, exodus of 37

pogroms *see* pogroms (Eastern Europe)
Fischer, Hans 166
Fitzpatrick, Brian 67
Flicker, Ursula 192
Fogel, Raizl 278, 281, 282
Folks Tsaytung (newspaper) 78
Folkspartei (Polish political party) 43
Footsteps in New York group (transition from Haredi) 297
Forward in Montreal group (transition from Haredi) 297
France 27, 111, 124, 137, 257, 270
  kehilot 43
Frances Barkman Home (hostel) 170
Frankfurter, Felix 115–16
Freedman, Leon 211, 213, 214
Freedman, Moses 10
Freedman, Rabbi Dr 120
Freedman, Shirley 127
Freemasonry 25–6
Freiberg, Freda 15–16
Friede, Anush 169
Friedman, Joel 278, 281, 283
Friendship (journal) 246, 266–7
Froy Advocate (play) 59
Frydman, B. 120
Frydman, Lew 246
fundraising
  Israel, for 182, 185, 268
    Six-Day War (1967) 273–4
  Jewish refugees *see* aid, welfare and fundraising (Jewish refugees)

Galatz (Romania) 13
Gawenda, Annie 176, 177, 274
Gawenda, Michael 195, 267
Gebirtig, Mordechai 93
General Jewish Workers Union in Russia and Poland *see* Bund/Bundists
Genia and Chaim Borensztajn Collection 295
George V (King) 27, 32
German Jewish Relief Fund 101–2
Germany 148, 227
  antisemitism 36, 134–5
  Beendorf concentration camp 146
  Bergen Belsen concentration camp 133, 134, 137, 146, 177
  Buchenwald concentration camp 134, 137, 167
  Dachau concentration camp 147
  Holocaust *see* Holocaust
  Kristallnacht pogrom (1938) 93, 94, 104
  Nazis *see* Nazis
  Ravensbruck concentration camp 146
  Russo-German war (1941-5) 111, 150
  Vajhingen concentration camp 147
  WWII *see* Second World War
Gesher group (transition from Haredi) 297
GEZERD *see* Society for the Establishment of a Rural Jewish Community (GEZERD)
'Ghetto Cabaret: A Night to Remember' 294
ghettos (Holocaust) 83, 111, 122, 129, 184, 187, 189, 215, 257, 278
  commemorations *see* commemorations (Holocaust)
  Lodz (Poland) 146, 147, 148, 186
  Shanghai 148–9
  Vilna (Lithuania) 148, 170
  Warsaw *see* Warsaw ghetto
Gilbert and Sullivan 56
  Mikado 29

INDEX

Giligich, Joseph 52, 78, 120, 129, 195, 196
  I.L. Peretz School 70–3, 199, 254, 265
Giligich Foundation 295
Ginter, Jacob 120
Ginter, Nosn 62
Ginter, Yankev 52, 60–2, 71, 77
  see also Yiddishe Bine (theatre group)
Goffin, Mary 127
Gold Medal (Australian Literature Society) 68
Goldberg, Abe 285
Goldberg, Cesia 285
Goldfaden, Abraham 199, 250, 251
  Di Kishefmacherin 63
Goldfaden's Cholem (play) 251
Goldfaden's Dream (play) 251
Goldhar, Pinchas 49–50, 51, 63, 66–8, 69, 73, 101, 129, 195, 246, 294
  The Australian Yiddish Almanac 66, 129, 246
  collected stories 66, 294
Goldman, Leon 256
Gomplewicz, S. 185
Gordin, Jacob 60, 62, 199, 250
  Mirele Efros 252
  The Slaughter 61
Gorman, E. (KC) 87
Gotlib, Mr 169
Great Depression 9, 31, 42, 49, 91, 167, 231
Great Synagogue (Sydney) 97, 122
Great War see First World War
Greenberg, Helen 285, 286
Grober, Chayele 251
  Oyf Fridlecher Erd 251
Grodski, Leon 6
Grodzenski, Wolf 77
Gryfenberg, Nachman 195, 266, 267

Melbourne Bund 267
gulags (Soviet Union) 150, 151, 169
  see also labour camps (WWII)
Gullet, H.B. 141
Gurewicz, Rabbi Joseph 102, 118, 210
Gurvis, Ida 168
Güssen concentration camp (Austria) 147

Haberfeld, Lusia 146
Habonim (Zionist youth group) 202, 257, 273
Haganah resistance (Palestine) 203
Hain, Taibella see Schwartz, Tess
Hallenstein, Lucy 41
Haredi community (Melb) 278–83, 296
  characteristics 279–80
  kindergarten see Divrei Eminah kindergarten
  matchmaking 282–3
  Pathways group (transition from Haredi) 297
  women/girls 279, 280, 281–2
Haredim
  emergence of 278—279
  matchmaking 282–3
  population 296–7
  transition from 297
Harrison, B. 120
Harrison Report (1945) 136
Hartman, Cyla 169, 233
Haskalah (Jewish Enlightenment) 194
Hatkhia (Zionist movement) 48
Hausner, Gideon 269
Hawaii 113
Haylen, Leslie 141–2
Hazomir Choir see Jewish Men's Choir

Hebrew Immigration Aid Society
  (HIAS) (US) 139, 157, 164
  established (1881) 105
Hebrew Standard of Australasia 110
here and now *(doykeit)* 9, 75–6, 80,
  214–15, 268
Here You Are and Don't Cry (review)
  200
Herzl, Theodor 80–1, 82, 211
Herzl Hall (Carlton) 84, 202
Heyes, Sir Tasman 160–1
HIAS *see* Hebrew Immigration Aid
  Society (HIAS) (US)
HIAS House (hostel) 169, 170
Hildebrand, Abraham 77
Hildebrand, Manye 77
Hilfsfond house (hostel) 170
Hiller, Maurice 120
Hirshbein, Esther Shumiatcher 47
Hirshbein, Peretz 47, 200
Hitler (Adolf) 97, 103, 116, 134,
  176, 212, 227, 270, 297
Holocaust
  Australian response to *see*
    immigration policy (post
    WWII); response to Holocaust
    (Melb Jewry)
  commemorations *see*
    commemorations (Holocaust)
  concentration camps *see*
    concentration camps (WWII)
  Einsatzgruppen (mobile death
    squads) 146
  Final Solution 112
  ghettos *see* ghettos (Holocaust)
  Jewish resistance 93, 147, 189
  labour camps *see* labour camps
    (WWII)
  reports about *see* reports about
    WWII
  survivors *see* survivors (Holocaust)
Holocaust Museum and Research
  Centre (Elsternwick) 192, 285, 290
  *Mameloshn: How Yiddish made a
    home in Melbourne* 287
Holt, Harold 159, 160
Holzer, Rachel 52, 58–9, 60, 78, 195
Honig, Yehuda 51, 120
  Kadimah 82
Hornstein, Sonia 168, 169
Horowicz, B. 184
Horowitz, Isaac 129
hostels 3, 164, 167–71, 254
  Bialystoker *landsmanshaft* 169, 182
  Frances Barkman Home 170
  HIAS/Camberwell House 169,
    170
  Hilfsfond house 170
  Radomer *landsmanshaftn* 169
  Warsaw Jewish Centre 169
House and Garden (magazine) 225
Hungary 111, 114, 115, 119, 138,
  158, 159, 279
Hurwitz, Isaac 21
Hutton, George 58–9
Hwa Lien (ship) 155

I Can Jump Puddles (book) 49
ICA *see* Jewish Colonisation
  Association (ICA) (UK)
I.L. Peretz School 51, 183, 185,
  254–5, 256–7, 284
  enrolments 254, 265
  establishment 33, 70–3, 199
  kindergarten 149, 199, 254, 265
  Sholem Aleichem School,
    absorbed into 265, 292
immigration policy (post WWII)
  152–61, 235, 237
  Chifley government 152–8
    Calwell, Arthur 121–2, 141,
      152–8, 159, 163

INDEX

political backlash 156–8
Displaced Persons Program 154–6
Iron Curtain embargo 158, 159
Jewish discrimination 153, 154, 156–8, 159–61
Menzies government 159
 Holt, Harold 159, 160
sponsorship *see* sponsorship
immigration policy (pre WWII) 1938-1939 94–7, 103
Calwell, Arthur 121–2
capital/financial support 40, 91, 96, 103, 104, 236
chain migration 13–16, 106, 152, 154, 158, 182
Department of the Interior 104
Evian conference 94
landsmanshaft see chain migration *above*
post WWII *see* immigration policy (post WWII)
Prime Minister's Department 38–9
relatives *see* chain migration *above*
1920s-30s 38–41, 91–2
sponsorship *see* sponsorship
White Australia policy 39
In Hartz fun Tel Aviv (play) 292
'In the City of Slaughter' (poem) 37
In the Heart of Tel Aviv (play) 292
India 270
international newspapers
 Jewish Telegraphic Agency 110
 reports about WWII 110–11, 112
International Refugee Organisation 157, 158
Irgun resistance (Palestine) 203, 204–5, 214

Isaacs, Isaac (later Sir) 27, 28, 32, 207
Isaacson, M. 120
Isaacson, Major Isidor 81
Israel 9, 25, 80, 201, 206, 247, 253
 Arab–Israeli conflict *see* War of Independence (Arab-Israeli)
 Begin, Menachem 214
 Ben Gurion, David 203, 209, 210
 Bund support for 215–16
 Declaration of Independence (1948) 202, 213
 celebrations 209–11
 Hebrew, revival of 215
 Herzl, Theodor 80–1, 82, 211
 International Choral Festival 261
 Kol Israel (radio station) 209
 Proclamation of Independence (1948) 209
 Sharett, Moshe 213, 233
 Six-Day War *see* Six-Day War (1967)
 What do you think of Israel? 218–19, 244
 Yiddishists in 215
'It is burning' (poem) 93, 294
Italy 137, 139, 148, 197
 kehilot 43
Ivriah Hebrew school 82
Ivriah Society (Palestine) 82

J. Waks Cultural Trust 289
J-Air (Jewish Australia Internet Radio) 290
Jabotinsky, Ze'ev 82, 202
Japan 240
 Darwin, bombing of 112
 Shanghai, occupation of 148
JDC *see* American Jewish Joint Distribution Committee (JDC)
Jedwab, Lou 130–1

Jerusalem (Palestine) 204, 269, 273
Jerusalem Post 110
Jew with a Violin (film) 200
Jewish Agency (Palestine) 121, 137, 203, 204
    King David Hotel, bomb attack on 204
Jewish Australia Internet Radio (J-Air) 290
Jewish Board of Deputies *see* Victorian Jewish Board of Deputies (VJBD)
Jewish Brigade (British Army) 137
Jewish Chronicle (UK) 110
Jewish Colonisation Association (ICA) (UK) 164
Jewish Community Council 237
Jewish Council to Combat Fascism and Antisemitism 230
Jewish Cultural Centre and National Library "Kadimah" *see* Kadimah centre
Jewish Frontier (US) 110
Jewish Herald see Australian Jewish Herald
Jewish Herald Special Service 111
Jewish homeland *see* Israel
Jewish Labor Committee (US) 122
Jewish Labour Movement (Poland) 133
Jewish Men's Choir 210, 261
Jewish nationalist movements
    Bund *see* Bund/Bundists
    Zionism *see* Zionism
Jewish newspapers (Aust) *see also* Yiddish newspapers (Aust)
    Australian Jewish Herald see Australian Jewish Herald
    Australian Jewish News see Australian Jewish News
    Hebrew Standard of Australasia 110

Melbourne Chronicle 246
    reports about WWII 109–10, 111
Jewish People's Relief Fund *see* United Jewish Overseas Relief Fund (UJORF)
Jewish Philanthropic Society 119
Jewish political party *see* Bund/Bundists
'Jewish Queen Lear' (play) 252
Jewish state *see* Israel
Jewish Students Societies 272
Jewish Telegraphic Agency 110
Jewish Welfare *see* Australian Jewish Welfare and Relief Society (AJWRS); Australian Jewish Welfare Society
Jewish Women's Guild 119
Jewish Young People's Association 86
Jewish Youth Council 119
Johan de Witt (ship) 155, 156
Johnston, George 260
    The Australians 260
Joint, the *see* American Jewish Joint Distribution Committee (JDC)
Jona, Dr Leon 84
Judean League (1923) 86–7, 88, 89
Judean Red Cross 119
Junior Auxiliary (Jewish Women's Guild) 119

Kadimah centre 46–53, 63, 77, 83, 84, 87, 88, 99–100
    annual reports 50, 190, 248
    Balaganeydn (cabaret) 294
    Carlton, move to (1932) 49
    conflicting ideologies *see* old versus new
    cultural hub, as *see* events and actvities *below*
    Elsternwick, move to (1967) 264

INDEX

establishment (1911) 46
events and activities 20–1,
  48–9, 50, 60–1, 63, 86, 128–30,
  199–200, 247–8, 293–4 *see also*
  Kadimah Hall
'Ghetto Cabaret: A Night to
  Remember' 294
hall *see* Kadimah Hall
Hatkhia, amalgamation with 48
I.L. Peretz School *see* I.L. Peretz
  School
Ladies' Auxiliary 119, 183
lebedike tsaytung 117, 212
membership 50, 128, 200, 248,
  262
new millenium, in the 292–6
politics and ideology 83, 87,
  88–9, 206
  Yiddishist control 47–8, 244
post WWII 247–8
presidents 21, 41, 47, 51, 76, 82,
  84, 290
response to Holocaust 117, 119,
  129, 130–1
'S'brent,' production of 93, 294
War of Independence (Arab-
  Israeli) 212
Welcome Society *see* Welcome
  Society
Kadimah Drama Circle 61
Kadimah Hall 49, 63, 64, 71, 77,
  184, 189, 210, 247, 248, 258
  Yiddish plays 199–200
Kadimah National Library 20, 46,
  47, 50, 68, 182–3, 193–4, 247, 262,
  294–6
  Bono Wiener Collection 295
  Dafner Family Collection 295
  Genia and Chaim Borensztajn
    Collection 295
  Jewish chidren's library 200

  Moishe Rabinowicz Centre 295
  Yasha Sher Reading Room 295
Kadimah Yiddish Radio Show 290
Kadimah Younger Set 48–9, 130
Kadimah Youth Organisation 130
Kahn, Yitzhak 51, 117, 246
Kalinski, Tomi 290, 292, 298
Kalisz (Poland) 16
Kaliszer *landsmanshaftn* 180
Kalman, Rachel 295
Kalus, S 185
Kalushyner, Baruch 261
Kaluszyner, Boruch 151
Kamenka, Eugene 156
Kaminska, Ester Rachel 252
Kaminska, Ida 251–2
Kaminska-Turkow, Ruth 251
Kaminski, Abraham Izaak 252
Karski, Jan 115–16
Katz, Dovid 297
Kazakhstan 151, 168, 256
  kolhoz (collective) 151
  labour camp 151
kehile/kehilot 42–5
  Australia, in 44–5, 46, 87, 181,
    232, 279
Keren Hayesod (Zionist fundraising)
  205
Keren Kayemeth (eco group) 183
Kersh, Yehuda 186
Keysor, Leonard 27
King David Hotel (Jerusalem) 204
Kipen, Israel 149, 240–1
Kiryat Bialystok (Israel) 183
Klezmania (folk group) 289
Kol Israel (radio station) 209
Kol Nidre 17
Kolt, Hymie 126, 194
Kovna (Lithuania) 79
Kowadlo, Ezra 202
Kremer, Arkady 75

Krongold, Henry 238
  UIA 274
Kronhill, Jacob 149, 195, 196, 217, 236
Kronhill Visiting Scholar in Yiddish Culture 286
Krynki (Poland) 21
Krystal, Cluwa 149, 195, 254

labour camps (WWII) *see also* concentration camps (WWII)
  Annaberg (Poland) 146
  Estonia 170
  gulags *see* gulags (Soviet Union)
  Kazakhstan 151
  Latvia 170
Labour Day parade 18
Ladies' Group (UJORF) 121, 167
Lady Lawyer (play) 59
Lamidey, Noel 157
Landau, David 147–8
Landau, Luba 147–8
landsmanshaftn 4, 106, 168, 169, 180–7, 206, 244, 246, 262, 268, 274
  Biale Podliaske 186
  Bialystoker *see* Bialystoker *landsmanshaft*
  Chelmer 168, 169
  Cracower 180
  Der Landsman (journal) 246
  Federation of Landsmanshaftn 185, 191
  Holocaust commemorations 193
  hostels *see* hostels
  Kaliszer 180, 186
  Lensziter 186
  Lodzer 184, 185, 186
  Lomzer 186
  Radomer *see* Radomer *landsmanshaftn*
  Vilner 186
  Warsawer 180, 186
  Zaglembie 186
  Zelichover 186
Lang, J.T. 141
language (Hebrew) 29, 56, 241, 257
  Hebrew *v* Yiddish 47–8, 71–2, 82–4, 188, 193–4, 215, 264, 299
  Ivriah Society (Palestine) 82
  schools *see* schools (Hebrew)
language (Yiddish) 46, 49, 56, 73, 76, 78, 82, 276–99 *see also* Yiddishism/Yiddishists
  Bund *see* Melbourne Bund
  commemorations (Holocaust) 188
  community surveys 276–7, 280, 283, 288
  demographics 283–4, 288–9
  endangered list (UNESCO) 276, 296
  fight for 193–8
    English *v* Yiddish 193–4, 196
    Hebrew *v* Yiddish 47–8, 50, 71–2, 82–4, 188, 194, 215, 264, 299
  future of 296–9
  Haredi community *see* Haredi community (Melb)
  identity, intertwined with 5, 55, 67, 76, 83, 181, 194, 257, 286–7
  libraries *see* Kadimah National Library; Peisach Kaplan Library
  Litvish (Lithuanian) 57
  newspapers *see* Yiddish newspapers (Aust); Yiddish newspapers (Poland)
  playwrights *see* playwrights (Yiddish)
  poets *see* poets (Yiddish)
  popular culture based on 288–91

– 328 –

INDEX

post-Holocaust era 286–8
'post-vernacular' age 288–9
post WWII immigrants 244
regional differences 180–1
    Litvish 57, 181
Ringelblum family 283–4
schools *see* schools (Yiddish)
Sof Vokh Oystralye (retreat) 291
theatre *see* theatre (Yiddish)
VCE subject 286, 290
writers *see* writers (Yiddish)
Yiddish Vokh 284
Larino children's home 102, 122
Latvia 63, 72, 150, 157
Laufer, Esther *see* Rosenberg, Esther
Lawson, Henry 30, 67
League of Rights 32
lebedike tsaytung (living newspaper) 117, 212
Lebns Fragn (journal) 215
Lederman, Arnold 239
Lederman, J. 100
Lederman, JH. 120
Lehi resistance (Palestine) 203, 204
Leivik. H 65
Lensziter *landsmanshaft* 186
Levita, Rachel 63, 64, 210
Lewin, I.M. 246
Liberal Party 224
    Menzies, Robert *see* Menzies, Robert
    Menzies government *see* Menzies government
Liberman, Chaim 238
Liberman, Jack 238
Liberman, Serge 178, 223
Life's questions (journal) 215
Lindsay, Norman 30
Lippmann, Walter 103, 120
    Jewish Welfare 261, 262
Lippmann family

    Australia, migration to 103–4
    Franz 103, 104
    Walter *see* Lippmann, Walter
Lipski, Ezra 3, 4 *see also* Café Lipski (Carlton)
Lipski, Sam 115, 130, 132, 190, 209, 212, 214, 227, 245
literature (Yiddish) 5, 48, 51, 52, 55, 71, 73, 76, 247, 248, 256, 266, 287, 292
    Australia, in 60, 65–8, 70 *see also* publications (Yiddish)
    writers *see* writers (Yiddish)
    YIVO institute (Vilna) 5
Lithuania 5, 72, 111, 157, 195, 240
see also individual towns
    Litvish Yiddish 57, 181
    Sugihara, rescue of Jews by 240
    Vilna ghetto 148, 170
Lithuanian Newspaper 110
living newspaper 117, 212
Lodge of Judah 26
Lodz (Poland) 5, 15, 16, 21, 47, 52, 60, 151, 185, 195, 253, 294
    ghetto 146, 147, 148, 186
    Peretz Yiddish School 290
Lodzer Centre 184–6, 196, 217, 233
    events and activities 185, 186
    financial assistance 185
    fundraising 185
    immigration assistance 185–6
Lodzer *landsmanshaft* 15, 180, 181, 184–5, 186
    Israel, in 185
Lomza (Poland) 63
Lomzer *landsmanshaft* 186
Lublin (Poland) 16, 195, 236
Lyons government 92
Mail (Adelaide) 113
Majdanek concentration camp (Poland) 146

Makow (Poland) 17
    Jewish population 5
Malkin, Dov Ber 248
Manger, Itzik 200, 250
    Megillah Lider 250
    The Witch 63
Manila (Philippines) 155
Mann, Leon 116, 127, 132
Manpower Australia 126
Margolin, Lt-Col Eliezer 27
Marks, Eva 150
Marshall, Alan 49, 67
    I Can Jump Puddles 49
Masel, Alec 89, 120, 152, 155
Mauthausen concentration camp (Austria) 147, 148
Mavar group (transition from Haredi) 297
McEwen, John 96
McPherson, William 103–4
Meadows, Julie 114–15, 124, 126
Medding, Peter 218, 219, 237, 241, 244
Megillah Lider (poetry) 250
Melbourne Bund 74–80, 81, 87, 183
    ALP, alliance with 79, 80, 121–2, 217
    decline of 267
    doykeit (here and now) 9, 75–6, 80, 214–15, 268
    establishment 76–7
    GEZERD, participation in 77–8
    Israel, support for 216, 274
    Kadimah *see* Kadimah centre
    leaders 267, 291
    response to Holocaust 116, 117, 121–2, 130
    Unzer Gedank 216, 246, 291
    Yiddish, preservation of *see* language (Yiddish)
    youth group *see* SKIF (Melbourne)
    Zionists v anti-Zionists 205–9, 216–17
Melbourne Chronicle 246
Melbourne Club 32
Melbourne Exhibition Building
    see Royal Exhibition Building (Carlton)
Melbourne Friends of Jerusalem's Hebrew University 84
Melbourne Hebrew Congregation
    see Melbourne Synagogue
Melbourne International Film Festival 260–71
Melbourne Jewish Advisory Board 85–6, 87, 88–9, 118 *see also* Victorian Jewish Advisory Board
    establishment (1921) 85–6
Melbourne Jewry
    Annual Independence Day 213–14
    communities *see* Melbourne Jewry (demographics)
    Haredi community *see* Haredi community (Melb)
    old *v* new *see* old *versus* new
    response to Holocaust *see* response to Holocaust (Melb Jewry)
    What do you think of Israel? 218–19, 244
        Six Day War *see* Six-Day War (1967)
    Zionists *v* Anti-Zionists 205–9, 216–17
Melbourne Jewry (a snapshot) *see also* Australia (a snapshot)
    1920s 5–7, 16, 23–4, 41, 44–5, 60–1, 69, 81–2, 85–6, 89, 245
    1930s 44–5, 52–3, 59, 60, 63, 68, 69, 70, 84, 89, 98, 245
    1940s 128, 199, 202, 232

INDEX

1950s 161, 186, 190, 198, 224, 226, 230–4, 243–4, 248, 250–3, 254–5, 259
1960s 192, 214, 230–2, 240–2, 246–7, 248, 250, 253, 259–68
1970s 192, 240–1, 242, 246–7, 250, 253, 261
1980s 187, 239, 260, 267
Melbourne Jewry (demographics)
  British born 6, 8, 24, 25, 122
  Carlton *see* Carlton (Melb)
  community surveys 276–7, 280, 283, 288
  immigration patterns 243–4
  northern suburbs 231–2, 238, 263 *see also* Brunswick (Melb); Moonee Ponds (Melb); Northcote (Melb); Thornbury (Melb)
  south-eastern suburbs 84, 191, 231, 255, 263–4, 265, 279 *see also* Elsternwick (Melb)
  statistics 28, 34, 128, 161, 189, 211, 213, 230, 243–4, 263–4
Melbourne Punch 31
Melbourne Synagogue 49, 85–6, 118, 119
  Bourke Street 17
Melbourne Town Hall 189, 190
Melbourne Yiddish Youth Theatre (MYYT) 250
Melburner Bleter (periodical) 246
Melman, Meir 251
memorials *see* commemorations (Holocaust)
Mendelssohn, Moses (1729-86) 194
Menzies, Robert 123, 124
  vision for Australia 224–5, 226
Menzies government 159
  Holt, Harold 159, 160
Michaelis, Archie 119, 122, 123, 207–8
Migdalek, Shmuel 147
Mikado (opera) 29
Mikhalevich, Beynish 77
Minister for Immigration *see* Calwell, Arthur; Holt, Harold
Minkowski, Chaja 92
Minkowski, Josek 92
Mir Kumen On Yiddish choir 289–90
Mirele Efros (play) 252
Mizrahi (political party) 43, 183
Mo' McCackie (stage character) 31
Moishe Rabinowicz Centre 295
Mokotow, Fay 250
Mokotow, Grisha 171
Mokotow, Mr and Mrs 171
Monash, General Sir John 27, 29, 31–2, 81
Monash University 272
  Kronhill Visiting Scholar in Yiddish Culture 286
  Yiddish program 286
Monson, Ronald 133
Moonee Ponds Jewish Centre 234
Moonee Ponds (Melb)
  Jewish Centre 234
  Jewish community 231
Morawetz, Paul 120, 152, 155
Moriah (school) 264
Mosley, Sir Oswald 32
Mother Courage and Her Children (play) 252
Mount Scopus College 185, 191, 237, 264
  Yiddish classes 196–7
Mrocki, Chana 261
Mrocki, Freydi 289, 292, 298
Munz, Hirsh 21, 67, 129
Mushin, Alec 120
MYYT *see* Melbourne Yiddish Youth Theatre (MYYT)

Nadir un Vayn Nisht (review) 200
Nasser, President 270
National Council of Jewish Women 98, 119, 183
National Origins Immigration (Johnson-Reed) Act 1924 (US) 12–13
Nazis 87, 103, 109 *see also* Hitler (Adolf); Second World War
    concentration camps *see* concentration camps (WWII)
    Einsatzgruppen (mobile death squads) 146
    Holocaust *see* Holocaust
    Kristallnacht pogrom (1938) 93, 94, 104
    Poland, campaign in 35, 110–12, 113, 114
Netanya (Palestine) 205
Netherlands 137
    kehilot 43
New York Post 110
New Zealand 84, 96, 272
New Zionist Organization 121
Newmark, Aaron 21
newspapers
    Hebrew Standard of Australasia 110
    international *see* international newspapers
    reports about WWII *see* reports about WWII
    Yiddish *see* Yiddish newspapers (Aust); Yiddish newspapers (Poland)
Niagara (ship) 104
Nirens, Aron 195, 240
North Judean League 119
Northcote Jewish Centre 233–4
Northcote (Melb)
    Jewish Centre 233–4
    Jewish community 231–2, 233, 238
Nusbaum, Motl 184

O'Connor, Vic 67
Oderberg, I.D. 84
Oifboy (journal) 246
Okno, Jewel 120
old *versus* new 200–1
    AJWRS, Yiddishist takeover of 162
    anti-Zionists *v* Zionists 205, 207, 209 *see also* Israel
    community leadership, struggle for 85–9
    establishment *v* Yiddishism 21–2, 24, 45, 55–7, 68–9, 72, 99, 116, 190, 263
Oliver, Moishe 77
On Peaceful Soil (play) 251
On the Cymbal (review) 200
Opatoshu, Joseph 65
Open Forum Group 130–1
Orwell, George 139–40
Oshlack, S. 120
OT-OZE *see* Union of Jewish Health Organisations (OT-OZE)
Otranto (ship) 90
Our Land (play) 206
Our little town is burning (song) 93
Our Thoughts (journal) 216, 246
Oyf di Moyrn fun Yerushalayim (play) 251
Oyf Fridlecher Erd (play) 251
Oyfn Tzimbl (review) 200
Oystralyer Lebn (newspaper) 69

Palais de Danse (St Kilda) 128
Palais Theatre (St Kilda) 252
Palestine (British Mandate) 13, 35, 37, 81–2, 83, 90, 116, 118, 202–9

INDEX

Arab-Israeli conflict *see* War of Independence (Arab-Israeli)
Balfour Declaration (1917) 48, 81
Ivriah Society 82
Jewish Agency 121, 137, 203, 204
Jewish insurgency 203–5, 207, 208
Jewish migration to 37, 81–2, 91, 203, 208
Jewish resistance groups
   Haganah 203
   Irgun 203, 204–5, 214
   Lehi 203, 204
official languages 83
UN partition resolution (1947) 205, 210
Yishuv community 203, 216
Palmer, Nettie 67
Palmer, Vance 67
Parasol, Kalman 202
Paris (France) 110, 178, 224, 235
   International Festival of Drama 252
Pat, Jacob 247
Pathways group (transition from Haredi) 297
Patkin, Aron 20–1, 51, 77, 78, 120
   Kadimah 21
Peisach Kaplan Library 182–3, 200
People's Newspaper 78
Peretz, Itzhak Leib 179, 249, 292, 293 *see also* I.L. Peretz School
Perlstein, Gedalia 202
Petrov spy affair 230
Picon, Molly 200
Pinski, David 61
   Yankl the Blacksmith 61
Pitt, Michael (Pitkowski) 15, 51
   Bialystoker Centre 183–4
PJRF *see* Polish Jewish Relief Fund (PJRF)

plays (Yiddish)
   Bay Nakht Oyfn Altn Mark 293
   Baymer Starbn Stayendik 252
   A Be Men Lebt 200
   Di Kishefmacherin 63
   Froy Advocate 59
   Goldfaden's Cholem 251
   In Hartz fun Tel Aviv 292
   Mirele Efros 252
   Nadir un Vayn Nisht 200
   Oyf di Moyrn fun Yerushalayim 251
   Oyf Fridlecher Erd 251
   Oyfn Tzimbl 200
   Scenes from Sholem Aleichem 251
   The Slaughter 61
   Tevye the Milkman 61, 292
   The Dybbuk 54–5, 64
   The Yellow Patch 62
   Tzvay Hundert Toyzent 62, 249
   Uncle Moses 251
   Unzer Erd 206
   Yankl the Blacksmith 61
   Zing Mayn Folk 251
playwrights (Hebrew)
   Ashman, Aharon 206
playwrights (Yiddish) 62, 249–50
   Aleichem, Sholem *see* Aleichem, Sholem
   Ansky, S. 54, 64, 249
   Asch, Sholem 249
   Goldfaden, Abraham *see* Goldfaden, Abraham
   Gordin, Jacob *see* Gordin, Jacob
   Peretz, Itzhak Leib *see* Peretz, Itzhak Leib
   Pinski, David 61
   Singer, Isaac Bashevis 250, 299
Poale Zion (Zionist group) 35, 43, 111, 183
poets (Yiddish) 245, 246, 253, 256, 287, 292

Birstein, Yossel 126, 246
Cykiert, Abraham 195, 246, 260
Einhorn, David 77
Gebirtig, Mordechai 93
Hirshbein, Esther Shumiatcher 47
Manger, Itzik *see* Manger, Itzik
Rosenberg, Jacob 148, 165, 176, 188, 193, 195, 229, 246
Shtern, Yisroel 294
pogroms (Eastern Europe) 37, 105, 180 *see also* Holocaust
   Kristallnacht (1938) 93, 94, 104
   Poland *see* Poland (pogroms)
   Russia *see* Russia (pogroms)
   Ukraine (1920) 8, 30
   WWI 37
Poland 5, 10, 100, 122, 138, 158, 195, 227 *see also* individual towns
   Annaberg labour camp 146
   antisemitism 12, 36–7
   Auschwitz concentration camp 114, 133, 137, 146–7, 148, 172–3, 177, 239
   Belzec concentration camp 112
   Bund *see* Bund/Bundists
   Catholic Church 93
   der alter heym 34, 44, 46, 51, 53, 100, 128
   Endecja (political party) 92
   kehile 43, 44
   kehilot 42–5
   Majdanek concentration camp 146
   Nazi campaign in 110–12, 118–19, 151
   pogroms *see* Poland (pogroms)
   pre-WWII Jewish population 150
   Second Republic 43
   Sobibor concentration camp 112
   Stutthof concentration camp 146, 170
   Treblinka concentration camp 112, 133, 143–6, 172–3
Poland (pogroms)
   1935/36, in 92–3
   Bialystok region 92
   Kielce (1946) 134
   Przytyk (1936) 92–3, 104–5
Polish Jewish Relief Fund (PJRF) 100–1, 102
   Welfare Society, disputes with 101
Polish Relief Society *see* Polish Jewish Relief Fund (PJRF)
Polish Youth Migrant Fund 122
Portnoy, Henry 261
Pose, Harry 127
post WWII Jewish immigrants
   assimilation 142, 154, 201, 226
   communities *see* Melbourne Jewry (demographics)
   employment and prosperity 225, 226, 227, 228–9, 231, 236–42
   home and family 223–4, 225–6, 234, 241
Pras Court (St Kilda) 263
press (Jewish) 10, 109–11, 112, 117, 119, 133, 135, 190, 251
   Australia, in *see Australian Jewish Herald*; *Australian Jewish News*
press (Yiddish)
   newspapers *see* Yiddish newspapers (Aust); Yiddish newspapers (Poland)
   Poland, in 65–6, 68
Prime Minister's Department 38–9
Princess Theatre (Melb) 55
Proclamation of Independence 1948 (Israel) 209
Protocols of the Elders of Zion (book) 37

INDEX

publications (Yiddish) 55, 60, 244–7, 284
   The Australian Yiddish Almanac 66, 129, 246
   beginnings 68–70
   Der Landsman (journal) 246
   growth of 244–7
   Lebns Frag (journal) 215
   Melburner Bleter (periodical) 246
   newspapers *see* Yiddish newspapers (Aust)
   Oifboy/Reconstruction (journal) 246
   post WWII 246
   Unzer Gedank (journal) 216, 246, 291
   Yiddishe Almanac (book) 246–7
Pushett, Jonas 101, 120, 162, 166, 195, 206
   Jewish Welfare 51
   Welcome Society 102
Pushett family 101
   Jonas *see* Pushett, Jonas
   survivors, meeting and resettlement of 166–7, 170
   Yankel 162–3, 166–7
Rabinowitz, Shalom *see* Aleichem, Sholem
radio (Yiddish) 151, 199, 260–1, 284
   J-Air 290
   Kadimah Yiddish Radio Show 290
   SBS Radio 260, 290
Rado, Erwin 115, 125
Radom (Poland) 34–6, 90, 91, 105, 180, 186
   newspapers *see* Yiddish newspapers (Poland)
   yeshivah 35–6
Radomer *landsmanshaftn* 180, 186
   hostel 169

Randa, Dasha 171
Randa, Dr Jack 171
Randa, Evichka 171
Randa, Tomik 171
Rapaport, Yehoshua (Shia) 101, 195, 245, 246
Ravensbruck concentration camp (Germany) 146
Ravitch, Melech 21, 67, 72, 78
   I.L. Peretz School 33, 70–1
Reading, Dr Fanny 98
REC *see* Refugee Economic Corporation (REC) (US)
Reconstruction (journal) 246
Redlich, Max 273
Refugee Economic Corporation (REC) (US) 164
Rene, Roy 31
reports about WWII
   Australian mainstream press, in 112–14, 132–3
   BBC, on 110–11
   concentration camps, about 131, 133, 134, 136
   individuals, news about 114–17
   international news 110–11
   Jewish press, in 109–10, 111–12, 118–19, 133–4
   underground reports 110–11
resettlement 15–16, 38
   interwar period 15–16, 38–9, 41
   Welcome Society *see* Welcome Society
   WWII and post war 122, 152, 161–5, 166, 167–71, 172, 187, 192, 206, 261, 290
   hostels *see* hostels
response to Holocaust (Aust govt) *see* immigration policy (post WWII)
response to Holocaust (Melb Jewry)
   meeting arrivals 165–7, 170, 192

public days of mourning 118–19
public fast days 118
public meeting/rallies 117–19
rescue and resettlement 161–71
unification in grief 116–17
welfare and fundraising 117, 119–22
Revisionist Zionist Organisation 43, 82, 84, 202
Revusky, Abraham 111
Riga (Latvia) 63, 150
Ringelblum, Pinye 151, 195, 260
    I.L. Peretz School 284
    Melbourne SKIF 257, 284
    Sholem Aleichem College 284
    Yiddish radio 151, 260, 284
Ringelblum family 283–4
Rintel, Moses 26
Ripps, Isaac 120
Rochman, Leib 248
Rodder, Mary 233
Rogozinski, Shimon 186
Romania 13, 25, 111, 119, 138, 159
Roosevelt, (Franklin) 118
Rose, A.S.100 100, 102, 120
Rose Court (St Kilda) 262–3
Roseby, Isaac 202
Rosenberg, Esther 148, 165–6, 173
Rosenberg, Jacob 148, 165–6, 176–7, 188, 193, 195, 229, 246
Rosenkranz, Shmuel 102, 109, 117, 202
Rosensaft, Josef 137
Rosenstein, Chaim 59, 65, 117, 129
Rothberg, Reuben 21
Rothkopf, Samuel 84
Royal Army Medical Corps 133
Royal Australian Air Force 123, 124
Royal Australian Navy 123
Royal Exhibition Building (Carlton) 192, 211
Royal Sydney Golf Club 32
Rubinstein, Bill 213
Rubinstein, Chaim 69
Russia *see also* Soviet Union
    Bolshevik Revolution (1917) 31, 48, 155
    Bund *see* Bund/Bundists
    pograms *see* Russia (pogroms)
    Red Army 131
    Russian Revolution (1905) 47
Russia (pogroms) 105
    Kishinev (1903) 37
    1890s, in 31, 37, 105
Russo-German war (1941-5) 111, 150

Samuel Myers Hall (St Kilda) 189, 210
Sanger, Rabbi Dr Herman 102, 120
'S'brent' (poem) 93, 294
SBS Radio 260, 290
Scattered and Dispersed (play) 61, 64
Scenes from Sholem Aleichem (play) 251
Schenk, Rabbi Max 208
schools (Hebrew) 241, 264–5
    Bialik College 82, 149, 185, 212, 264
    Ivriah Hebrew School 82
    Moriah 264
    Mount Scopus College 185, 191, 196–7, 237, 264
    Talmud Torah schools 71, 183
    United Jewish Education Board 71, 265
    Yavneh 264
    Yeshivah/Beth Rivkah 264
schools (Yiddish) 52, 60, 70, 71, 196, 217, 254–7
    Adass Yisroel 264, 281
    CYSHO schools (Poland) 71, 78, 254

INDEX

Divrei Eminah *see* Divrei Eminah kindergarten
I.L. Peretz School *see* I.L. Peretz School
Israel, in 215
Sholem Aleichem *see* Sholem Aleichem schools
Schwartz, Tess 6–7
Scullin government 19, 32
Second World War 50, 59, 63, 83, 101, 123, 127, 153, 167, 212, 247–8
   aftermath *see* aftermath (WWII)
   Allied forces *see* Allied forces (WWII)
   Australian Jewish enlistment 122–6, 131
   Commonwealth Munitions 127
   concentration camps *see* concentration camps (WWII)
   Hitler (Adolf) 97, 103, 116, 134, 176, 212, 227, 270, 297
   Holocaust *see* Holocaust
   Japan *see* Japan
   Jewish Brigade (British Army) 137
   Manpower Australia 126
   Nazi–Soviet non-aggression pact (1939) 78
   Red Army 131
   reports about *see* reports about WWII
   Russo-German war (1941-5) 111, 150
secular/socialist political party *see* Bund/Bundists
Segaloff, Ben 261
Seltzer, Dov 250
Sforim, Mendele Moykher 83
Shaiak, Gedalia 246
Shandler, Prof Jeffery 287

Shanghai
   Jewish refugees 141–2, 155, 236, 240, 254
   Shanghai ghetto 148–9
Sharett, Moshe 213, 233
Sharp, Pinchas 261
Sher, Israel 51, 101, 120
   Kadimah 21
Sher, Shulamis 249
Sher, Yasha 52, 63, 116, 129, 199, 249, 255
   Yasha Sher Reading Room 295
   Yiddish radio 260
Shifman, Menachem 202
ships (refugee)
   Cyrenia (ship) 170
   Derna 166
   El Misr 169
   Hwa Lien 155
   Johan de Witt 155, 156
   Niagara 104
   Otranto 90
   Ville d'Amiens 155, 166, 168
Shoah Foundation 143
Sholem Aleichem: 100 and not yet dead (tribute) 293
Sholem Aleichem College 185, 266, 284–5
   Yiddish instruction 285–6
Sholem Aleichem School 183, 255–7, 260, 286
   closure 292
   enrolments 256, 265
   I.L. Peretz School absorbed into 265
Sholem Aleichem Sunday School 199, 237, 255, 285
Shtern, Yisroel 294
Shulman, Avrom 297
Shulman, R. 120
Shuster family 232

Siberia (Soviet Union) 151, 168
    labour camps 150
Silman, Myer 51, 77, 120
Silman, Yides 77
Simonsen, Frances Alda 29
Sing My People (play) 251
Singer, Isaac Bashevis 250, 299
Six-Day War (1967) 270–5
    fundraising 273–4
    rallies 271–2
    recruitment 272–3
SKIF (Melbourne) 151, 250, 257–8, 260, 266–8, 284, 285, 290, 291
    Chavershaft (journal) 246, 266–7
    concerts 258
    membership 257
SKIF (Sotsyalistisher Kinder Farband) 257, 258
Slonim, Charles 166
Slucki, David 267, 268, 286–7
Smith, Issy 27
Smith's Weekly 31
    antisemitism 30–1, 140
Smorgon family 236
Sobibor concentration camp (Poland) 112
socialism/socialists 47, 77, 79
    Poale Zion 35, 43, 111, 183
Socialist Children's Union (SKIF) 257, 258
Society for the Establishment of a Rural Jewish Community (GEZERD) 77–8
    Communist faction 78
Sof Vokh Oystralye (retreat) 291
Sokol, A. 120
Sokolowicz, Aron 147, 174, 192, 195
Sokolowicz, Cyla 174
Solvey, Joe 212
Sotsyalistisher Kinder Farband (SKIF) 257, 258

South Africa 25, 96
Soviet Union 77, 80, 270 *see also* Russia
    gulags *see* gulags (Soviet Union)
    Jewish refugees 150, 151, 168, 169
    Nazi–Soviet non-aggression pact (1939) 78
    war with Germany (1941-5) 111, 150
sponsorship
    interwar years 14–15, 92, 96, 103–4, 106
    post WWII 154, 159, 162–3, 236
St Kilda (Melb) 169, 191–2, 199, 231, 255, 256, 263, 279
    aged care homes 261–2
    Bialystoker Centre *see* Bialystoker Centre (St Kilda)
    Café Scheherazade 236–7
    Palais de Danse 128
    Palais Theatre 252
    3rd St Kilda Scout Group 124
    Samuel Myers Hall 189, 210
    schools (Yiddish) *see* Sholem Aleichem schools
    Welfare House 169, 257
St Kilda Synagogue 85–6, 87–8, 102, 202
St Kilda Town Hall 191
Stalin (Joseph) 118, 297
Stalingrad (Russia) 131
Star, B. 72
State Jewish Theatre (Warsaw) 251
State Zionist Councils 272
    Victoria 51, 190, 191, 204, 214
Steinberg, Dr 129
Stern gang (Palestine) *see* Lehi resistance (Palestine)
Stock, S. 120
Storch, Heniek 151

INDEX

Stutthof concentration camp (Poland) 146, 170
Sugihara, Chiune 240
survivors (Holocaust) *see also* aftermath (WWII)
  citizenship/permanent residency 137–8, 139
  commemorations *see* commemorations (Holocaust)
  community of survivors 171, 175–9, 181, 187
  landsmanshaftn see landsmanshaftn
  nightmares 172–9
  personal stories 115, 133, 136, 143–8, 193
  post-war world, in 134–8
  Sugihara, Chiune, saved by 240
  why Australia? 138–9
synagogues 71, 72, 130, 191, 209, 232–3, 265, 273
  Beth Israel synagogue 88
  Carlton Synagogue 86, 88, 101, 102, 118, 196, 210, 217, 233
  East Melbourne Synagogue 85–6
  Great Synagogue (Sydney) 97, 122
  Melbourne Synagogue 16, 49, 85–6, 193
  Northcote, in 232
  St Kilda Synagogue 85–6, 87–8, 102, 202
  Thornbury, in 232–3
  women, role of 280
Szabinski, L. 72
Sztajer, Blima 143–4, 146
Sztajer, Chaim 143–6
Sztajer, Hela 144, 146
Sztajer, Laibl (Leon) 143

Taft (Tafipolsky), Yasha 15
Talmud Torah schools 71, 183
Tashkent (Uzbekistan) 178
teachers (Yiddish) 51, 199, 254, 285, 286
  Ajzenbud, Moshe 150, 246
  Burstin, Symche 150, 165, 195, 230, 257
  Charak, Danielle 147, 200–1, 261, 267
  Dafner, Alex 250, 261, 290
  Giligich, Joseph *see* Giligich, Joseph
  Kalinski, Tomi 290, 292, 298
  Kaluszyner, Boruch 151
  Krystal, Cluwa 149, 195, 254
  Mrocki, Freydi 289, 292
  Munz, Hirsh 21, 67, 129
  Ravitch, Melech *see* Ravitch, Melech
  Ringelblum, Pinye 151, 195, 257, 260, 283, 284
  Sher, Israel 21, 51, 101, 120
  Star, B. 72
  Szabinski, L. 72
  Wasserman, Genia 151, 195, 256
  Zeleznikow, Avram 148, 192, 195, 230, 235, 236–7, 243, 244
Tel Aviv (Israel) 209, 215
Temple Emanuel (Sydney) 208
Ten Million (poem) 77
Tevye the Milkman (play) 61, 292
The Advertiser 204
The Age 208
The Argus 58, 113, 208
  concentration camps 132–3
  King David Hotel, bomb attack at 204
  Kristallnacht pogrom (1938) 93
  reports about WWII 112
The Australian Yiddish Almanac (book) 66, 129, 246
The Australians (book) 260

The Bulletin (magazine) 267
   antisemitism 30–1, 140
The Dybbuk (play) 54–5, 64
The Herald 98
   antisemitism 98, 140–1
The Kingdom of Shylock (pamphlet) 31
The New York Times 37, 110, 135
The Shop on the Main Street (film) 252
The Slaughter (play) 61
The Sydney Morning Herald 59, 112, 113
The West Australian 113
The Witch (play) 63
The Yellow Patch (play) 62
theatre (Yiddish) 20, 35, 50, 51–2, 54–5, 57–65, 70, 78, 128–9, 206, 289, 292, 293
   actors *see* actors (Yiddish)
   David Herman Theatre *see* David Herman Theatre
   international impresarios 58, 248, 250–3
   MYYT 250
   plays *see* plays (Yiddish)
   playwrights *see* playwrights (Yiddish)
   post WWII 248–53
   Yiddishe Bine *see* Yiddishe Bine (theatre group)
Thornbury (Melb)
   Jewish community 231–3
Thornbury Synagogue 232–3
3ZZ and 3EA *see* radio (Yiddish)
trade unions *see* unions
Treblinka concentration camp (Poland) 112, 133, 143–6, 172–3
Trees Die Standing (play) 252
Triwaks, H. 248
Truman, President H. 136
Tsen Milion (poem) 77
Tsezeyt un Tseshpreyt (play) 61, 64

Tsukunft (Bund youth group) 76, 250, 257
Turkow, Rosa 250–1
Turkow, Zygmunt 250–1
Two Hundred Thousand (play) 62, 249
Tzvay Hundert Toyzent (play) 62, 249

UEC *see* United Emergency Committee (UEC)
UIA *see* United Israel Appeal (UIA)
UIA Young Adults 272
UJORF *see* United Jewish Overseas Relief Fund (UJORF)
Ukraine 38, 111, 292
   pogroms (1920) 8, 30
Ukrainian Jewish Relief Fund 30
UN Educational, Scientific and Cultural Organisation (UNESCO) 276, 296
UN Special Committee on Palestine (UNSCOP) 205
Uncle Moses (play) 251
Undzer Shtetl Brent (song) 93
Unemployment *see* business and employment
UNESCO *see* UN Educational, Scientific and Cultural Organisation (UNESCO)
Union Club 32
Union of Jewish Health Organisations (OT-OZE) 121
Union Theatre (Melbourne) 206
unions *see also* Bund/Bundists
   Australia 18–19, 31
   Poland 9, 18, 35, 75, 79
United Australia Party
   Bruce government 19
   Lyons government 92
United Carpet Mills Pty Ltd 14
United Emergency Committee (UEC) 119–20

INDEX

United Israel Appeal (UIA) 185, 233, 248, 268, 270–1, 272
   Keren Hayesod 205
   Young Adults 272
United Israel Emergency Appeal 274
United Jewish Education Board 71, 265
United Jewish Overseas Relief Fund (UJORF) 100, 120–1, 162, 206
   AJWRS, merge with *see* Australian Jewish Welfare and Relief Society (AJWRS)
   Ladies' Group 121, 167
United Jewish Relief Fund *see* United Jewish Overseas Relief Fund (UJORF)
United Nations
   Declaration of Human Rights 160
   General Assembly 205
   partition resolution (1947) 205, 210
   UNESCO 276, 296
   UNSCOP 205
United States 12, 65, 253, 270
   antisemitism 27–8, 140
   Eastern European Jews' migration to
      1881-1914 25
      1921-1925 37
   Jewish refugees (WWII) 96, 139
   welfare organisations
      HIAS 105, 139, 157, 164
      JDC 105, 121, 139, 164, 236
      REC 164
United Woollen Mills Pty Ltd 14
UNSCOP *see* UN Special Committee on Palestine (UNSCOP)
Unzer Erd (play) 206
Unzer Gedank (journal) 216, 246, 291
USSR *see* Soviet Union

Uzbekistan 150

Vajhingen concentration camp (Germany) 147
Verneuil, Louis 59
   Lady Lawyer 59
Victorian Association of Ex-Servicemen 191
Victorian Jewish Advisory Board 98, 122–3, 207
   establishment (1936) 88
   King David Hotel, bomb attack on 204
   representation on 88–9
Victorian Jewish Board of Deputies (VJBD) 185, 189, 190, 191, 217, 237, 244, 272
   Appeals Committee 192
   establishment of Israel 208
   Jewish Heritage Committee 192
   Yiddish language 196
Victorian Jewish *Year Book* 186
Victorian State Zionist Council 51, 190, 191, 204, 214
Vietnam War 271
Ville d'Amiens (ship) 155, 166, 168
Vilna ghetto 148, 170
Vilna (Lithuania) 5, 52, 72, 74, 79, 195, 253
   Jewish population 5
   YIVO institute 5
Vilna Troupe 52, 57–8, 64
Vilner *landsmandshaft* 186
Vilner Trupe *see* Vilna Troupe
VJBD *see* Victorian Jewish Board of Deputies (VJBD)
Voice of Israel (radio) 209

Waislitz, Yankev 55, 58, 60, 62, 63, 64, 78, 206, 250
   tribute to 293

Vilna Troupe 52, 57–8
Waks, Jacob 79–80, 155, 163, 195, 235
   J. Waks Cultural Trust 289
   Melbourne Bund 291
Waks, Mina *see* Fink, Mina
Waks, Yankev 117, 120
Waks House 291
War Effort Circle 119
War of Independence (Arab-Israeli) 205, 210, 211, 212, 214
   Six-Day War *see* Six Day War (1967)
Warsaw ghetto 146, 189, 190, 256
   uprising 131, 147, 187, 188–9, 190, 191
Warsaw Jewish Centre 169, 233
Warsaw (Poland) 16, 72, 105, 143, 178, 195, 253
   Folks Tsaytung 78
   ghetto *see* Warsaw ghetto
   Jewish population 5
   kehile 43
   State Jewish Theatre 251
   Vilna Troupe 52, 57–8, 64
Warsaw Yiddish Art Theatre 57
Warsawer *landsmanshaftn* 180, 186
Warshawski, B. 129
Warszawski, Binem 117, 120
Warszawski, Rabbi 120
Wasserman, Genia 151, 195, 256
Waten, Judah 67–8, 230
Wein, Sarah 114
Weinberg, I. 185
Weisberg, Theo 126–7
Weissberg, Shmuel 60
Welcome Society 11, 20, 21, 41–2, 102
   Women's Auxiliary 41
welfare *see* aid, welfare and fundraising (Jewish refugees)

Welfare Appeal 185
Welfare House (St Kilda) 169, 257
Welfare Society *see* Australian Jewish Welfare Society
Werder, Felix 261
Werdiger, Nathan 239
West Melbourne Stadium 213
White, T.W. 94
White Australia policy 39
Whitlam government 240
Wiener, Bela 77
Wiener, Bono 147, 186, 192, 195
   Bono Wiener Collection 295
   Lodzer Centre 196, 217
   Melbourne Bund 267, 273
Wiener, Pintche 147
Wiernik, Yankel 133
Wilenski, Motl 196
Wisse, Prof Ruth 277
WIZO *see* Women's International Zionist Organisation (WIZO)
Wolf, Friedrich 62
Women's International Zionist Organisation (WIZO) 84, 130, 183, 273
   WIZO Younger Set 119
Woods, Frank 191
World Coordinating Committee of Bund Organizations 217
World Jewish Congress 121
World Zionist Organization 80, 272
writers (Yiddish) 47, 51, 53, 57, 60, 65–6, 101, 244–7, 256, 292
   Ajzenbud, Moshe 150, 246
   Aleichem, Sholem *see* Aleichem, Sholem
   Bennett, Shmuel 34–5, 36, 46, 49, 51, 53, 90, 104–5, 180
   Bergner, Herz *see* Bergner, Herz
   Cykiert, Abraham 195, 246, 260
   Frydman, Lew 246

INDEX

Giligich, Joseph *see* Giligich, Joseph
Goldhar, Pinchas *see* Goldhar, Pinchas
Hirshbein, Peretz 47, 200
Horowitz, Isaac 129
Kahn, Yitzhak 51, 246
Leivik, H. 65
Lewin, I.M. 246
Munz, Hirsh 21, 67, 129
Opatoshu, Joseph 65
Peretz, Itzhak Leib *see* Peretz, Itzhak Leib
Rapaport, Yehoshua 101, 195, 245, 246
Ravitch, Melech *see* Ravitch, Melech
Rosenberg, Jacob 148, 165, 176, 188, 193, 195, 229, 246
Rosenstein, Chaim 59, 65, 117, 129
Sforim, Mendele Moykher 83
Shaiak, Gedalia 246
Shtern, Yisroel 294
Shulman, Avrom 297
Steinberg, Dr 129
Warshawski, B. 129
Waten, Judah 67–8, 230
Zable, Arnold 197, 237, 249, 254–5, 268
WWI *see* First World War
WWII *see* Second World War
Wynn, Samuel (Shloyme) 15, 50, 53, 81, 101, 119, 195, 210
   Kadimah 21, 41, 47, 51, 84
   Keren Hayesod 205–6
   Zionist Council 51

Yaffe, Sam 120
Yankev Waislitz on the World Stage (tribute) 293
Yankl the Blacksmith (play) 61
Yasha Sher Reading Room 295
Yavneh (school) 264
Yeshivah/Beth Rivkah (school) 264
Yeshivah Centre (Melb) 233
Yiddish Book Center (US) 294
Yiddish newspapers (Aust) 47, 55, 66, 244–7, 254 *see also* Jewish newspapers (Aust)
   Di Yiddishe Nayes see Di Yiddishe Nayes (newspaper)
   Di Yiddishe Post 30, 69, 199, 245
   lebedike tsaytung 117, 200, 212
   Oystralyer Lebn 69
   Yiddish weekly 30, 69
Yiddish newspapers (Poland) 46, 47, 60, 61, 68–9, 179
   Folks Tsaytung 78
   Radomer Lebn/Radomer-Keltser Lebn 36
   Radomer Shtime 36
   Radomer Tsaytung 36
   Trybuna 36
Yiddish Sunday and Afternoon School *see* I.L. Peretz School
Yiddish Vokh 284
Yiddish Week 284
Yiddishe Almanac (book) 246–7
Yiddishe Bine (theatre group) 54, 62, 64 *see also* David Herman Theatre
   The Dybbuk 54–5
   Tzvay Hundert Toyzent 62
   The Yellow Patch 62
Yiddishism/Yiddishists
   Bund *see* Melbourne Bund
   culture *see* culture and identity (Yiddish)
   doykeit (here and now) 9, 75–6, 80, 214–15, 268
   education *see* schools (Yiddish); teachers (Yiddish)

established Jewish community, and *see* old *versus* new
Ginter home 62
identity *see* culture and identity (Yiddish)
Israel, in 215
Kadimah *see* Kadimah centre
language *see* language (Yiddish)
PJRF *see* Polish Jewish Relief Fund (PJRF)
radio broadcasting *see* radio (Yiddish)
UJORF *see* United Jewish Overseas Relief Fund (UJORF)
Yiddishkeit 22, 36, 51, 52, 58, 70, 101, 201, 253, 257, 268
    meaning of 19–20
Yidl mitn Fidl (film) 200
Yishuv community (Palestine) 203, 216
Yisroel Shtern project 294
YIVO institute (Vilna) 5
Yom Kippur 17
Young Jewish Social Club 86
Young Judean Zionist Society 86
Youth Aliya Committee 119
youth groups 85, 124, 201–2, 214
    Bund *see* SKIF (Melbourne)
    Jewish Students Societies 272
    Jewish Young People's Association 86
    Kadimah Younger Set 48–9, 130
    UIA Young Adults 272
    Victorian Jewish Youth 191, 272
    Young Jewish Social Club 86
    Zionist *see* youth groups (Zionist)
youth groups (Zionist) 201–2, 214
    Australian Zionist Youth Council 272
    Betar 202, 257
    Habonim 202, 257, 273

Young Judean Zionist Society 86
Yugntruf Yidish Vokh (US) 291
Yugoslav War Crimes Committee 133

Zable, Arnold 197, 237, 249, 254–5, 268
Zaglembie *landsmanshaftn* 186
Zalbe, L. 185
Zamosc (Poland) 293
Zbar, A. 117
Zeleznikow, Avram 148, 192, 195, 230, 235–7, 243, 244
Zeleznikow, Masha 235, 236
Zeleznikow, Yankel 235
Zelichover *landsmanshaftn* 186
Zeltner, Myer 120
Zerman, Bernie 126
Zilberman, Max 167
Zing Mayn Folk (play) 251
Zionism
    Agudas Yisroel 35, 43, 121
    Balfour Declaration (1917) 48, 81
    Eretz Israel *see* Israel
    growth of 29, 80–4
    Poale Zion 35, 43, 111, 183
    World Zionist Organization 80, 272
Zionism/Zionists (Aust) 61, 77, 85, 116, 201, 241
    Bnei Akiva 202
    growth of 81–4, 86, 87
    Hatkhia movement 48
    Israel *see* Israel
    Kadimah battleground 47–8
    language *see* language (Hebrew)
    leaders 51, 77, 84, 111, 202, 208
    Melbourne Friends of Jerusalem's Hebrew University 84
    origins 80–1
    Poale Zion 35, 43, 111, 183

INDEX

Revisionist Zionist Organisation 43, 82, 84, 202
schools *see* schools (Hebrew)
State Councils *see* State Zionist Councils
WIZO 84, 119, 130, 183, 273
youth groups *see* youth groups (Zionist)
Zionist Federation of Australia 84, 88, 118, 272
Zionists *v* Anti-Zionists 205–9, 216–17
Zionist Congress (1897) 80–1
Zionist Federation of Australia 66, 84, 118, 272
Zuben, Deborah 170–1
Zufi, Reene 261
Zygielbaum, Shmuel 115
Zylberman, Bobbi 261
Zylberman, Michael 261
Zylberman, Mira 261

ABOUT THE AUTHORS

Dr Margaret Taft is a Research Associate at the Australian Centre for Jewish Civilisation, (ACJC) Monash University, and author of *From Victim to Survivor: The Emergence and Development of the Holocaust Witness 1941–1949* (2013) and, with Andrew Markus, *Walter Lippmann, Ethnic Communities Leader* (2016). Margaret has been researching Yiddish Melbourne for the past eight years as part of a major study undertaken by the ACJC. She is a Yiddish speaker and daughter of Holocaust survivors whose early years were spent in the post-war immigrant community of Northcote.

Professor Andrew Markus is the Pratt Foundation Research Professor of Jewish Civilisation at Monash University and a Fellow of the Academy of the Social Sciences in Australia. He has published extensively on Australian immigration and race relations. Andrew heads the Scanlon Foundation social cohesion research program which in 2017 conducted its 10th national survey. He is also the principal researcher on the Australian Jewish population and Yiddish Melbourne research projects. Andrew is a post-war immigrant from Hungary who arrived in Australia in January 1957.